Family Studies

Family Studies: An Introduction provides a comprehensive understanding of contemporary family living. While many argue that 'the family' is the most important thing of all, many families are left to suffer poverty, disability, abuse and divorce with remarkably little support. Today, as always, there is a widespread variation and diversity as well as rapid change in families in Western societies. Rejecting the traditional model of 'the family', this book argues that we should listen to what children, adolescents, husbands and wives, mothers and fathers tell us about their experiences.

The chapters are designed to work as individual units of study in courses on family living. Each chapter:

- highlights key issues
- summarises the most relevant research in the area
- suggests activities as a basis for student projects
- recommends further reading

The author argues for the foundation of family studies in schools, colleges and universities in order to help all members of society understand and be better prepared for the many roles and challenges in childhood, partnering and parenting. Real sexual equality may be achieved by encouraging men to participate more in the unpaid work roles of parenting, especially housework and child care. Government has a role here in creating equality in both paid and unpaid work, especially by giving men legal rights to parental leave. Fundamental changes in paid and unpaid work, family relationships and human services are essential for us to generate a society in which families, in all forms, are put first.

Jon Bernardes is Principal Lecturer in Sociology at the University of Wolverhampton.

LONDON AND NEW YORK

Family Studies

An Introduction

■ Jon Bernardes

First published in 1997
by Routledge
11 New Fetter Lane, London EC4P 4EE

Simultaneously published in the USA and
Canada
by Routledge
29 West 35th Street, New York, NY 10001

Reprinted 2000

*Routledge is an imprint of the
Taylor & Francis Group*

© 1997 Jon Bernardes

Typeset in Janson and Futura by Keystroke,
Jacaranda Lodge, Wolverhampton

Printed and bound in Great Britain by
TJ International Ltd, Padstow, Cornwall

British Library Cataloguing in Publication Data
A catalogue record for this book is available
from the British Library

*Library of Congress Cataloguing in Publication
Data*
Bernardes, Jon, 1952–
    Family studies : an introduction / Jon
Bernardes.
        p.   cm.
    Includes bibliographical references and
index.
    ISBN 0–415–16468–0 (hc.) — ISBN
0–415–16469–9 (pbk.)
    1. Family. 2. Family—Research. I. Title.
    HQ515.B47   1997
306.85—dc21   96–47497
                                        CIP

ISBN 0–415–16468–0 (hbk)
ISBN 0–415–16469–9 (pbk)

Contents

To assume that a form, because it is a variant, is abnormal, is to evade the task before us. The first job of science is, after all, to study what IS, not what might be, or could, or should be.

(Adams, 1971, p. 82)

The scientific study of the family is still in its infancy. I have attempted briefly and I know inadequately to touch on certain of the aspects of family life that . . . have seemed to be important for future research. These are: first, to push further the effort to describe, analyse, and classify the patterns of family life; second, to recognise that the family as a going concern depends more on the natural unity that arises and develops through the personal interaction of its members than upon any attempt to enforce the family obligations which the law imposes.

(Burgess, 1926, p. 9)

Acknowledgements

There are a great many students and colleagues who have contributed to the development of ideas contained in this book. I extend my deepest thanks to you all for having helped me over so many years to develop and test different ideas and arguments. I hesitate to identify individuals for fear of doing an injustice to those I omit; but I do especially thank Maria Alvarez (University of Santiago, Chile), Pierpaulo Donati (University of Bologna, Italy), Wilfried Dumon (University of Leuven, Belgium), David Keddie (University of Southampton), Irene Levin (University of Oslo, Norway), Li Qiang (People's University of China, Beijing), David Morgan (University of Manchester) and Kari Moxnes (University of Trondheim, Norway). I am also grateful to various reviewers and editors for encouraging the writing of various articles in the past. At Routledge, Mari Shullaw has been especially helpful.

Several organisations have, in supporting my work, contributed to this book. The University of Wolverhampton has enabled me to teach a great many students on a great many courses about a great many aspects of family living. Staff at the Learning Centre, Shropshire Campus of the University of Wolverhampton have been particularly helpful and tolerated the large amount of work I have generated for them. The British Council has supported visits to family scholars in Chile, China and numerous European countries; these contacts have been invaluable in developing this text.

Most important, however, are members of my immediate family: my wife and partner, Carole; my daughter, Eleanor; and my son, Jacob.

Using this book

I hope that this book will be useful to students, decision-makers, professionals and lay people. I have attempted to construct this as a textbook that may be followed from start to finish or used selectively.

The style of this text is to pose more questions than answers. A textbook is where things start, not where they finish, and should therefore be about encouraging and facilitating learning. The key is not to tell you 'the way it is' but rather encourage you to discover the way to learn about families. Use this text to learn *how* to look, rather than learn *what* to see.

In each chapter, I have picked out key issues and where possible suggested activities students may wish to take up as projects or exercises. These exercises can be used in a variety of ways. At the simplest level, the reader might wish to spend a few moments thinking about an issue. At a more complex level, especially within educational settings, readers might engage in collective discussions or conduct small or large surveys; many of the exercises may be treated as the bases of essay or project questions. At the end of each chapter, a useful exercise is an attempt to list the six main points of the chapter.

I hope that this book includes many topics and items which are ignored in more traditional textbooks. Having said this, choices have had to be made and editing had to be fierce. The effort, then, is to provide a sense of the rich complexity of everyday family lives. This means that I have omitted a very great deal that I should have liked to incorporate – perhaps next time. I should be happy to receive any suggestions as to 'omissions' although I do not guarantee to reply to all letters.

For members of everyday families, I hope that this book will probe and challenge. I would be glad if it 'changes your ideas' in some small way. 'Changing ideas' need not be too painful; above all one needs to be open and responsive and consider the possibility of how new ideas may relate to, or influence, your own 'family life' .

For decision-makers, I want to encourage 'social problems' of all kinds to be seen anew. Of vital importance is the consideration of new and different policy responses arising from these new perspectives. I have tried to suggest, where possible, new avenues for decision-making or policy changes.

For professional groups of a wide range, I want to suggest ways in which you can 'deal with families' in new and hopefully 'better' ways. Also of vital importance, though, is recognising the possibility that 'families' may be better able to deal with their own problems or the problems of other families. Allowing families to explore such possibilities with guidance and support may enhance and expand professional credibility.

Chapter 1

Family lives

Introduction

Most people in Western industrialised societies, and probably most people world-wide, consider family living as the most important aspect of their lives. In the first report of the Research Centre on Micro-Social Change, Scott and Perren observe that, 'Family events were by far regarded as the most important aspect of people's lives' (1994, p. 263). A report for the European Commission demonstrated that 96 per cent of the population identify family living as the single most valued aspect of life across the European Union (Commission of the European Communities, 1993b, p. 60).

The most serious problem for anyone wishing to study family lives is their own closeness to the topic. This is not a matter of bias but rather the strength of beliefs about family lives. For most of our lives, 'our family' is the most important thing of all. Most of us are born into families and spend, whether we choose or not, most of our childhood and teenage years within 'our family'. Even single people living alone can readily identify both immediate and more distant members

1

of 'their family'. Thereafter, most of us set up some kinds of partnerships that may 'become a family' with the birth of children. We then begin another period within a family as a partner and parent, perhaps divorcing, re-marrying and becoming a new parent. Even when our children have left home, we may find ourselves again closely involved as grandparents in gift giving, family celebrations or child care. It is also within families that 'we first experience differences, divisions and hierarchies, which in "the family" are structured around gender and age' (Ribbens, 1994, p. 213).

> If 'family life' is so important, why not educate people for family lives, as we educate them for paid work?

In view of the centrality of family lives and the passion with which we believe family living to be important, it would be reasonable to expect the study of family living to be the most important academic discipline in our schools, colleges and universities. This is simply not the case. Whilst Family Studies is common in the USA and exists in some European countries, there are no departments of Family Studies in the UK. This textbook is aimed at developing and establishing the discipline of Family Studies in the UK.

The meaning of 'the family'

Most academic commentators seem to believe either that 'the family' does exist or that it is a good enough description of what does exist to continue to use the term. In recent years some scholars in the UK and USA have begun to question whether anything corresponding to the popular image of 'the family' exists at all.

> Ask half a dozen people what they think 'the family' is and how common it is in modern societies.

Despite a common-sense belief that 'no two families are the same', there is a clear and popular belief that something called 'the family' or 'the nuclear family' does exist. When asked, people are often puzzled as to why anyone should ask the question because the answer is 'so obvious'. The majority will, if pressed, present an image surprisingly like sociological definitions of 'the nuclear family'. Despite enormous real world variation and diversity, a common and popular image of 'the nuclear family' portrays a young, similarly aged, White, married heterosexual couple with a small number of healthy children living in an adequate home. There is a clear division of responsibilities in which the male is primarily the full-time breadwinner and the female primarily the caregiver and perhaps a part-time or occasional income earner.

There is something very strange about this image: it is quite simply unrealistic. Most simply put, this image of 'the family' omits the rich detail of everyday living and certainly ignores any possible 'negative' side of family living. It is equally clear that this simple model of 'the family' has not reflected the realities of people's lives at any stage in recorded history. Dalley suggests that, 'within . . . the ideology of familism, non-family forms are deemed to be deviant and/or subversive' (1996, p. 27). This model does not allow for divorce, single parenthood, family abuse, sickness or impairment, cultural and ethnic diversity, poverty, homelessness and very many other important variations. The model of 'the nuclear family' does not reflect my experiences as a son, a husband, a father. This model does not speak of the experiences of those I know and love: relatives, friends, wife, children.

The power of 'the family'

The idea of 'the nuclear family' is remarkably powerful; as Muncie and Sapsford observe, the 'idea of the nuclear family clearly retains a potency such that all other forms tend to be defined with reference to it' (1995, p. 10). This idea is attractive to opinion leaders because it asserts the correctness of clear gender divisions, parental responsibility for children and the privacy of 'the family'. Ordinary people resist giving up the idea of 'the family' because it is so simple and justifies so much behaviour. We do not need to worry about the justice of women doing all the child care and housework or the justice of male dominance in paid work and many positions of authority (see Bernardes, 1990).

Everyday people have little choice but to accept the kinds of statements made in public and religious life. One of the key means by which ordinary people continually receive the idea and image of 'the family' is through religion and associated morality. A wide range of religious tracts contain notions of 'the family', just as they contain notions of God and faith. This itself has important links to 'scientific' arguments about biology and universality. These views also coincide with conservative beliefs, especially ethnocentric views emphasising the superiority of White Western societies. Even in the more secular Western societies, religious beliefs remain as foundations of widely accepted social beliefs.

> Try and go for a whole day not using the term 'the family'.

Generations of competent social scientists have accepted the existence of 'the family'. This is both a puzzle and an indicator of the enormous power and strength of beliefs about 'the family'. Considering debates about 'the family' involves considering central and fundamental issues about the nature of society. Not least are issues of sex and gender, paid work versus unpaid family work, who takes responsibility for childrearing, the purpose of 'the family', and changes in family life associated with socio-historical events. These, and many more issues, are central to the way social science is undertaken in Western societies. Despite a popular idea that social science is critical, even radical, social science is generally remarkably conservative in relation to family life. This conservatism reflects popular ideas about 'the family' contained in biology, history and morality.

Sociology

The main academic discipline supporting the existence of 'the family' has been sociology. Grand theorising in sociology requires 'the family' so that even the most basic explanations about the nature of society can be undertaken. For example, traditional sociology sees 'the family' as the key institution responsible for rearing children to become mature adults able to undertake paid work in the formal economy. Similarly, the division of labour within the ideal model of 'the family' is widely used to justify male preoccupations with paid work and female preoccupations with attracting men, marrying, bearing and rearing children. The classic sources in the UK remain the work of Willmott and Young who documented the nature of the 'extended family' in the working-class East End of London (Young and Willmott, 1957) and the much smaller immediate family (now popularly known as the 'nuclear family') to be found when families moved to new housing estates (ibid.) or into the suburbs (Willmott and Young, 1960). The idea of the shift to the nuclear family was also supported by those from the anthropological side of sociology and these themes were developed in textbooks in the 1960s (see Harris, 1969).

The existence of 'the family' has been taken for granted by those of the Left and Right, Marxist and conservative sociologists alike. For many sociologists, any query over the use of 'the family' appears rather trivial and tends to be dismissed. The failure to question the idea of 'the family' has allowed all sorts of mistaken ideas to persist, such as the naturalness of monogamy (whereas many societies permit polygamy), the inevitability of female inferiority (which many feminists dispute), the right of many men to control and abuse women (which many women dispute), and the right of parents to control and punish children (whereas some forms of punishment are illegal in some European countries).

Many theorists have made clear that 'the nuclear family' is an 'ideal type' or 'a theoretical construction, derived from intuition and observation' (Goode, 1970, p. 7). To use an ideal type is a normal and conventional means of pursuing sociology. Gelles has recently made the point that, 'Ideal types are abstractions, and no phenomenon exists in the real world that can perfectly match the ideal type' (1995, p. 12). The very same author ends his wide ranging American text-book by confusing an ideal type abstraction with an everyday stereotype, 'Perhaps the greatest strength of the family is that it inspires so much concern and debate' (ibid., p. 511).

The problem for sociologists is two-fold. First, the term 'ideal' is very often taken to mean the 'normal' which people should aspire to achieve. In this sense, the simple existence of an ideal type is taken by lay people to mean that this is the 'best' form of family living which people should adopt. Second, though, sociologists have rarely if ever enquired whether this ideal type reflects any part of everyday family living because it has been so 'obvious' to them as everyday actors. Sociologists take the popularity of the stereotype in everyday life to confirm the accuracy of their ideal type and everyday actors take the sociological ideal type to confirm the accuracy of their stereotype.

Gather a montage of images of 'the family' from newspapers and magazines.

This language trap can have dramatic results in some instances. It is most clearly seen in cases where authors shift from treating 'the family' as an ideal type or abstraction to arguing that 'the family' does exist. This is best seen in the remarkable American claim of Talcott Parsons in 1971. In a society with widespread poverty, a large range of ethnic minorities and a large working class, Parsons claimed:

> It is of course a commonplace that the American family is predominantly and, in a sense, increasingly an urban middle-class family . . . there has emerged a remarkably uniform, basic type of family. It is uniform in its kinship and household composition in the sense of confinement of its composition to members of the nuclear family.

(Parsons, 1971, p. 53)

5

Biology and universality

The power and 'obviousness' of the popular stereotype of 'the family' is rooted in popular understandings of biology. Clearly, the sexes are very different in their roles in biological reproduction. Women conceive and suckle infants, these are indeed biological facts. It is very easy indeed to point to other species that engage in similar divisions of labour. From this it is a simple matter to create an image of a 'biological family' of lifelong monogamy between male and female, where the female is responsible for the rearing of the children. If this image of the 'biological family' matches both popular stereotypes and sociological ideal types, then they all become more convincing and reinforce one another.

This argument can be taken much further to add a moral dimension. Clearly, a phenomenon determined by nature will also be universal to the species. The arguments then become mutually reinforcing. If 'the family' is assumed to be natural or biological, researchers will tend to believe it is universal. If 'the family' is assumed to be universal, researchers will tend to assume that it is natural or biological in origin. These kinds of arguments have enabled all sorts of groups (from those framing civil laws to the makers of religious texts) to claim that one sort of 'the family' is natural and that other living arrangements are somehow 'unnatural'.

Nearly all accounts of 'the family' include a discussion of universality. The source for modern debates about the universality of 'the nuclear family' is one of the major figures in the development of modern sociology, George Murdock. After examining evidence from 250 societies throughout the world, Murdock asserted that:

> The nuclear family is a universal social grouping. Either as the sole prevailing form of the family or as the basic unit from which more complex familial forms are compounded, it exists as a distinct and strongly functional group in every known society.
>
> (Murdock, 1965, pp. 2–3)

In the many discussions about the universal nuclear family, few scholars reject Murdock's thesis. As Reiss (1965) points out, however, it seems that Murdock actually observed the universality of sexual reproduction. This is clear when Murdock argues that 'the nuclear family' may be 'the basic unit of which more complex familial forms are compounded'. Would there be any cases for which the 'nuclear family' was not basic? Murdock himself seems to believe that single parenthood and polygamy are somehow basically examples of 'the family'.

> Ask six people which parts of human behaviour are 'biological' and which are 'learned'.

The way in which sociologists exploring family living have drawn upon popular understandings of biology was clearly seen in one of the major works on 'the family' in the UK. Ronald Fletcher's influential book, *The Family and Marriage in Britain*, first published in 1962, asserts that, 'The family is, and always has been, the most intimate and one of the most important of human groups. With qualifications of negligible importance, it can be said to be universal' (1973, p. 35). Fletcher goes on to assert that, 'The human family is centred around . . . biological propensities and needs: mating, the begetting of children, and the rearing of children'. This illustrates the error of linking biological reproduction with a particular social form of 'the family'. Clearly, there are many different ways of reproducing and rearing children, of which the Western notion of 'the family' is only one form.

In this way, the power of 'the family' draws upon deeply held personal feelings we each have about ourselves as biological beings. It is inevitable that it takes some great courage to overcome what are assumed to be 'natural' feelings and proclaim, for example, a dislike of children or a preference for a homosexual lifestyle. This again links morality and a sense of the superiority of Western industrial societies to issues of biology; all three become mutually reinforcing and extremely difficult to challenge.

History

Popular understandings of history contribute a fourth element reinforcing the power of 'the family'. Looking at the economic and political power of the West, few historians have doubted that the appearance of 'the nuclear family' had some key part to play in this development. Most accounts emphasise the population shift in the seventeenth and eighteenth centuries from rural extended families to densely packed small nuclear families in the new booming industrial towns of Britain and elsewhere.

Historians, like sociologists, tend to work with an extremely broad brush and look to identify trends and patterns. Shorter wrote an extremely wide ranging book in which he claimed to describe and explain *The Making of the Modern Family* (1975). In a single book, Mitterauer and Sieder identify, describe and explain the rise of one particular form of family, that is *The European Family*, associated with the modern period (1982). In adopting such broad brush approaches, historians inevitably avoid or neglect the complex details of ordinary everyday lives and few have doubted that 'the family' exists, is universal and is generally a good thing.

Historians have demonstrated the mechanisms by which industrial societies have developed to become 'more advanced'. In all of this, it is has been important to argue that the particular family form labelled as the 'nuclear family' somehow 'fits' modern industrialisation. These ideas are also attractive in that policy-makers in many developing nations seem intent on moving towards a 'nuclear family' form. They are doing so in the belief that this will be part of the necessary social changes to achieve the magic of economic development to bring about the kind of Western 'consumer societies' seen and envied by many developing nations.

Most analyses suggest that industrialisation involves a shift from rural extended families to isolated urban nuclear families. This shift mirrors the dramatic change in production techniques from patterns in agriculture and 'outworking' to labour concentrated in factories. Pre-industrial relationships are all-encompassing, involving almost feudal ties of housing, food, loyalty, property rights and so on. Manufacture requires more specialised labour and obtains this by simply offering attractive wages that lure workers and their immediate families into the new urban towns.

List the advantages and disadvantages of having a large 'extended' family.

There are two kinds of problems with these analyses. First, they are deeply ethnocentric, ignoring other cultures and minority cultures within European societies. Second, we must ask whether the pictures of the past we have may reflect the hopes and wishes of the literate classes rather than the realities of families. Detailed historical work has suggested that pre-industrial households were surprisingly small and that 'nuclear family forms' were probably more common. Anderson has suggested that a household size of less than five people was common in England from 1700 through to 1900 (1980, p. 23). Goldthorpe charts the historical development of family relations in Britain and America but opens with a critical note, 'family life may be more diverse than we think, and we can easily generalise too readily from personal experience' (1987, p. 2). Another rare, yet much more explicit, contrary view is given by Smith who argues that historians have taken part in the 'construction of a myth of a transition from extended to nuclear families associated with industrialisation' (1993, p. 338). Smith attributes the development of this myth to the use of particular concepts and ideas from within history as a discipline and especially the adoption of the notion of 'ideal types' from European social theory.

The power of the image of 'the family' rests upon the way in which it has rarely been challenged and frequently been supported by disciplines as different as sociology, biology and history. The assumption of the existence of 'the family' within these disciplines has corresponded to a popular stereotype of 'the family' held by those practising these disciplines. In this way, a more or less 'closed circuit' has developed in which the idea of 'the family' has gained more strength and support despite any contrary evidence. Virtually all text-books feel obliged to review biology, universality, history and the shift from extended family forms to modern nuclear forms of 'the family'. Once these arguments are accepted as reasonable, it is remarkably difficult to think of anything other than 'the family'.

Does 'the family' exist?

The simple problem that arises out of the popularity of the image of 'the family' is that very few scholars have ever bothered to ask if it exists or ever has existed (see Bernardes, 1985a, 1986b). It is important, here, to go beyond simply asserting that 'it' does not exist because of widespread variation and diversity and rather examine hard statistical evidence. In 1925, Bowley and Hogg found that the 'conventional family' (of a wage earning man, his wife and three dependent children) accounted for only 5 per cent of all families in the northern counties of the United Kingdom (1925, pp. 8–9). Using 1978 Government statistics, R. and R. N. Rapoport found that only 20 per cent of UK households contained single breadwinner families (1982, p. 478). Rimmer and Wicks argued that such a family type only accounted for 15 per cent of households in 1981. In 1984, Westwood noted that such a model represented only 5 per cent of UK house-holds (1984, p. 248).

In the US, Ramey found that only 13 per cent of families corresponded to the 'nuclear family model' of father as sole breadwinner with mother at home rearing the children (1978). There have been few estimates since but in 1989, Ricketts and Achtenberg claimed that only 7 per cent of the US population lived in such a situation.

At first sight it may appear that 'the nuclear family' has declined rapidly in the last few years. This is probably because most scholars feel comfortable with the idea that there has been a rapid change rather than with the point that 'the family' may never have existed. The Rapoports, in acknowledging a 'lag between behaviour and the appropriate conceptual models' (Rapoport *et al.* 1977, p. 129), suggested that behaviour had changed fairly recently. Perhaps clearest is Peter Laslett's argument that, 'there is now no single British family' (Laslett, 1982, p. xii) after asserting that, 'This [nuclear family model] had prevailed almost universally in our country until the 1950s' (p. xi). It is vital to note that evidence for the existence of 'the nuclear family' was not produced by those promoting these ideas. The point is not so much whether 'the family' once existed, but rather how can sociologists have ever believed that there existed a single form of 'the family'.

> How clearly does an 'ideal type' model of 'the family' have to match reality to be useful?

Work on the 1981 Census suggested that less than 2 per cent of families corresponded to the model of 'the nuclear family'. This takes no account of chronic illness, stage of childrearing, behavioural problems and other similar items mentioned in the preceding section (see Bernardes, 1986b). With increasing family diversity, it seems certain that this percentage has declined to a negligible proportion in the 1990s.

A great deal of the 1991 UK Census was published by 1994 but very little material relates directly to defined 'families'; future tables may include the relevant material. There were 21,897,322 households in the UK in 1991; some 1,503,888 of these households contained one adult male and one adult female with between one and three dependent children where only one of the adults was in employment. This suggests that only 14.6 per cent of households contained this particular household form. This proportion will include, however, unmarried adults, unrelated adults and children, chronically sick persons (some 8 per cent of all age groups), and all the other variations that can be thought of. It seems very likely indeed that the proportion of households matching a stricter definition of 'the nuclear family' will be a small fraction of 1 per cent (see details of the 1991 Census in OPCS 1992a, 1992b). Putting the point most simply, even the roughest analysis suggests that the nuclear family is so rare as to render the whole idea of the nuclear family entirely redundant.

Are all families 'nuclear' for a brief period?

One common response is to argue that whilst 'the nuclear family' may not be in the majority at a particular moment in time, it is none the less a 'stage' through which all families must pass. In this argument, both the Left and Right re-assert the central importance of the model of 'the family' as a key focus of analysis.

Whilst it does seem likely that very many do pass through a stage in which there are two adults and one or two children this does not represent a 'common experience'. Clearly, the experience of poor Black parents with learning difficulties will be rather different to that of wealthy aristocratic parents. When you begin to appreciate the enormous richness and diversity of life, especially by way of social class, gender or ethnicity, then, clearly, people come to that 'stage' by a wide variety of different routes. Similarly, it is also clear that the outcomes of that 'stage' are extremely varied, ranging from abuse and divorce to different 'types' of marriage. In view of this, it seems extremely unlikely that the superficial appearance of there being two adults and two children tells us anything at all about what actually goes on in that 'stage'.

Second, there is a more basic conceptual flaw that reflects rather outdated understandings in sociology. The mistake is to believe that people have similar experiences in a given situation. This is simply not true, women after childbirth face similar tasks and challenges but their experiences are very varied and diverse indeed. Some will be rich, some poor, some experience postnatal depression, others may be almost euphoric.

Pick a 'family event' (such as childbirth or a child's first day at school) and explore how differently people experienced this.

Variation and diversity in families

Knowledge about the extent of variation and diversity in family forms has existed for some time. In exploring a 'Framework for Family Studies', Weeks summarises the efforts of Rapoport and Rapoport to identify five types of diversity (see Weeks, 1986; Rapoport and Rapoport, 1982):

1   Organisational Diversity in Families. Primarily a result of diverse patterns of internal domestic labour or patterns of working outside the family home. This form of diversity will be influenced by the extent and nature of unpaid work within a family.
2   Cultural Diversity in Families. There are very clear, but often completely neglected, variations in behaviours, beliefs and practices as a result of culture, ethnicity, political and religious affiliations. It is important to realise that there may be very wide variations within White groups just as there are wide variations within and between a wide range of 'non-White' groups.
3   Social Class Diversity in Families. There are obvious variations resulting from marked differences in the availability of material and social resources. These will range from simply having enough food to attitudes towards whether infants should be reared by their mothers or paid

'nannies', or whether children should or should not be sent away to boarding schools.

4   Cohort Diversity in Families. It is clear that particular historical periods mean that people born within that period will have quite different experiences to those born in different periods. The obvious cases are periods of war and civil disruption (such as the 'Troubles' in Northern Ireland) and, less clear, historically located events across Europe such as the rise in divorce, single parenthood and cohabitation.

5   Family Life Course Diversity. This form recognises how life changes dramatically with events in the course of life, for example, having children, whether a child is a baby or teenager.

It is vital to recognise that the five forms of diversity taken together mean that it is extremely unlikely that families will pass through 'essentially similar' phases. A special edition of the *Journal of Family Issues* (1995) makes it clear that cultural diversity results in members of different cultures having more or less entirely different experiences of the society in which they appear to 'live together'. Ingoldsby and Smith (1995) have presented some sense of the enormous range of variation and diversity in *Families in Multicultural Perspective* which, whilst American in orientation, surveys history, cross-national and ethnic variation in terms of kinship, mate selection, household labour, gender and material wealth (to identify but a few variables). In the UK, for example, it is not likely that a poor African-Caribbean couple having their first child have the same experiences as a wealthy public-school educated couple. Similarly, within similar levels of wealth and resources, it is unlikely that a dual-working nominally Christian couple will have the same experiences as a male-breadwinner orthodox Jewish couple.

At a more detailed level there are many things that make families special: wealth, housing, transport, poverty, age, death, disability, unemployment, ethnicity, education, paid work, whether both parents work, number of children, twins or multiple births. Are babies different to toddlers or teenagers? Are all 'couples' much the same or do they merely appear much the same until they 'split up'? Are all husbands breadwinners? Are all wives homemakers? Are we all always fit and healthy? Does sickness or disability make a difference? Do parents always love each other and their children? Do children always 'get on with' their parents or other children in their family? Do we all have similar hopes, ideals and interests? Are we all decently non-violent? What about domestic murder, child abuse and child sexual abuse? What about the shared private worlds of sexual behaviour or the even more private individual worlds of innermost thoughts, beliefs and secrets.

> Identify the changes caring for a housebound person would make to your own life.

In the face of this complexity, it is easy to avoid serious research and rely on popular stereotypes of 'the family'. When looked at in detail, family lives are enormously varied and diverse. When you begin to consider this, it is clear that 'the nuclear family' does not exist except as a powerful image in the minds of most people. For a serious study, the important thing about families is how different they all are, not how they all match a model of 'the family'.

In one view, the extent of variation and diversity might appear to invalidate the idea of Family Studies, suggesting the need to focus upon, say, social class or culture. This approach, however, is that of traditional sociology which has led to the relegation of the importance of family life.

In exploring 'Family Life and Racial and Ethnic Diversity', Sjoberg *et al.* (1995) review the impact of large scale bureaucracies upon families and argue that variation and diversity present a major theoretical challenge for Family Studies. Variation and diversity suggest the urgent need for the development of a scientific academic base from which to begin to understand the enormously complex origins of many contemporary 'family problems'. Many of these problems cannot be properly understood using the focus of class or culture but come into focus when using the framework of family living as a whole area. For example, it has been easy for many groups to label single parent or Black families as somehow deviant from the point of view of dominant White culture. Only when you begin to look in terms of widespread variation and diversity does the 'normality' of single parenthood and the efforts of Black people to assert a cultural identity become clear.

International comparisons and developments

It is very easy indeed for a member of one society to believe that other societies are much the same. Much of the literature available on family living is American and completely ignores Europe. Similarly, much of the work undertaken on aspects of family life in the UK completely ignores other member states of the European Union (see Bernardes, 1991). This was most clearly brought home to me when two visiting American scholars asked where the Department of Family Studies was located in my university; it had simply not occurred to them that such departments might not exist in the UK. Conversely, it is extremely important for those in the UK to consider the possibility that other societies may 'do things differently'. In the case of the location and importance of studying family life, we must recognise that things are very different in other societies.

Nearly all European states, the USA, Australia and many other countries have some form of Family Studies in schools and universities. The term 'Family Studies' has very rarely been used in the UK; two exceptions are a project by the British Library and the University of Southampton that initiated a Panel Review on Family Studies in 1983, reporting in 1986 (see Weeks, 1986), and a recent textbook by Morgan (see Morgan, 1996). Despite this effort, there are no academic departments of Family Studies, no government ministries or departments of family life. There are no journals of family life and no national bodies.

In the USA, the National Council on Family Relations (NCFR) holds annual conferences attracting thousands of delegates. European conferences on family life have been supported by the Council of Europe, the European Commission and the United Nations. The work of The Confederation of Family Organisations in the European Community (COFACE) has been important in stimulating developments within the European Commission (see COFACE, 1987, 1989). The 1989 'Council of Ministers Responsible for Family Affairs' led to the setting up of the European Family Policy Observatory that reports annually. In these debates, the UK Government has no representative from a 'Ministry of the Family' to despatch. Whilst some UK academics may attend, they tend to represent particular areas of expertise (such as childhood or fatherhood) rather than a wide ranging concern with family living.

> Why isn't family life at the heart of all UK Government policy?

There is a clear sense in which the European Union nations, the USA and Australia are prepared to think seriously about family life in public debate and policy-making. Britain, on the other hand, resists radical ideas. Rodger argues that, 'British social policy compares unfavourably with other European countries because it lacks an explicit family policy' (1995, p. 5); for Rodger, this lack of family policy suggests that much social policy constitutes a form of moral regulation rather than coherent policies which support and enhance families. This view is supported by the tendency to over-react to evidence that comes to public attention when serious problems (child sexual abuse) or changes (divorce and single parenthood) have already occurred. No amount of public debate can resolve these problems; rather our attitude to, and commitment to, family life must change.

Contemporary trends in families

Whilst the whole of this book is largely about the rich variation and diversity of contemporary family trends, it is useful to draw together a selection of the key trends that preoccupy commentators or perhaps suggest significant challenges of modern societies. Bjornberg notes an emerging pattern throughout Europe involving 'sinking birth-rates; later marriages; older parental age for the birth of the first child; fewer children per family unit; and a growing rate of cohabitation, divorce and of single parenthood' (1992b, p. 2). There are also rising numbers of births outside marriage and increasing rates of female paid work. The Commission on Social Justice argued that this transformation of domestic relationships had created three new sets of demands:

> For families, a renegotiation of the relationships between mothers, fathers and children. For employers, new demands for flexible work patterns, support for child care and other measures to accommodate caring work within the home. For the government, a fundamental review of the social security system, child care and social services.
>
> (1994, p. 79)

Population

The population is ageing and household size is decreasing to a European Union average of 2.6 persons in 1991 (Eurostat, 1995). In the past twenty-five years, European nations have moved from situations of population growth to levels below replacement level, that is, where not enough babies are born to keep the total population size stable. In 1970, only Denmark had a birth rate below replacement level; by 1993 the European fertility rate had dropped to 1.44 children per woman. Total fertility rates in both Spain and Italy (traditionally high fertility countries) have dropped below 1.3 children per woman; Italy has now dropped to 1.21, probably the lowest fertility rate in the World (Eurostat, 1995). Britain stands at 1.8 children per woman, only Ireland exceeds 2.00 in the European Community (McGlone and Cronin, 1994; Eurostat, 1995). This means that most of Europe is now on or below population replacement levels.

Cohabitation

Buck and Scott's analysis of UK households reveals that whilst cross sectional work tends to suggest gradual changes in household composition, the British

Household Panel Surveys 'show high levels of gross change' (1994, p. 61). The clearest and most dramatic change relates to levels of cohabitation.

The United Kingdom is second only to Denmark in cohabitation rates. In Denmark the number of cohabitations may exceed marriages this century (Kiernan and Wicks, 1990; COFACE, 1987). In 1994-5, 23 per cent of un-married women aged between 16 and 49 years were cohabiting in the UK (Central Statistical Office, 1996). Recent estimates by Buck and Scott suggest that more than 70 per cent of newly formed couple relationships involved cohabitation rather than legal marriage. In looking at these couples at a later date, it was clear that large numbers had subsequently married (1994, p. 61).

Marriage

Marriage is a major turning point in the lives of most members of Western societies. Even when couples have previously cohabited, with their marital partners or others, the event of marriage holds great symbolic significance in the wider society. In legislating for the form and nature of marriage, society expresses clear views about sex and sexuality. In virtually all Western societies, marriage can only be contracted between men and women and thereby conveys an overwhelmingly heterosexist image. In the same vein, marriage in Western societies is monogamous with polygamy being illegal, despite its legal acceptance in many other societies.

Marriage rates in the UK stand at 5.9 per 1,000 population in 1993 compared to 7.1 in 1981; the European Union average was 6.1 in 1981 and 5.3 in 1993. In the UK, the median age at first marriage has increased – for women from 21.4 years in 1971 to 26 years in 1994–5 when the male median age was 28 years (OPCS, 1994; Central Statistical Office, 1996). Teenage marriages have declined significantly from 32.5 per cent of females under 20 years marrying in 1966 to 6 per cent in 1993 (OPCS, 1994; Central Statistical Office, 1996).

Childbearing

A feature of the 1980s related to cohabitation is the separation of marriage and childbearing. The proportion of children born outside marriage in the UK has increased dramatically from 12 per cent in 1980 to over 30 per cent in 1992 compared to a European Union average of 20 per cent (Eurostat, 1995). In 1987, 68 per cent of such births were registered by both parents; 7 out of 10 of these were registered as living at the same address (i.e., cohabiting). Again Denmark is the exception in the European Union with nearly 40 per cent of births outside marriage; the UK is similar to France in exceeding the European Union average (Kiernan and Wicks, 1990; COFACE, 1987).

Most children (even in Denmark) are still born to women in their first marriage; 70 per cent of children were born to women in their first marriage in the UK in 1987. In 1985, 78 per cent of United Kingdom children under 16 were living with both natural parents who were legally married to one another compared to 83 per cent in 1979 (Kiernan and Wicks, 1990; COFACE, 1987).

Divorce and re-marriage

One of the major shifts in modern Western societies is the instability of marriage. In previous centuries it was simply not possible for the majority to contemplate divorce. This does not mean that their marriages were some-how more stable or lasting, simply that they did not divorce and thus have the opportunity to re-marry. Paradoxically, the availability of divorce has meant that there are now more marriages then ever before, many individuals marry-ing more than once in their lives.

Divorce rates in the UK have risen since 1981 from 2.8 per 1,000 population to 3.1 per 1,000 population in 1993 compared to a European Union average of 1.5 per 1,000 population in 1981 and 1.7 per 1,000 population in 1993 (Central Statistical Office, 1996). In the 1980s about 150,000 couples a year divorced; each year around 150,000 children under 16 have parents who divorce. If the divorce rates of the mid-1980s continue, then 37 per cent of marriages are likely to end in divorce: one in five children will experience a parental divorce by age 16 years (Central Statistical Office, 1994).

Whilst the UK closely resembles the USA in divorce, it is also not too different from other European Countries: Denmark has a high rate but Germany and France are close behind. In the UK over half of men and women who divorce are likely to re-marry within five years. By 1991, 36 per cent of all marriages involved re-marriage for one or both partners. A substantial number of women bearing children alone will later marry (Kiernan and Wicks, 1990; COFACE, 1987).

Stepfamilies

One of the consequences of high divorce rates is that of the creation of increasing numbers of stepfamilies that may involve either cohabitation or re-marriage. Utting estimates that in 1991 there were nearly half a million stepfamilies in Great Britain which included 800,000 stepchildren and a further 300,000 children born to both parents (Utting, 1995, pp. 23–4). Given continuing trends, it is estimated that 1 in 15 children will live in a cohabiting stepfamily before their sixteenth birthday whilst 1 in 18 will live in a married stepfamily before their sixteenth birthday and, of course, many children will experience both situations.

Single parents

A major issue that receives regular public attention is that of single parenthood, both as a result of divorce and as a result of unmarried pregnancy. Many of the ills of society, especially those related to delinquency, are associated with single parents. On the other hand, especially in the UK, there is overwhelming evidence that single parents are amongst the poorest of families and struggle to rear their children as best as they can.

In 1994–5, 22 per cent of all families with dependent children in the UK were lone parent families, compared with 7 per cent in 1972 (Central Statistical Office, 1996). In the European Union, the UK has one of the highest proportions of lone parent families, second only to Denmark (Kiernan and Wicks, 1990; COFACE, 1987; Roll, 1992). But what distinguishes the UK from Denmark is the level of unemployment of single mothers; of those single mothers with children under 4 years of age, 50 per cent worked full time and 17 per cent part time in Denmark compared to 7 per cent full time and 10 per cent part time in the UK (Lewis, 1993, p. 11).

Family poverty

In a 1993 conference paper, Stitt and Grant quoted Rowntree himself (writing in 1901): 'That in this land of abounding wealth, during a time of perhaps un-exampled prosperity, [so many people] are living in poverty is a fact which may well cause great searching of heart' (1993, p. 25). Stitt and Grant find that 'in Britain in the 1990s, more people are living in absolute poverty than at any other time over the last 100 years'. In terms of Primary Food Poverty (the percentage of families with children spending less than the estimate of minimum weekly food needs) across Europe, Grant and Stitt (1994, p. 11) found 30 per cent in the UK compared to 20 per cent in Ireland, 20 per cent in Spain, 15 per cent in Germany and 13 per cent in Belgium.

In 1994, Kempson *et al.* explored *Hard Times? How Poor Families Make Ends Meet.* Not surprisingly, this detailed study found that very many families face a continual struggle to make ends meet. This is seen in continual dilemmas and attempts to 'juggle' limited budgets to provide food, housing, heating, clothing and other necessities; the resulting stress has negative impacts upon the physical and mental health of all members of poor families.

Single parent families feature significantly among poor families. Among the various legislation to support single parent families, the UK Child Support Act of 1993 set up the Child Support Agency to, among other things, pursue absent fathers for payment of child maintenance. This Act has proven to be highly controversial and Clarke *et al.* found that, 'A year after the implementation of the Child Support Act, it was very difficult to find any evidence of benefits – either financial or emotional – to the children concerned' (1994, p. 112). This is largely due to the fact that whatever maintenance is obtained is lost from income maintenance payments; Clarke *et al.* go further to point out that, 'a number of children could anticipate being worse off financially, if their fathers were no longer able to afford the informal financial help they had been giving because of having to pay more maintenance through the Child Support Agency' (ibid.).

In exploring the way in which poverty effects children, Kumar argues that:

the number of children living in families with incomes below 50% of the average increased from 1.4 million to 3.9 million between 1979 and 1991 ... it is now incontrovertible that many families with children were not merely worse off in real terms but absolutely as well.

(1993, p. xxi)

Social class

Social class is a broad concept usually taken to mean differences between social groups based largely upon material wealth and power. Whilst social class is usually judged by the occupation of the male breadwinner, families are the common unit of analysis since the incomes of any working individuals generally determine how well all family members live (see Morgan, 1996, pp. 46–9). Whilst critical of the way in which 'most models of class use occupation as the basis for beginning classification' (1996, p. 52), Morgan is quite clear that social class is a key feature in distinguishing families from one another.

There are many studies of social class that emphasise differing family behaviours by way of social class or changing behaviours within social classes related to changing external circumstances. Perhaps the best known studies are those of Willmott and Young in the 1950s and 1960s (see Young and Willmott, 1957 and Willmott and Young, 1960). One long standing theme in British sociology has been movements between social classes, in which families are usually seen as the groups that 'move' from one class to another (see Pawson, 1993). One key aspect of all these debates has been the way in which the social class of a family is usually defined in terms of the male occupation; this has attracted a great deal of debate and criticism from feminist researchers as summarised by Roberts (1993).

In terms of trends, the major debate in recent years has been centred on whether or not there is an emerging 'underclass', usually taken to mean families which are in some sense disconnected from the world of work and much of the rest of society and enmeshed in poverty and 'deviant' behaviours such as delinquency or single parenthood (see Morgan, 1996, pp. 60–1). It is far from easy to give hard and fast figures about social classes and their changing composition but it does seem clear that there are major trends related to marriage patterns, divorce, single parenthood and consequent impacts upon the income and wealth of many millions of households in the UK. Whilst social class is a feature of many European societies, it is extremely difficult to compare the nature of social classes for historical and cultural reasons.

Families and work

Paid work

Another very popular concern in the UK is with working women, most especially working mothers. The UK has one of the higher proportions of paid working mothers in Europe but, on closer examination turns out to have quite low levels of mothers in full-time paid work. Female economic activity rates increased from 10 per cent of married women in 1931 to 51 per cent by 1994–5 (Central Statistical Office, 1996). Over half (52 per cent) of married couples with children have partners who are both in paid work.

The majority of mothers of very young children do not take up paid work in the UK and the majority of those with school-age children have part-time or flexible-shift paid work. In discussing a number of social problems, many commentators have blamed mothers who work for somehow neglecting their children. This is a rather odd criticism in a society that overwhelmingly favours paid work above unpaid work and places many families in the situation where both partners need to work to achieve a bearable standard of living.

Unpaid work

Most Western societies emphasise paid work as being much more important than unpaid work. Many of the tasks associated with successfully rearing a family are the products of unpaid work. Despite the rise of female economic activity, most household tasks (for example, cooking, cleaning and washing) are still done by the woman even when she takes up paid work. In the UK, recent shifts in welfare policy, especially those relating to community care, have increased the burden upon unpaid carers (Kiernan and Wicks, 1990).

Ageing population

One of the remarkable successes of Western industrial society is that of the general improvement of health. More people survive adulthood, especially women surviving childbirth, and both sexes are surviving serious ailments because of modern medicine. One key issue, often seen as a demographic problem or even as a 'demographic time bomb', is the relatively recent rise in the number of people surviving into old age. Various studies have suggested that this trend will continue into the future creating a very large number of elderly people. There has been an increasing number of three- and four-generation families. In the UK, the number of people aged over 85 will double between 1981 and 2001, from half a million to over 1 million. There are 6 million family carers of elderly or disabled people (Kiernan and Wicks, 1990, p. 22). Most old people have one or more living children, the majority have grandchildren and surviving siblings.

In a materially based society, it is usually the simplest and crudest issue about later-life families that preoccupies us: how can we support so many economically inactive people? The key indicator is usually identified as the 'dependency ratio', or the number of economically active people (those in paid work) in comparison to the economically inactive (those in unpaid work, children, the unemployed, those sick and disabled, the elderly).

Multi-racial societies

The UK contains distinctive multi-cultural communities including White races (European immigrants and refugees), a range of Oriental and Asian peoples (direct from the Indian Sub-Continent or arriving through expulsion from Commonwealth nations in Africa), and a range of African-Caribbean and African peoples. Recent estimates put the 'non-White' population at around 6 per cent of the UK population or well over three million people. Particular regions, such as the South East (9.9 per cent), the West Midlands (8.2 per cent) and Greater London (20.2 per cent) had far higher proportions of non-White ethnic groups in 1991. Given this richness and history, it is indicative of widespread racism until recent times that there are surprisingly few studies of what might be loosely called 'ethnic family life'.

We are still very much at the stage of identifying and confronting the myths and prejudices built into common racist assumptions about African-

Caribbean or Asian families as is shown most clearly in the study *Young Mothers* by Anne Phoenix (1991). Several researchers have echoed American work in identifying teenage single motherhood as a 'Black problem', although American research has suggested that the key variable is teenage motherhood rather than ethnicity. In the UK, Phoenix has challenged the idea that 'there are particular cultural values among Black "West Indian" women which predispose them to become mothers in their teenage years' (1991, p. 16). It seems much more likely that teenage motherhood is most common amongst the poorest and most disadvantaged. Black teenage motherhood, then, seems to reflect racism and inequality in society at large rather than particular cultural values.

In 1995, Ingoldsby and Smith presented an American model of how to go about the study of *Families in Multicultural Perspective*. Aimed at the American discipline of Family Studies in high schools and universities, this text none the less includes valuable material about families across the world in historical context, issues around comparative method and studies of families in various countries. In the UK, Elliot devotes an entire chapter to the issue of 'Ethnic Differentiation, Gender and Family Life' noting that 'the diversification of ways of life associated with the development of non-European communities in Britain has been accompanied, not by the celebration of diversity, but by intense anxiety and conflicts' (1996, p. 73). Ingoldsby and Smith make clear that 'understanding differences in cultures, societies, and families helps to broaden and deepen our knowledge and appreciation of all families, and can also help us to learn more about our own societies' (1995, p. xi); it is to be hoped that such an approach might also reduce intolerance and conflict.

Convergence to diversity

Rapoport argued that we are seeing the acceptance of a 'Diversity Model' throughout Europe, including Britain. 'With the diversity model, each particular family form – conventional, dual worker, single-parent, reconstituted, etc. – is seen as providing the structure of a lifestyle' (Rapoport, 1989, p. 60). Such an argument is perhaps over optimistic in the context of the UK where public debate still rages around the sanctity of 'the family'.

In the 1993 edition of the American journal, *Family Relations*, devoted to the issue of family diversity, Fine laid down a series of arguments about family diversity. Demographic changes make increasing family diversity inevitable and it is vital to grasp that there is great diversity within apparently single types of families. There are many different kinds of single parent families ranging from UK royalty to the poorest Black disabled single mother. Studying diverse families demonstrates how adaptable family living is and how sensitive families are to popular images and definitions. In general, Fine argues that the concepts and techniques developed by White, English speaking academics may not be applicable to other cultures even within Western societies.

Why study family lives?

In 1996, Morgan's book entitled *Family Connections: An Introduction to Family Studies* was the first UK book to identify Family Studies. Towards the end of a wide ranging survey of work, stratification, gender, care, the body, time and space, food, and home, Morgan clearly endorses the importance of the study of family lives. Morgan, however, sees Family Studies as having two possible forms of development: either as a discrete topic area or as a means to 'see a family dimension in all or most other areas of social inquiry' (1996, p. 186). Whilst certainly sympathetic with Morgan's position, especially that which suggests we focus upon 'Family Practices', it does seem clear to me that more progress is likely to be achieved if an attempt is made to build a discrete topic area. This is necessary in my view, not so much for academic coherence (although this is an issue) but in terms of public profile. Only this is likely to generate the sort of changes by which family issues will come to be taken more seriously by academic, public and political parties alike. There is a wide range of contemporary family trends that occupy considerable energy in the form of public debate and government action. More to the point, these trends relate to activities that the vast majority of us are likely to engage in during our lives. The need to bring together these concerns is an obvious and potentially fruitful means of addressing a number of contemporary social problems.

Ask ten people if it is important to study family lives.

An emphasis upon 'the nuclear family' coincides very well with emphases upon heterosexuality, monogamy, individualism, free market policies and minimal government. This model rejects as abnormal, physical and sexual violence. Recent evidence suggests that such abuse is far more widespread than previously thought; it seems increasingly probable that such abuse is part of the 'ordinary routine' of many families. This model also denies men and women genuinely equal places in the economic, political and cultural spheres, not to mention family life.

'Family life' is much more important than any social science textbook, political tract or religious faith suggests. I want to argue here that 'family life' is the key to understanding human society. More than this, understanding 'family life' is the key to improving society, creating a just and decent world, ensuring a more certain and more peaceful future.

Most of what we 'know' about 'family life' is an illusion. This leaves us deeply ignorant about what is the most important aspect of our lives. Society can only generate sound social policies on the basis of accurate knowledge about child care, the context of crime, the care of the sick or whatever else. With better knowledge about what 'families' actually do (and what they cannot do), we may be able to better support 'families'. Rather than the traditional view of agencies doing things to and for families, the exact reverse may be possible. With a detailed understanding of 'family lives', people may begin to realise that they do not have to be self-sufficient. We can all give and receive support with no loss of standing in the community. The acceptance that we all 'have problems' in 'family lives' may enable us all to live better and more fulfilled lives.

> List three areas in which popular concerns suggest the need for modern families to 'do better'.

A detailed understanding of the nature of 'family living' may help the service professions: police, social work, health, law, teaching. Rather than deliver services to families, we may encourage families to help their own members and members of other families. Exposing the criminal to the victim is a recent idea but it could be taken further. We could give criminals a clear sense of the harm they do by exposing them to the families of victims and of other criminals. Similarly, all parents have a vast store of working practice they had to gather afresh. Family life education in schools could ease or even avoid many of the crises of confidence all parents experience.

The development of Family Studies, then, is a task of some urgency. Not only do we need to catch up with many nations with which we compare ourselves but we also need to make up for the neglect of family life. Studying family lives is also much more difficult than generally believed. The development of Family Studies, then, is a formidable task and a potentially invaluable one.

Suggested reading

Gittins, D. 1993 (Second edition): *The Family in Question – Changing Households and Familiar Ideologies*. Basingstoke: Macmillan.

Morgan, D. H. J. 1996: *Family Connections: An Introduction to Family Studies*. Oxford: Polity.

Muncie, J. *et al.* 1995: *Understanding the Family*. London: Sage.
Rapoport, R. N. *et al.* (eds) 1982: *Families in Britain*. London: Routledge and
    Kegan Paul.

Chapter 2

Theorising
family lives

Introduction

Most of us experience family living in a variety of ways for most or all of our lives. In view of this, it would be reasonable to expect the social sciences to take theoretical issues around family lives as the major preoccupation. In fact, family living is absent from many of the social sciences; even in sociology, the study of family living is far from a central concern. How can it be that something so central to all our lives, so powerful in driving our hopes and ambitions, is banished to the sidelines?

Most sociologists, and especially those studying family lives, have failed to recognise that their task is far more demanding than any other discipline. The idea of 'the family' is so powerful that it supports a wide ranging family ideology. This family ideology presents to us images of what is 'right and proper' in family life and what is somehow 'wrong'. Because of the nature of family ideology, sociologists have also failed to recognise a considerable number of practical and theoretical difficulties facing any who wish to study family lives.

The difficulty of theorising families

As a scholar and teacher, I spend regular sessions each year explaining to students that 'the family' does not exist and all those things we think of as 'new problems' have existed for centuries or longer. Dual-worker families are probably the norm throughout history and throughout the contemporary world. Single parent families have always been common in periods of industrial development. Polygamy as an ideal or reality has probably been far more common throughout human history than monogamy; polygamy is still a major form of partnering across the world. Abuse and violence between intimates are as old as any human mythology.

For far too long, lay people and social scientists themselves have allowed to flourish the idea that understanding society is easy. I have never accepted this. When you look at the differences and similarities between children, partners and parents, it is rather like watching millions of dice (so beloved of statisticians). Not only do the dice give untold numbers of different results but they are different sizes, colours, weights and have different systems of numbering.

List differences and similarities in family backgrounds and statuses between yourself and four other people.

We must recognise that society is, by definition, much more difficult to understand than any natural scientific topic. The objects of natural scientific enquiry do not much care what the scientists think, and only sometimes respond to what they might do. On the other hand, ordinary people are likely to select and seize upon popular accounts of what some family sociologists and others think and say about family living; for example, debates about divorce, single parenthood, or children and television watching. This can most obviously be seen in media images and in the pronouncements of moral and political leaders on divorce, violence, parenting and so on (see Durham, 1991).

Studying human societies involves formidable difficulties of accurate measurement, as in the natural sciences. When you add language, creativity, the ability to shape the environment with tools, then, clearly, human societies are far more complex than any natural scientific phenomenon.

It is important, then, to realise that the challenge of theorising family living is considerable. Our subjects are far less predictable than natural scientific phenomena, interact with our analyses and may even change their behaviour according to what we say. Within the social sciences, it is likely that studying family lives is quite simply the most challenging topic because it is a topic so close to us all and deeply intertwined with our own sense of self.

Why have theory?

In exploring what is meant by family theory, Smith argues that:

> Family theories structure how we think about families, what we observe, how we interpret this knowledge, and how we use the information in programs and policies that affect family life. Consequently, theories have a profound effect on what we know about families.
>
> (1995, p. 8)

Whilst a clear and simple point, it is surprising that the potential difficulties of family theories have rarely been explored. In greater detail, the need for theoretical development arises for two reasons.

First, the nature of most current theorising is extremely limited. Traditional models of 'the family', for example, omit reference to stress, strain and abuse as part of everyday family lives. If these negative aspects are included at all, they tend to be seen as 'problems'. In this way both divorce and single parenthood are seen as problems whereas they may be, for some of those involved, solutions to intolerable situations.

Second, we need to develop a means to penetrate everyday common-sense or popular stereotypes. Because family living is so much part of all our lives, we tend to believe that we somehow 'know something' about the topic. This belief is perfectly adequate for our daily living, in which we make a wide range of assumptions about the nature of 'the family' to get on with our own lives. In the scientific study of family living, however, relying on our untested common sense is simply not acceptable. At various times, authority figures have denied the possibility of violence or abuse in marriage, marital rape, or the abuse of men and children by women.

Cheal suggests that theoretical approaches may help us achieve five things (see Cheal, 1991, p. 19):

1   Theoretical approaches provide us with concepts that we can use to analyse and communicate our observations. The concept of 'the family' has 'shaped' the way we see family life. The need now is to develop alternative concepts.
2   Theoretical approaches suggest questions to ask. Theoretical approaches reveal things previously 'hidden' from view. The emphasis upon 'the family' has focused upon questions about the sexual division of paid and unpaid work and the 'normality' of a particular structure. This has left a great deal of family living hidden from view, such as ordinary misery, abuse, or marital rape.

3   Theoretical approaches provide ways to answer questions with orienting assumptions and guides to observation. The traditional notion of 'the family' justifies female inferiority, especially in paid work; it has also justified men taking remarkably little part in childrearing and unpaid labour. Traditional work has also emphasised the way children are socialised by their parents and has neglected the impact children have upon parents.

4   Theoretical approaches help us interpret. Theoretical approaches should clarify events, producing a sense of order, structure or meaning. This should permit us to 'see' more clearly. This needs to be handled very carefully; it is tempting to believe that understanding is related to developing a clear and complete 'explanation', such as the model of 'the nuclear family'. It seems extremely unlikely that such a limited and simple model can ever do justice to the enormous variation and diversity of everyday family living. A theoretical approach that helps us to interpret should yield a sense of the enormous richness and complexity of family living.

5   Theoretical approaches involve value judgements as to the purpose and application of social scientific knowledge. This is an important claim by Cheal and one that is rarely taken seriously by those studying family life. Because the idea of 'the family' is so superficially 'true' and 'obvious', few have realised that adopting this model involves taking very clear value stances. The value stances involved tend to be sexist, racist, heterosexist (favour heterosexuals over homosexuals), and ableist (favour those who are not sick or impaired), to mention but a few.

The task of theoretical development, then, has several major aims. First will be the critical examination of traditional theorising and the rejection of the value of the simplistic model of 'the family'. Second, we need a means by which to penetrate everyday common sense about family lives and begin to explore what families are really like. Third, to achieve these two goals, some alternative means of understanding family lives is called for.

Theoretical difficulties: family ideology

The main problem in theorising family life is that of family ideology. It is surprising in many ways that so many sociologists have failed to recognise the depth and power of family ideology. The nature of the difficulty presented by family ideology can be seen in the way in which 'the family' is located in sociological theorising. Notions of 'the family' are embedded in accounts of the biological bases of sexual inequality, explanations of the process of industrial change involving the shift from 'extended' to 'nuclear family' types. Given this centrality, it is possible that critical re-evaluations of 'the family' have been largely unthinkable on the part of those whose careers are based in the validity of such theorising.

Mannheim distinguished two levels of ideology, the 'particular' and the 'total'. In the 'particular' level of ideology Mannheim identified the kinds of views that might be held by an opponent, where it is possible to express scepticism. A more difficult form of ideology, is 'total' ideology by which Mannheim meant the ideas of an era or socio-historical group (Mannheim, 1972, pp. 49–50). At this level it is far more difficult to express scepticism. In referring to this aspect of family ideology, Morgan argues that:

> What ideology does, in effect, is to select from the range of possible ways in which a society might handle the relationships between the biological and the cultural, particularly in the sphere of childbirth and parenthood, and to proclaim the method so selected as the method, as natural and inevitable.
>
> (Morgan, 1985, p. 295)

Try telling friends, loved ones or relatives that 'the family' does not exist. Watch out for some odd reactions.

To this conception of family ideology, a further note from the work of Barrett needs to be added; ideology is not just a set of abstract ideas but is expressed in everyday actions (see Barrett, 1980, p. 30). This is extremely important and is the means by which ideology is reproduced or passed from one person to another and continually reinforced. For example, it is not just that many people think of women as the most appropriate carers of children but rather that we all act on this belief in our daily lives. Men may hesitate or not know how to engage in certain tasks or, in public, men may be discouraged from comforting a lost child whilst a woman may 'naturally' take up this role. Examples of family ideology can be found in a wide range of everyday practices, from images on supermarket products to who picks up dirty laundry (or who drops it in the first place).

Levin noted that, 'If one has a closed and non-problematicised concept of family, certain types of interpretations of social reality are made. . . . The concepts we use decide what we see' (1990, p. 18). Family ideology supported by family sociology, has ensured that we have paid attention to White, middle-class, two parent families. At the same time, family ideology ensures that some aspects of social existence are simply not seen or become invisible. For example, traditional family theorising has ignored the possibility of widespread abuse or unhappiness in 'the family'.

As Dalley notes, 'As an ideological construct, "the family" – the central focus of familism – underlies all contemporary forms of social organisation of daily living . . . it is the standard against which all forms are measured and, importantly, judged' (1996, pp. 26–7). Family ideology is so deeply embedded in our minds that few people can support the idea that 'the family' does not exist for any length of time. One reason for this may be found in the rather limited nature of previous conceptualisations of 'family ideology'. The best place to 'see' family ideology is in a busy supermarket. Look for gender inequality, age inequality, abuse, stress, anger.

Seeing ourselves as individuals

Family ideology plays a vital role in sustaining an individualistic mode of thought. Ribbens notes how the 'core notions of "the individual" and "the family" can be seen as both polarised and intertwined' (1994, p. 46). 'The family' is regarded as the fundamental 'natural' human grouping. Family ideology involves the development of extreme individualism. Being a 'father' is distinct from being a 'mother'; the roles of 'son' or 'daughter' depend upon age, sex and blood relationships. 'The family' is seen to contain unique positions occupied by individuals. More than this, Dalley argues that family ideology relates to a particular form of 'possessive individualism' (1996, p. 34); this form of individualism is often dangerous for families in that men especially may put their own interests before those of members of their family.

> Try and think of a way in which to rear children so that they do not become so extremely individualistic (see Ribbens, 1994, Chapter 3).

Seeing ourselves as different

Family ideology supports the way in which we all see ourselves as unique and different. The creation of difference, and inequality, rests upon distinguishing individuals by the apparently 'objective facts' of age, gender, biological relationships. It is hardly surprising that many feminists have shown a deep hostility towards 'the family' in that it is an idea that underpins the creation of gender difference and inequality (see, for example, Barrett and McIntosh, 1991).

Try to think of other ways to distinguish people, other than age, sex, or blood relationships. Other important differences of class and race often draw upon assumptions about 'family' in different classes and races.

Deceiving ourselves

Family ideology allows us all to deceive ourselves into believing in our own normality by creating and sustaining an image of 'the family'. This is the danger of the typical model: it is so vague and imprecise as to match everyone. This vagueness means we can each believe that all families are much the same, they are all 'normal', and therefore we do not need to explore everyday 'family living' (see Bernardes, 1985b). Attention is given to the idol of 'the family' as a fixed, apparently objective entity rather than to the complex realities of everyday life. In this way, the concept of 'the family' masks lived experience with an attractive but essentially false idol.

Explore the way in which religions elevate 'the family'.

The social construction of realities

The idea of the social construction of realities within family life is a development of Berger and Kellner's work on 'Marriage and the Construction of Reality'. This develops the point that marriage contributes to our sense of certainty and identity (1971, p. 23). Berger and Kellner focus upon language as the medium by which 'the social' is constructed, especially in generating a shared 'sense of reality'. Among the conversations available to individuals, marriage occupies a 'privileged status among the significant validating relationships for adults in our society' (1971, p. 24).

Summarising this process, Berger and Kellner argue that:

> the process is . . . one in which reality is crystallised, narrowed and stabilised. Ambivalences are converted into certainties. Typifications of self and others become settled. Most generally possibilities become facticities. What is more, the process of transformation remains, most of the time, unapprehended by those who are both its authors and its objects.
>
> (1971, p. 28)

Whilst developed in connection with marriage, these forms of analysis all seem to apply equally well to the relationships between parents and children, especially explaining the way in which children often share (if not agree with) parental understandings of the world.

Is this moment real? How do you know? Who would you ask? Who first taught you about 'realness'?

Backett's study, *Mothers and Fathers: A Study of the Development and Negotiation of Parental Behaviour* emphasises human interaction in 'family life as a mutually created shared reality' (1982: p. 35). Askham's study, *Identity and Stability in Marriage* concludes that 'marriage is in many ways a compromise between stability-maintaining and identity-upholding behaviour, and that on the whole married people perform this balancing act very skilfully' (1984, p. 183). Again, this idea of a mutually shared reality and striking compromises seems to apply equally well to parenting. Our first and most important experiences occur within, and are largely determined by, family life. Subsequent major life experiences – dating, marriage, parenthood – are also largely determined by family ideology.

The way in which realities and ideologies are constructed within family lives effectively mystifies our own lives. Not only are certain practices presented to us as real but alternatives are also closed off as unnatural. For example, the way in which I respond to two particular females and a male is not only a professional and methodological problem, but is also in a very important sense a theoretical problem. To describe and assess those relationships in terms other than 'wife' or 'partner', 'daughter' and 'son' would be to move outside the bounds of conventional reality. Both as an everyday actor and as a sociologist, I cannot avoid my own realities; these people are my wife, son and daughter. The process of the social construction of realities and ideologies that I have experienced has structured my relationships with other human beings in ways that I cannot avoid or deny.

Social structure

The final theoretical aspect of studying family lives concerns the most basic of sociological concerns: social structure. The questions are 'how is society possible?' and 'what enables us to occupy a place within society?' To put the case most simply, 'family life' is the key in constituting social structure and maintaining social order.

Dalley argues that 'the ideology underpinning domestic relations becomes a major organising principle upon which social relations outside the domestic group are based' (1996, p. 27). Within family living the social construction of realities presents to us people, power, inequality, love and obligations as real. This makes our own lives possible and structures our most basic relationships with one another. It is these relationships between us, from a simple nod of acknowledgement to a lifelong marriage, that create social structure.

In structuring our most basic relationships with parents, siblings, lovers, children and kin, 'family living' also serves to instruct us in the conduct of personal relationships. Family ideology structures human relationships along the lines of age and gender and the wider dimensions of power, authority, deference and respect (Bernardes, 1985b, pp. 285–7). In establishing the pattern of parental authority, the idol of 'the family' serves as a basic instruction for many later relationships in education, work, dealings with bureaucracies and citizenship more widely. In linking the creation of gender to family living, Morgan proposes what he calls a simple model in which, he argues: 'Family constructs gender, family obscures gender, family modifies gender; gender constructs family, gender obscures family, gender modifies family' (1996, p. 72). The point to take is that gender and family are inextricably linked and it is difficult for most of us to even think about one without making assumptions about the other.

Try 'breaking the rules' of social structure. Think of treating adults like children, children like adults, mothers like fathers and fathers like mothers. What differences emerge?

Within social structure, there are elements of social control. In critically exploring 'Models of the "underclass family"' including both the fatherless underclass family and the criminal underclass family, Rodger argues that 'the supervision of families considered to be anti-social has been a characteristic of most welfare systems' (1996, p. 133). The demonising of such family forms is one of the main components upon which many modern forms of social control are built. That is to say that the continual exploration of such 'underclass families' is part of a much wider system of social control which influences us all.

There is a further problem to consider. Most accounts of social structure tend to emphasise the way actors recognise one another, interact and even co-operate. There is another side here, that of the 'hidden social structure', usually unspoken of in sociology, of fear and intimidation that keeps us all in certain locations at certain times or leads us to avoid certain locations at certain times. Most conventional accounts of social structure focus upon the explicit and openly understood rather than the implicit and hidden elements of fear and intimidation. It is important to see that the growing recognition of family abuse brings out into the open some aspects of the 'hidden structure', although there remains a good deal still left hidden.

The point to grasp is that family life relates to our own sense of 'who we are' and how we 'fit into' the lives of others. Critical analysis of family lives inevitably involves examining our beliefs about ourselves (which we usually call reality), our beliefs about others (which we often call ideology), our position in society (location) and the nature of society itself (or social structure).

Modernist theorising: 'the family'

The bulk of family theory is North American, especially from the United States itself. Family Sociology and Family Studies in the USA go back at least into the moralistic period of prohibition in the 1920s, through the anti-Communist moralism of the 1950s up to the present day.

Until recently, in the UK there were relatively few texts that drew upon family theory in any depth. The works of David Morgan (1975, 1985 and 1996) stand out as rare and thorough accounts of family theory in the UK although these use largely American source material. A Canadian, Cheal, identifies a post World War II 'convergence' towards the view that 'systematic' and 'scientific' work would eventually generate a single theory of 'the family'. In all this, Cheal locates as a key problem the assumption that there is some 'universal core to family life, which can be given an objective definition as "the family"' (Cheal, 1991, p. 8).

Modernist family sociology has been deeply positivist. Positivism is the traditional, natural science-based approach in the social sciences that assumes the existence of facts, stability and order, which seeks to be objective and detached. Perhaps the easiest way to think of positivism is that it involves the assumption that everything is 'out there'. The world is external, objective, factual and requires technical expertise from us to capture, analyse, describe and explain it. Positivism in the area of family living usually places a heavy emphasis also upon rationality, the idea of a clearly structured 'system' and the idea of the 'purpose' or 'function' of behaviour and institutions within that system.

Within American traditions there is a wide range of what are often called 'Systems Theories' that take as their basic concept the idea that 'the family' is akin to an organic system 'striving to maintain balance as it confronts external pressures' (Smith, 1995, p. 11). 'Family Systems Theory' emerged in America after World War II and draws upon the then-emerging ideas from the physical sciences which view families as a 'set of elements' which interact among themselves and with their environment. A similar view, that of 'Human Ecology

Theory' focuses more upon the interaction with the external environment. A theoretical approach drawing upon both the idea of systems and ecology is that of 'Family Development Theory' which addresses the interactions of family members in relation to their external environment and internal processes (such as childbirth and childrearing) but does so in a distinctive developmental frame that treats family life as involving a predictable time related sequence of events. In the more complex theoretical work in America, a good deal of work around family living has drawn upon wider theoretical positions relating to interaction, exchange and resource theories. It is interesting to note that in a recent wide ranging survey of family theories, Klein and White (1996) shift very little from a traditional modernist stance of taking the existence of 'the family' for granted. Towards the end of their review, the authors do move to using 'families' or 'the family group' instead of 'the family' but the central assumption is still that of an institution which, despite some change and diversity, remains essentially of a uniform type.

Functionalism

The main approach to the analysis of family life has been functionalism which, whilst often criticised in the USA and UK, remains at the heart of most modernist approaches to family life (see Smith, 1995, pp. 9–11). The central idea of 'function' relates to activities necessary for the maintenance of the species, society or social group. These functions include such things as sexual reproduction, economic production, education, religion and recreation and much more, all of which have to be undertaken for a society to achieve a stable existence. This approach was refined by Murdock (1949, p. 10) who emphasised the four key functions of 'the family' as being: sexual, economic, reproductive and educational. Functionalism lays down a general 'systems' theory of human society drawing on the ideas of biological imperatives such as reproduction and the maternal 'instinct'.

The key element of functionalism that has been so attractive is that it provides a very clear value platform. Smith argues that:

> This perspective views society as an organism that strives to resist change and maintain itself in some sort of balance or equilibrium. . . . Stability and order are considered natural and desirable, whereas conflict and disorder are evidence of deviance and dysfunction in the system.
>
> (1995, p. 9)

In this way, functionalism is a remarkably conservative set of ideas that generates clear rules about what is 'functional', and therefore 'good' for society, and what is not 'functional' ('dysfunctional' in the jargon), and is therefore 'bad' for society.

> Explore the 'values' reflected in the idea of the 'function' of female inferiority.

The functionalist view of 'the family' was further developed in the post-war period by Parsons. Parsons identified two essential functions of 'the family' as childhood socialisation and the maintenance of adult personalities (see Morgan, 1975, pp. 26–7, for details). This version of functionalism became the central means of discussing family life in human society. Morgan has said of Parsons: 'It would not be too much of an exaggeration to state that Parsons represents the modern theorist on the nuclear family' (Morgan, 1975, p. 25).

Morgan makes clear that Parsonian functional analysis must be seen as having a 'political dimension' (1975, p. 58). Parsons drew upon popular stereotypes of 'the family' rather than properly collected evidence to create an extremely attractive and relatively simple 'explanation' of society. Identifying key components of a system and listing their 'functions' makes for a very simple model of society. The simplicity of this model means that functional explanations have very rapidly become part of ordinary everyday common sense.

Parsons suggested that 'the nuclear family' of a married couple plus children is best suited to, indeed is a functional prerequisite of, large scale industrialisation (see Morgan, 1975 and 1985). Associated with this model were all sorts of ideal models of behaviour connected with mothering, gender, dependency, emotional and instrumental roles (see Bernardes, 1985b; Durham, 1985; Fitzgerald, 1983).

Despite a common rejection of functionalism by sociological authors, grouping social situations into a single class or 'thing' and attempting to identify the 'purpose' of this thing is still popular in most forms of thought and theorising. Having grown up with the notion of 'the nuclear family' it is extraordinarily difficult not to 'adjust' what we see to fit the idea of 'the family'. Without 'the nuclear family', functionalism would not have been theoretically workable, nor would it have had the same strong appeal to scholars (Bernardes, 1981, p. 13).

Postmodernist theorising: family pathways

The term postmodern family life was developed by Stacey 'to signal the contested, ambivalent, and undecided character of contemporary gender and kinship arrangements' (Stacey, 1990, p. 17), and Morgan has recently concluded that the focus on the issue of family practices gives some sense of the 'flow and fluidity [which] is probably part of a post modernist understanding' (1996, p. 200). Taken together, these seem to capture the image of family living that I wish to explore here along with theoretical strategies developed to study such family lives.

Postmodernism is the area of theoretical work that has developed new tools and approaches that seek to understand family lives in new ways. Perhaps it is most easily thought of as looking at family lives 'in here' (in our heads). Cheal characterises postmodernism as 'an approach that engages in sceptical reflection on the culture of modern society or, in other words, modernity and its dominant world view, namely modernism' (Cheal, 1991, p. 5). In exploring what might be involved in a sociology of postmodern families, Cheal argues that 'Post modernist thought in sociology begins from contemporary experiences of pluralism, disorder and fragmentation, which were not predicted by the modern paradigm of universal reason' (ibid., p. 9). There have been several precursors to postmodern analysis of family living, amongst which the recognition of variation and diversity, Marxist-inspired critiques and feminism have been most important.

There is one simple and central problem with adopting the label of postmodernism in that most characterisations of postmodernity emphasise the notion of 'relativity' in which 'ideas are relational and from a standpoint; there is no final authority for any argument' (Klein and White, 1996, p. 203). This seems to me to be a classic modernist formation in that some final external truth is sought; moreover, it is based in the tradition in which value-freedom is regarded as both possible and central in scientific practice. The problem, is, of course, that critiques of postmodernism can say that a particular position is 'simply your view' and a postmodernist has to admit that this is indeed the case whereas a modernist will seek to assert that something is undeniably 'true' or 'a fact'.

A textbook seeking to introduce and establish Family Studies is hardly the place for an extensive philosophical discussion of theoretical positions. For the present purposes, the author simply wishes to argue that the modernist position that there is some final authority, some final fact or some final truth is itself simply a point of view. What remains important is that views and values are the basis upon which theoretical positions are built and sustained. For my own part, I see this as not only a piece of respectable honesty but as an important tenet of scientific research. Embracing relativity and the importance of values does not harm a theoretical position; on the contrary, such openness strengthens it. In what follows, I seek to make very clear the point that our values influence what we see and that one of the important subjects for a scientific researcher is the nature of such essential values. In the present case, the author's one essential value is, I very much hope, crystal clear – we should elevate the importance of family living in our scheme of things to the point where we seriously consider 'putting families first'.

There have always been a few scholars who have been uncomfortable with modernist family theory. In 1942, the American feminist, Bernard, argued that 'The family as an institution in our culture shows differences as important as those observed in other cultures' (1942, p. 245). In 1958, Bott (a Canadian working in the UK) argued that 'the family' was 'vague and confusing, for its precise empirical referents are seldom made clear' (1964, p. 193). Perhaps the best known protest, though, was from a political scientist, Moore, in 1958. Moore explored the rather optimistic views that suggested that 'social arrangements corresponding rather closely to the modern family may be expected to remain with us indefinitely'. To this, Moore responded that:

> In reading these and similar statements by American sociologists . . . I have the uncomfortable feeling that the authors, despite all their elaborate theories and technical research devices, are doing little more than projecting certain middle-class hopes and ideals onto a refractory reality.
>
> (Moore, 1965, p. 161)

By the mid- to late 1970s there had emerged a minor but significant literature testifying to variation and diversity in family patterns. The point about such literature is that 'traditional theorising' was inevitably inappropriate: many of these apparently new family structures or behaviours (such as divorce, cohabitation and communal families) did not 'fit' neat ideas of function and system. Indeed, unmarried cohabitation and divorce were seen as 'dysfunctional' in that they threatened the stability of marriage and, it was believed, the stability of society. Despite the popularity of cohabitation and the significant rise of divorce, traditional theory has retained the emphasis upon formal marriage rather than the process of partnering.

Variation and diversity

In terms of criticising traditional family theory, the work of the 'Radical Psychoanalytical' school was important (see Morgan, 1975, Chapter 4). Laing's *Politics of the Family* (1976) and Cooper's *Death of the Family* (1971) suggested that 'the family' may not be the best place to rear children in psychological terms. The general theme of Laing and Cooper was that such limited and intense relationships, especially focused around authority and power, were damaging to children. At the same time there were many experiments in lifestyles: communes, alternative marriage styles, the emergence of homosexuality and related lifestyles, and dual careerism.

> List all possible forms of variation and diversity in family lives.

In the USA, the work of Marvin Sussman was central in making popular the idea of variation and diversity in marriage and family styles. Sussman edited two special editions of the *Journal of Marriage and the Family: Non-Traditional Family Forms in the 1970s* in 1973 and 'The Second Experience: Variant Family Forms and Life Styles' in 1975. Each of these two collections brought together the work of scholars working on a wide range of variation and diversity in family living.

In the UK, the Rapoports championed the idea of 'Diversity in Parental Situations' (a chapter title) in 1977 in which they explored divorce, infertility, single parenthood, adoption, fostering, communes, dual-worker families, step-families and families with handicapped children. In 1982, the same authors edited a collection, *Families in Britain*, in which their own contribution explored 'Families in Transition' by way of a wide variety of factors (R. and R. N. Rapoport, 1982). The notion of family diversity is often introduced as a qualification to general debates which are still about 'the family' (for examples, see Kiernan and Wicks, 1990 and Utting, 1995). Dallos and Sapsford have more recently explored a range of varieties of family lives in the UK, including lone parent families, extended families, communes and the kibbutzim, gay and lesbian relationships, and change and the family life cycle (1995, p. 127).

Marxism

From a rather different source comes a range of work that draws upon the inspiration of Marx in a variety of ways. This work tends to be much more rare in America and more common in Europe. In her wide ranging review of American family theory, Smith, for example, does not even mention Marx or Marxism (Smith, 1995). For Marx himself, the key issue was that of social class rather than family or gender but he did make it clear in his essay on 'Private Property and Communism' that gender equality is essential to develop an egalitarian, socialist society (see Sydie, 1987, p. 89). The main work drawn upon in Marxist accounts of family life is *The Origin of the Family, Private Property, and the State* written by Engels using extensive notes made by Marx from Lewis Morgan's 'Ancient Society' published in 1877 (see Sydie, 1987, p. 95). In drawing upon the work of a Victorian anthropologist, it is hardly surprising that some of the ideas are rather general and make assumptions about 'savagery' and 'civilisation' which modern readers might find odd if not simply objectionable.

In terms of more recent debates, a long standing concern of twentieth-century Marxist authors has been that of the 'Domestic Labour Debate', that is, the unpaid work undertaken within families to maintain the ability of workers to supply labour to employers and the economy more generally. Much of this debate has been within rather sterile terms around the idea of 'surplus value', where some commentators have argued that 'domestic labour does not provide surplus value and is not therefore, in the strict Marxist sense, productive labour' (Sydie, 1987, p. 105). More influential has been the work of Zaretsky in his *Capitalism, the Family, and Personal Life* (1976) which focuses upon the separation between 'the economy' and 'the family' (Cheal, 1991, p. 94). Zaretsky explores and rejects the idea that modern welfare states have invaded or replaced 'the family' to argue that the ideal type of family remains autonomous and fulfils major roles in supporting capitalism.

It is important to realise that Marxist work has not generated popular theoretical approaches to the study of family life in America or Europe. What Marxist work has done, however, is to underpin critiques of modern capitalism and supply many radical thinkers with concepts, especially those around inequality, which have been the basis from which to develop new radical approaches, among which are some elements of feminist work on family living. One such example is the recent work of Delphy and Leonard who have developed the idea of 'The Family As An Economic System' (Chapter 5 of Delphy and Leonard, 1992) in which they present an analysis of the Western family which 'focuses upon the social relationships associated with its economic structure: upon the hierarchy of production, distribution and consumption of resources within family-based households and on the hierarchy of transmission of wealth between kin' (1992, p. 105).

Feminism

The single most important phenomenon to influence family theorising has undoubtedly been feminism. There are a very wide range of feminist perspectives that generally share a focus upon the subordination of women with some kind of commitment to ending that inequality. Feminist critiques brought fresh critical vision to what predominantly male scholars have usually regarded as a 'safe' and 'uncontroversial' area. Feminist analysis has also clearly brought to public attention some of the pluralism, disorder and fragmentation to which Cheal refers. Morgan argued that, 'Undoubtedly, one of the main challenges to the mainstream sociology of the family has come from the body of writing associated with the Women's Liberation or radical feminist movements' (1975, p. 134).

The starting point of much contemporary feminism is to identify the major obstacle to equality for women as male power and oppression, often expressed in the concepts of gender inequality and patriarchy (see Beechey, 1979). This was neatly summarised by Hartmann who in 1981 identified 'The Family as the Locus of Gender, Class and Political Struggle', a theme that was echoed by Meyer and Rosenblatt's (1987) feminist analysis of American family textbooks. In the UK, Rodger has argued that 'The issue at the heart of feminist work on family life is the failure of existing theoretical perspectives to adopt a normative stance on the inequalities of power and control which shore up the institution of the family' (1996, pp. 21–2).

There are a wide range of types of feminist work reflecting a range of theoretical and political positions. Smith contrasts liberal feminism, which holds that men and women have the same abilities and will become equal if only given the same opportunities; radical feminism, which focuses on the need to eliminate patriarchy; and socialist or materialist feminism, which draws upon Marxist notions of the material or largely economic origins of female inequality (see Smith, 1995, pp. 22–5). It is noteworthy that, unlike much conventional sociological theorising which has often been developed by men, nearly all types of feminism have taken up issues around family life at some time. Each of these different kinds of feminism tends to take up different aspects of family life in different ways although there are some common roots.

The unequal status of women is often linked to the idea of biological inequality related to motherhood within 'the family'. The era of what is some-times called the 'second wave' of feminism began somewhere around 1968. In 1971 Germaine Greer published *The Female Eunuch* and Shulamith Firestone published its Marxist sister *The Dialectic of Sex* (1972). Also important in the 1960s was work like Hannah Gavron's *Captive Wife* (1966). The first UK Women's Refuge for victims of male domestic violence was set up in Chiswick in 1971. By 1975, in the USA, Brownmiller had constructed a feminist theory of rape. This theory was based on seeing rape as an expression of patriarchy. It is men who rape women, not the other way around, and therefore rape can be seen as men clearly demonstrating their dominance over women.

In all of this early work, the existence of 'the family' was taken for granted by feminists as it had been by modernist theorists. In 1974 Oakley sought to develop an argument to 'liberate housewives' in which she insisted that, 'The family must be abolished' (1974b, p. 222). Gittins moves between writing as if 'the family' exists (indeed her book title is *The Family in Question*) to asserting that 'if one thing should have become obvious by now, it is that to speak in terms of "the" family is totally misleading. There is no such thing' (1993, p. 167).

Ask five males and five females what they think about 'Women's Liberation'.

Much feminist research throws light on family life as the site of much female experience. Delphy and Leonard, for example, explore *Familiar Exploitation*, that is, the way in which women are exploited in their performance of 'family roles' (1992). More recently, Ribbens has focused upon the everyday activities of *Mothers and Their Children* in building a feminist sociology of motherhood (1994). Feminists have also engaged in studies of health, social policy, sexuality, language, masculinity and much more. Such studies have revealed areas previously regarded as insignificant to be centrally important.

Thompson and Walker review the impact of feminist scholarship upon American Family Studies and conclude that feminists have focused upon five themes: gender, social change and gender equality, feminist practice, the centrality of women's lives, and challenging 'the family'. The authors conclude that 'the discipline has created a legitimate place for feminism, but this place is often at the margins. . . . It is only in the domain of housework that feminism has moved to the centre' (1995, p. 847). This appears to somewhat underplay the role of feminism. With regard to family living, the work of feminists has been especially important in identifying, and making visible, the central importance of two topics that had been completely ignored by male scholars studying family living. Within a conventional model of 'the family', both motherhood and housework were assumed to be completely 'natural' and non-problematic; feminist scholarship has begun to reveal these topics to be far more problematic and challenging than earlier work suggested.

An example of the insights that can be gained from adopting a postmodern feminist perspective comes from a recent study of DeVault (1991) who looks at the role of cooking and meals in the construction of families. Taking a modernist account, the role of the mother in preparing meals is taken for granted and, consequently, very few sociologists have even looked at the topic although it is a daily experience for the vast majority of families. The key importance of such daily activities is brought out by the postmodernist perspective. Using such an approach, DeVault demonstrates how the interaction around meals serves to develop and reinforce all kinds of sex role and age related behaviours between children and parents. Almeida goes one step further in arguing not only that feminist scholarship has best challenged gender issues around family living, but that 'feminist family theory is best equipped to include ideas of diversity' (1994, p. 1). It is important to note that feminists have explored issues around race and ethnicity, social class, and culture with regard to family life (see Almeida, 1994, for American examples). In the UK, Elliot (1996) devotes chapters to the exploration of ethnicity and race, paid work and unemployment, ageing, family violence and AIDS.

Family discourses and practices

One way to grasp the enormous power of modernist family theorising is in the area that has become known as 'family discourse'. Cheal summarises this area, 'Social Scientific . . . concepts of "the family", are commonly derived from folk models. . . . When these categories become objects of attention in discussions and debates they acquire common meanings within a shared way of talking, or discourse' (1991, p. 20). This is to look at the models people have in their heads and their shared language(s). Feminist work, both inside and outside academic circles, has brought the unequal status of women to public attention and raised numerous issues around abuse, wages for paid work, safety on the streets and much more. This has had the effect of shifting the nature of family discourse and set the conditions for theoretical development.

Gubrium and Holstein's book *What Is Family?* (1990) is at the forefront of this theoretical development. This book is deeply critical of the traditional family sociology so often repeated in UK textbooks and political rhetoric. The whole point of the book is to reject the usefulness of the concept of 'the family' and begin the enormous task of developing an alternative approach to understanding family life. Gubrium and Holstein argue forcefully that we must replace the idea of a thing called 'the family' with a conception of the processes associated with 'being family'.

Several scholars have sought to avoid the problem of assuming a model of the 'typical family' by avoiding the idea of 'the family' altogether and using, instead, the concept of household. In pioneering work in 1967, Bender argued that a household may be thought of as a 'residence group that carries out domestic functions' whilst 'a family' should be seen essentially as a 'kinship group' (Bender, 1967, p. 493).

This argument was taken much further by Ball who proposed the adoption of the concept of 'living together' in 1972 to signal a 'cohabiting domestic relationship which is (or has been) sexually consequential', that is, involves sexual activity and possibly the birth of children (1972, p. 302). Ball argues that this approach is 'one which says nothing about families per se' and is therefore likely to yield new insights into family living without imposing sociological definitions of what is or is not 'a family' or, indeed, 'the family'.

In the intervening period, the concept of household has come to be adopted by a wide range of researchers to pursue pragmatic research aims. Several feminists have worked on the distribution of resources within households, obtaining important data about gender inequalities in control over resources (see Brannen and Wilson, 1987). Most recently, Buck *et al.* (1994) have provided the first report of the Research Centre on Micro-Social Change into The British Household Panel Survey. Whilst these have proved to be valuable means to generate research material, it has to be noted that they have not, in the main, expanded our understanding of family living as such. Simply replacing the concept of 'family' with that of 'household' has not generated new or radical reinterpretations of the nature of family living.

> Explore five households, list the differences and similarities.

The first obvious reason for this is that the concepts of household and family are quite distinct in everyday thought and language; the head of the household and the head of the family may overlap but are different ideas. In this sense, adopting the term 'household' instead of 'family' runs all the risks of simply re-importing another popular concept that is not primarily designed for sociological analysis.

Second, it is clear that a great deal of the sentiment and related sense of connection, exchange and obligation goes well beyond the household. Much of the debate about family obligations is about people caring for people in other households (see, for example, Finch, 1989).

Third, the notion of household does not enable analysts to study how people use family language, such as 'a good father' or 'not really a family' whereas it is likely that it is this ordinary everyday language that holds the key to understanding just how powerful ideas around family living are.

An interesting and linked proposal comes from Morgan who centres his most recent book on the issues of family practices 'If we talk about "family practices" we are referring to certain practices which participants tend to think of as being in some way "different" and which may colour other practices which overlap with them. Thus "family practices" might overlap with and interact with "gendered practices"' (1996, p. 11). Bearing in mind the way in which discussion, concepts and discourse relate directly to practices, the notion of family practices fits well with the notion of family discourses. Morgan discusses family practices in the contexts of gender, the body, food and the home. For the present purposes, family practices may be best thought of as behaviours linked to family living which, in their very existence, demarcate family living from other non-family forms of living or being.

Family pathways

Unlike scholars who talk confidently about 'the family', I have long believed that we know remarkably little about family living. For example, how is a researcher to even define a sample or group for study without drawing upon his/her own beliefs about what families are?

One important and very productive approach has been that of studying the 'life courses' of individuals, that is, the way our lives develop and change along with personal events such as marriage, the birth of a child or death of a partner. Cohen speaks of the individual life course as 'like a bus journey, with boarding and embarkation points . . . these stages are not fixed' (1987, p. 3). This has, for example, enabled researchers to focus more upon dilemmas about returning to paid work at stages in the life course for women or the issue of middle-age. In the UK, this approach usually focuses upon individuals' life courses within assumed models of the normal 'nuclear family'.

Morgan argues in support of the shift to the notion of the life course as this represents an important shift away from 'models of the life cycle (which) tended to suggest a relatively fixed series of stages' (1996, p. 142). For Morgan, 'The idea of the life course was chosen because it more adequately suggested linkages between changes in households and changes in individuals' (ibid.). Whilst this is certainly progress, a further step needs to be made in order to link 'external' social structural changes to changes in households and changes in individuals and add a much clearer sense of the way in which individuals and groups not only follow courses in their biographies but also have to make these courses through various forms of social structures. This may be accomplished by adopting the notion of pathways, that is, the coming together of individual life courses upon family pathways (Bernardes, 1986a). The proposal is that we should think of individual life courses meeting, sometimes being or becoming interdependent, even combining and perhaps later parting. An individual is not merely born nor simply becomes older. An individual occupies and moves through different structures relating to, for example, being a baby, a child, a teenager, a single adult, a spouse, a parent. Many of these involve important 'rites of passage' such as leaving home, marriage, becoming a parent. At all times the individual has to negotiate a pathway through these structures. In exploring mothering, Ribbens argues that 'the everyday experience of bringing up children in family units requires a constant and subtle negotiation to achieve some balance, and the responsibility for this balancing act is largely the mother's, as primary mediator within the family' (1994, p. 166). Whoever takes the major responsibility, it is clear that all family members are continually negotiating their own pathways.

We need to always remember that the way in which, as Unger and Sussman (1990) remind us, such life courses and pathways link families to other subsystems of the community. This model allows us to escape from the static picture of 'the family' for a much richer appreciation of variation and diversity. It is vital that we do not shy away from the way people use terms about family – indeed, the model of family pathways is all about treating everyday terms as a proper subject for investigation in itself rather than substitute a new sociological concept (such as household). With this model, we can look at how people express ideas of family, which may or may not include those outside their households, especially parents and extended kin. Thus, resources in a household may be diverted to a student living away from home who occupies another household.

It is important to add that an individual's life course is multidimensional and can be sensibly seen in terms of, say, health, education, career, hobbies, sport, etc. Morgan has recently emphasised the importance of time and space, noting 'that there is not, even within a given culture, one time and one space but a multiplicity of times and spaces, all weaving and interacting with each other' (1996, p. 139). In developing a similar critique of the life course as too rigid, Germain proposed a similar model which is:

> based on the concept of non uniform pathways of development. This model incorporates new family forms, human diversity (race, ethnicity, culture, gender, sexual orientation, and physical/mental states), and environmental diversity (economic, political, social). The model includes temporal orientations (historic, individual, and social time) to examine the influence of life transitions, life events, and other life issues on family development and transformations over time.
>
> (1994, p. 259)

The present approach of utilising Family Pathways certainly includes all of these areas as well as seeking to add that an individual's life course, at any given point in time and space, may be party to several pathways with other and perhaps differing sets of individuals. A child may relate to mother, father or siblings but may also develop an important shared pathway with a group of teenage contemporaries.

Plot your own life course and life events and assess how 'close' you were (or are) to parents, siblings and others.

Groups of individuals whose life courses coincide on the same pathway may refer to themselves as 'a family' for some time. Researchers must ask at what point and why people refer to situations as 'family'. The most obvious situation is where the term 'the family' is used by an individual to refer simultaneously to a small unit (perhaps a one parent situation) as well as a larger grouping of kin (perhaps including non-biologically related 'aunts', 'uncles').

Bearing the model of Family Pathways in mind presents families as enormously complex and difficult to study. The portrayal is not of ideal types or typical patterns but a sense of the uniqueness of pathways. Many of us find ourselves facing similar experiences, such as parenthood, but come to these events from very different routes and respond quite differently. Nunnally suggests that 'most families encounter external or internal stresses at different points in the life span of each member. These stresses vary from one family to another depending on many factors in the environment and the family' (Nunnally *et al.*, 1988, p. 13). We share the necessity of facing and coping with similar events or situations, this does not mean that we all experience those situations in the same way. This begins to hint at the enormous richness of variation and diversity in human family living which is precisely the objective of developing alternative theorising about family lives.

Suggested reading

Cheal, D. 1991: *Family and the State of Theory*. Hemel Hempstead: Harvester-Wheatsheaf.

Delphy, C. and Leonard, D. 1992: *Familiar Exploitation: A New Analysis of Marriage in Contemporary Western Societies*. Cambridge: Polity.

Ingoldsby, B. B. and Smith, S. (eds) 1995: *Families in Multicultural Perspective*. New York: Guilford.

Rodger, J. J. 1996: *Family Life and Social Control: A Sociological Perspective*. Macmillan: London.

Chapter 3

Family Studies

Introduction

The previous chapter began from a critique of modernist family
sociology and moved to develop a new theoretical approach
from postmodernist perspectives. It may be tempting to believe
that simply adopting a new approach will be sufficient to
develop a new discipline of Family Studies. The point about
modernist theorising, however, is that it did great harm in a
wide number of ways, as feminists and many others have
pointed out. This suggests the need to pay considerable attention not only to the tools we use in Family Studies, but also to
the way in which we use these tools.

Sociologists have to recognise their responsibilities and,
within this, their political role. It is paradoxical that a discipline
often criticised for being too politically biased has refused to
accept its political role in discussing 'the family'. This chapter
proposes the adoption of the idea of Family Citizenship as a
counter to 'the family' and as a recognition of family living as a
political entity.

51

Before exploring how sociologists may come to terms with their responsibilities, this chapter sets out with an exploration of the neglect of family abuse. Mostly simply put, without some sense of responsibility, traditional modernist work only 'looked for' what it believed existed; in short, it was impossible to discover the unknown. It is significant that much of what has been 'discovered' is due in large part to the work of feminists both inside and outside academia. Feminists have, in the main, not felt constrained by traditional theories or ideas and have engaged in free criticism on a wide variety of fronts.

On the other hand, many feminists have felt rather ambiguous about emphasising the pleasure and joy found by many women in families. This is hardly surprising, the introduction of joy and pleasure rather detracts from an attempt to demonstrate how oppressive families can be. This is yet another area awaiting a much wider exploration. It seems clear that many adults not only fulfil their 'sexual needs', as well as their 'reproductive destinies', in families but may also enjoy these activities. There is often discussion of the 'love of children' but this is rarely explored in detail; it remains to discover what pleasure parents derive from their children. Very few textbooks or accounts of 'the family' deal with pleasure or enjoyment in this way.

As Dobash and Dobash note, the progress made on family abuse is paradoxical: 'the past two decades have seen both radical change and no change at all' (1992, p. 1). Whilst we seem able to continue to uncover new and ever more startling 'facts' about abuse, and whilst some social movements have created new facilities (such as Women's Refuges), the study of family abuse has not radically changed or shifted approaches to the study of family life. The issue of family abuse demonstrates how modernist accounts of 'the family' obstruct attempts to engage in radical rethinks.

Modernism is a view of the world characterised by progress, certainty and clear orthodoxies. Modernist textbooks have only weak links with experience. There is no place in accounts of 'the normal family' for anger, resentment, inequality, stress, depression, physical or sexual violence. There is rarely much discussion of sexuality beyond reproduction.

In portraying 'normal families' in this way, modernist family sociology has played a part in oppressing both victims and perpetrators of family abuse. In portraying the image of 'the normal family', modernism has provided a popular yardstick by which so many people measure their own personal success or failure (see Bernardes, 1993). Since violence is seen as 'not normal', victims, perpetrators and third parties have all colluded in 'keeping the secret', so characteristic in accounts of family abuse (see *Feminist Review*, 1988; Blume, 1990).

The modernist position has also been used, as Armstrong observed, to take women's attempts to 'speak out' and turn these into an industry which 'individualises and medicalises survivors and marginalises feminist politics' (1991, p. 29). Within modernist accounts, it is practically unthinkable that the majority of women may be at risk of abuse. Part of this theme can be seen in the readiness with which the media has taken up the notions of 'ritual abuse' as a means of explaining why apparently normal people have engaged in abuse (see McFadyen *et al.*, 1993).

> Whilst concern is growing, many seem to think that abuse within families is a 'private' matter and the state should not intervene. Conduct a mini survey of attitudes.

Even accepting lower estimates of abuse begins to implicate our friends, neighbours, colleagues and loved ones. Using La Fontaine's work (see 1990, p. 44), with a group of 100 men and women, somewhere between 1 and 25 adults may have experienced child sexual abuse. Between 1 and 25 adults might now be abusing their partners or children or elderly relatives. These are good reasons to reject the idea that only 'particular types of people' are victims or abusers; we are all potential victims and abusers.

Images of 'the normal family' have tended to support denials of accounts of abuse as they emerged. At various stages, commentators have denied the possibility of the abuse of wives and partners, the physical abuse of children, or the sexual abuse of women or children. This in part reflects the sociological confirmations of the value of monogamy and the insistence that adults can find all their needs satisfactorily met within marriage. Currently, most commentators express doubts about the possibility of frequent marital rape, the sexual abuse of children by children, or the sexual abuse of children by women. In all of these denials, ideas of 'what is normal' draw heavily upon images of parents and children built into popular stereotypes of 'the family'. In adopting the stereotype of 'the family' as adequate and then reinforcing this stereotype by using it as a central theoretical model, modernist family sociology has contributed to considerable social harm.

Practical difficulties: methodology

Theoretical development often results from debates between sociologists of different backgrounds. The study of 'family life' is rather different. Few sociologists have not experienced some kind of 'family life' and most will have an ongoing involvement in it. There have been attacks upon, and defences of, 'the family' (see Berger and Berger, 1983; Mount, 1982) but the most interesting feature of this literature is the way in which all parties accept the existence of 'the family'.

This acceptance of the existence of 'the family' reflects a number of practical problems in studying family living. Any attempt to develop a new Family Studies must recognise and find resolutions to all of these problems.

Our own closeness

'Family life' is where our personal experience begins and is of prime importance in influencing our development as individuals. Our experiences of 'family lives', both as children and as adults, are direct and immediate.

> Is the study of family life possible, given that we are all so familiar with our own family lives?

This familiarity is a real disadvantage: it is difficult to 'get out of' the subject and adopt a critical stance. We are each someone's son or daughter and most of us are likely to be, or become, partners and parents. In studying 'family life', one cannot 'go in' from 'the outside' because most of us are already 'family members'.

Sociological views about 'family life' are surprisingly like everyday common sense. Anderson has described this difficulty:

> One source of difficulty lies in the special force in this field of the paradox with which every sociologist has to contend, namely that he [or she] knows at the outset too much about what he [or she] is supposed to be studying.
>
> (1971, p. 8, notes in brackets added).

Models of normality

Whilst we all like to think of ourselves as somehow 'special', we also like to think of ourselves as essentially 'normal'. Some part of that personal sense of normality comes from our own understandings of 'normal family life'.

'Family life' is so morally central in modern societies that it is easy not to notice the way that our lives are judged in terms of normality. Ball made the point explicitly in 1972, 'a major source of those traditional social problems with families as their focal points are directly derivative from the concepts and definitions of the family itself' (1972, p. 295). Since most of us are involved in marriage and parenthood, we are faced with our own normality and the normality of those close to us: parents, partners and children. Normality is measured in dating, heterosexuality, marriage, reproduction and child rearing. The media, the building industry, consumption goods, education, transport and much else is ultimately directed towards 'the family'.

Our own language

The key problem about language for anyone studying family lives is the very familiarity (note use of 'familiar') of the terms. 'Family' language is ubiquitous in occurring in a host of different situations involving different meanings all at the same time. Religious institutions often use terms such as father, mother, sister and brother; trades unions and socialist groups often use the terms brother and sister to signify solidarity. We talk of 'a family' of people, of animals, of plants. These metaphors can be bizarre, such as references to a 'mother ship' or 'father Thames' or 'fatherland' (which is defined in the *OED* as 'mother country'!). You can talk of 'a family' that is unlike 'the family' although it does not happen to be 'my family' but is none the less part of 'the human family of mankind'.

We are bound by the limits of our language: if we do not have a word for it we cannot know what it is. 'Family' language already exists: 'mother', 'father', 'family', 'son', 'daughter'. Built into each of these terms are models of behaviour: you can convey a lot by saying 'She is the mother of four . . . '. The reverse of this is cited by Levin and Trost (1992) who report the consternation of Norwegian social workers when a Sami woman (a 'Lapp') reported the father of her child to be her nephew. There is no incest here, simply different rules and language for biological and social fatherhood.

Our problem is whether we can go beyond these terms. It is even worse than this: if you argue that we can go beyond the limits of everyday language, say with a special vocabulary (like natural science builds for itself), will anyone else understand? Does it make sense for me to suggest that 'the family' does not exist?

Language related to 'the family' makes real communication almost impossible. Exploring two related ethnic groups, Birdwhistell found that despite sharing a common language the groups diverged in the meanings attached to this language. One group may never be aware of the other group's different meanings despite interaction, even inter-marriage (1966, p. 206). This is possible because of the tendency to view individual behaviour as odd rather than indicating a different culture.

I suggest that the bulk of language and interaction is about misunderstanding and resolving apparent conflicts and contradictions. Very often this 'resolving' means that we may arrive at two quite different understandings without realising it. We have no way of knowing if we do inhabit the 'same world'. Language may function to obscure contradictions and mask conflicts; we may continue passing back and forth an idea until we agree, compromise or simply give up.

> Try describing your own mother or father to someone without using the term 'mother' or 'father'. At some point the other person will guess and suddenly appear to understand.

Dorothy Smith has recently expanded the appreciation of the problem of language with regard to studying family lives. Smith suggests that language around family living is much more than expressions of values but that 'the family' is an 'ideological code' like a genetic code that reproduces itself even in the work of those who try to avoid it (Smith, 1993, p. 53). What is surprising, however, is that sociologists have generally failed to recognise the enormous problems of language involved in the study of family life. Clearly, any theoretical development must find a means of examining the use of language around family living rather than treat language usage as adequate.

Invisibility

In 1967, Mayer argued that we are likely to know surprisingly little about the married lives of other people because the greater part of marriage is unseen or 'invisible' (1967a). Mayer later suggested that the invisibility of marriage and family life results from the 'assumptive world' within which we operate (1967b). We do not need to 'see' the marriages of other people because we make assumptions about what 'goes on' within marriage or 'family'.

> How much of your own family life is invisible to others? How far do you go in keeping your own family private and unseen? How much would you rely upon what you told a researcher?

Privacy

Marriage and 'family life' are intensely private affairs in contemporary societies. Donald Ball related deviance to the degree of privacy. The more private an area of behaviour is, the more likely there are to be clear public social norms and extensive private deviance (1975). This suggests that norms relating to 'family life' may be clear because conformity may be minimal.

> What sorts of things do you do in private that you do not reveal in public? Be honest, at least with yourself.

There are, then, a wide range of practical difficulties in developing better analyses of family living. Many of these difficulties are seemingly imponderable and may not be easily 'solved'. The search for clear and obvious solutions is, of course, part of the modernist project and is often rejected by postmodernist theorists. In the area of developing Family Studies, it seems likely that these difficulties should be addressed, at the very least, by adopting new and radical perspectives.

Responsibilities in postmodern sociology

In the previous chapter, the notion of Family Pathways was adopted in an attempt both to reject the adequacy of the image of 'the family' and facilitate further exploration of family living without re-imposing an ideal type. The key strategy of this theoretical device is to place the responsibility for determining what is or is not 'a family' with participants within families rather than with sociological observers.

This is an important step, but this theoretical construct should not be thought of as adequate in itself. The lesson to be taken from modernist theorising is that the cultural, religious, professional and personal values embedded in theorising have long been implicit and denied. Traditional views of 'the family' have been conservative, racist, 'class-ist' and heterosexist. In developing new forms of theorising and a new postmodern sociology of family living, a key strategy is that of exploring a wide range of values.

It is important to proclaim the key value upon which this postmodern sociology of family living is based. Quite simply, family living is accepted as the most important thing in most of the lives of most members of society, as several recent studies have revealed (see opening paragraphs of Chapter 1). Consequently, the development of a postmodern sociology of family living is seen as the most urgent and important task of sociology. I believe that this venture represents a critical test of the practical value of 'doing sociology'; it is my hope that the development of sociology in this way can at least contribute to the well-being of the majority of those living in families.

Our ignorance

At the outset, we must accept the depth and breadth of our own ignorance about the nature of family living, both as scholars and as everyday people. If the model of 'the family' is an ideal that fails to reflect the realities of everyday family living, then it follows that most of what we believe we 'know' about 'family life' is at best unproved, at worst entirely wrong.

Understanding our ignorance rests on recognising the error of believing that you can study family life in isolation and the error of believing that such a study will have no practical effect. This has several implications for sociology. First, there is an essential error in the way we split up features of social life for study (for example, class, ethnicity, family, education, crime) and thereby fail to look at the essential unity of people's lives. Second, there is a further error in that we often study surface appearances or even presume features to exist (for example, 'the family') rather than seek the underlying actuality: what is actually going on (Bernardes, 1986a). In this sense, we need to critically re-evaluate all that we believe we know about family living; some knowledge will turn out to be reliable but a great deal will need revision.

Value freedom examined

Our ignorance is largely a result of the failure of many sociologists to come to terms with the issue of values. Sociologists have often denied their role in generating and upholding particular value positions. In the case of the study of 'the family', the strength and power of values adopted by largely White male sociologists is extremely clear. What was presented as a simple 'objective description' contained within it wide ranging values relating to the superiority of paid work and the inferiority of women and children.

> Are you ever truly value free?

I am sure that there is no such thing as a value-free sociologist nor can there be a piece of sociological research that is entirely free from human values (Shipman, 1981, especially Chapters 2 and 12). I am equally sure that there is no such thing as a value-free natural scientist. The search for objectivity and value freedom is an illusion. Medicine, science and religion all assert objectivity and value freedom. These are merely labels used by authority to give credibility to some ideas whilst discrediting other ideas. In this respect, sociologists need to pay far more attention to the issue of their professional responsibilities.

Confronting responsibility

Despite the claim by David Cheal that our task in destroying the 'orthodox consensus about the normal family . . . is now complete' (1991, p. 153), there is still widespread use of the term 'the family'. There then emerges a paradox when evidence that the model may not match the reality of family life generates pleas to uphold 'traditional family values' rather than stimulate new theoretical approaches (see Durham, 1991). So the very idea of 'the family' is continually reiterated and reinforced. In her recent work towards a feminist sociology of childrearing, Ribbens makes a similar point: 'the terms of sociological agendas and descriptions can have a major impact on the whole meaning of every-day reality within which people are operating, although this may rarely be recognised as sociology' (1994, p. 38).

As a practising sociologist, my greatest horror and shame is that I cannot appeal to any authority to discredit work that I know to be positively dangerous. It is ideas that people and societies really care about, are willing to defend to the death or persecute others in the name of. Compared to those who design, manufacture and sell intentionally and unintentionally harmful technology, our job is much more dangerous. People can choose to use science and technology to pollute the world, wage war, oppress or imprison. What we deal in, ideas themselves, are the bases upon which people make choices, including those of polluting the world, waging war, oppressing or imprisoning others.

The responsibility is awesome and many might say we are best to deny or avoid this responsibility. We have been doing this for decades, as economists, psychologists, political scientists, historians and sociologists. We have wreaked havoc and harm in people's lives. I know primarily about the harm done by stereotypical images of 'the family' but the ideas of 'normal personality', 'rational economic decisions' and so on have all wreaked as much harm.

Exploring values

The idea of 'the family' has been remarkably oppressive and harmful. People interact on the basis of ideas about social structure, 'the ways things are'. We must recognise our own location as everyday people who interact to create and sustain our own identities and realities. These activities in everyday lives have shaped the views of sociologists as sociologists. For sociologists, however, the use of language tends to involve 'doing things' to other people both at the personal level and at the more impersonal level (see Bernardes, 1987).

In exploring crime and the family, Utting highlighted our current values and priorities:

Each year vast sums are committed to researching the cause of different diseases and in support of experimental interventions designed to prevent them. If only comparable resources could be devoted to preventing the social cancer caused by crime, the savings in public health as well as wealth would surely more than justify the costs.

(1993, p. 75)

Whilst focused especially on *Crime and The Family*, Utting's point applies much more widely. We simply do not invest the kind of resources in studying family living to reflect the public rhetoric.

As philosophers have shown over the millennia, there are no easy answers here although the themes of respect and tolerance do emerge in most attempts to establish ethical positions. Respect and tolerance are fine, of course, until those you have respected and tolerated refuse to respect and tolerate you or, indeed, members of their own families. There is much in the traditions of many cultures which Western feminists find deeply offensive, just as those cultures find the emphasis upon the freedom of women deeply offensive. Similarly, the value placed upon children varies enormously throughout the world.

Make a list of 'family values' which you would like to see adhered to in your own society.

The values of sociologists

Sociologists are widely known for 'being political'. I am not a member of any political group and do not adhere to the values of any one political party although I do vote in national and sometimes local elections.

Like many sociologists, I detest gross inequality, especially when it is visited upon the weak and innocent (such as the young and the old). At the same time, I recognise that a considerable amount of sociology has failed to recognise that many people support that inequality. In a wider sense, we must recognise that human beings are extremely complex and often contradictory. It is not obvious, for example, that revealing widespread abuse and violence will be well received. Put most simply, if family abuse is widespread then many of our audience will be both abusers and survivors and it will be in their interests to deny or downplay the research. This, of course, is precisely what has happened in the recent decades of exploring forms of family abuse and is perhaps one reason why abuse is often still seen as 'deviant' or 'abnormal'.

I have spent a great deal of my career interested in and working around issues connected with family living. This is because I share a feminist view that to understand family living is also a means to understand major systems of oppression and inequality. It is therefore possible that 'new understandings' of family life will be significantly liberating. It must be remembered, however, that 'changed understandings' risk creating damage and harm.

Suppose we generate a new theoretical approach to liberate women and children. What guarantee have we that such work will not, in its turn, harm or threaten people in some other way? Can we, as sociologists, go around tinkering with people's understandings of the world when what people understand often determines what they do and to whom they do it?

In all of this, I have my own sets of values and beliefs. It is dishonest of any scientist to claim that he or she does not cherish certain values in preference to others or to claim that such values will not slant the work. The author's values are, as I suspect are all value positions, ambiguous. Whilst critical of excessive wealth and power, I have spent a career climbing a salary scale. Whilst sympathetic to all kinds of categories of 'charity', I retain much of my income for disposal by myself and immediate family (!) I am a heterosexual, nominal Christian, White male with a female partner, and two children, having shared one relationship for twenty years.

> Can a White, heterosexual male understand the family lives of non-Whites, females or lesbians?

Every effort will be made to pay due regard to all kinds of discrimination including those based upon age, sex, gender, ethnicity, religion, social class, disability and sexual orientation. Every effort will be made to pay due regard to the location of the UK, first, in the European Union and, second, in occupying a particular location within the wider community of the world. I take it for granted that such comparative work can be of value in spotlighting peculiarities about the way any particular nation or society may do things. I also take it for granted that such comparisons may reveal 'lessons we can learn from'.

In determining to take a stand, I can think of no better argument than that of Stacey who has developed most of what might be thought of as a postmodern study of family living. In 1993, Stacey argued that 'Family Sociologists should take the lead in burying the ideology of "the family" and in rebuilding a social environment in which diverse family forms can sustain themselves with dignity and respect' (1993, p. 547).

Developing a new Family Studies

As mentioned previously, whilst Family Studies does not exist in the UK, it is a common discipline in the USA, Europe and Australia. Much of what goes under the label of Family Studies draws heavily upon the modernist tradition and seeks to find solutions to particular family problems or, indeed, problem families. In recent years, however, a small number of authors, from very widely different backgrounds, have made pleas to develop a new form of Family Studies.

In 1988, Wesley Burr and his colleagues argued that:

> We believe that the family realm has a much greater effect on the human condition than most people realise, and if more of us were to realise that our field is a basic discipline that deals with a profoundly important part of the human condition, it may help us usher in a period of unusual creativity in the next several decades.
>
> (1988, p. 205)

Burr *et al.* attempted to lay down a definition of the 'family realm' to establish 'family science'. Whilst I do not agree with their particular formulation, I do agree about the centrality of family life.

In 1990, Gubrium and Holstein suggested 'a new direction, a new programme for "family studies" ' (p. 162). The key to their approach is the recognition that 'the family' is 'as much idea as thing' (p. 163). This approach has been a central part in developing a postmodern approach to Family Studies.

This book has a clear mission: stating the case for the establishment of a postmodern Family Studies in the United Kingdom and laying down the essential components of this new discipline. Parties of all kinds have common interests in family life. All agree that people should be given every chance to best prepare themselves for marriage and parenthood. It is in all our interests to support and enhance marriage and parenting. Further generations are vital to us all; the happiness of current generations is also vital to us all. The happiness and well-being of spouses, parents and children must be a prime goal for us all.

There are fierce debates about the morality of divorce, abortion, marriage, single parenting, childrearing and many other things. The job of social science is not morality; we have another role to play. It is our job to study the reality of such situations rather than engage in moral debate. It is our task to understand how to minimise the pain, suffering and misery of family life and how to maximise the joy, pleasure and love of family life.

Do your elected officials (local and national) believe that families are the most important things of all? Ask them.

Family practices and Family Citizenship

In that modernist family sociology contributed to a widespread family ideology, it was taking a distinct political stance and contributing to defining a political entity of 'the family'. In developing postmodern Family Studies, it is important to replace this political entity. It is also vital to do so in an explicit and open fashion. A clue to how to proceed comes from the European experience, especially the role of Family Associations (see p. 68) and the way in which such associations ensure that families (rather than 'the family') are given a prominent role in political debate. For the present purposes, the notion of Family Citizenship will be adopted to replace a central political notion of 'the family' (see Bernardes and Keddie, 1994).

Marshall identified three elements of citizenship: civil corresponding to legal equality; political citizenship corresponding to freedom of political association and representation; and social citizenship corresponding to the guarantee of minimum standards of living (see Rees, 1996). These are important as elements but all relate to individuals and, as Lister has pointed out, largely to 'he' or men; women are accorded a secondary citizenship especially in their much lower level of economic power through wage earning (see Lister, 1989 and 1991; Rees, 1996).

Central here is the notion of family practices as recently developed by Morgan to signal practices 'which participants tend to think of as being in some way "different" and which may colour other practices which overlap with them. Thus "family practices" might overlap with and interact with "gendered practices"' (1996, p. 11). Citizenship, as currently understood and used simply does not address those practices but rather operates in such a way as to emphasise possessive individualism rather than any familial elements of individual living.

In 1991, Donati presented a paper at the European Union Conference on 'Children, Family and Society'. Donati reviewed a set of commonly recognised 'family problems' that have arisen in a period of rising affluence and wealth. In a subsequent paper, Donati posed the question and answer: 'The question: "What do families need?" should be given a reply which is very simple and extremely complex at the same time: families need to be fully recognised as families' (Donati, 1993, p. 209). That is, we should begin to give families a specific and real location and role in civil, political and social debate, especially ensuring that the interests of families as families are included in debates about policy formation and change.

Finch and Mason's survey confirmed that family relationships continue to be of great importance in the lives of ordinary people; built into these notions are sets of beliefs about responsibility, obligation and rights (see Finch, 1996). What arises out of these analyses is that the extent to which family members actually practice rights and responsibilities depends upon circumstance and individual's views, this of course reflects the work of Gubrium and Holstein (1990) and the development of that work in Morgan's notion of family practices (1996). In developing the notion of Family Citizenship, it is important to note that social agencies seem to be able to seek to influence individuals' beliefs; they may do this so as to emphasise possessive individualism or in such a way as to emphasise Family Citizenship in an effort to enhance and protect families.

The key issue is to look, as Lister does, at the 'share' of wealth directed to dependants in families rather than to individuals. Lister argues that the key symbol here is the protection of Child Benefit and the way in which this may be seen as a badge of citizenship; in short, Lister sees Child Benefit as marking citizenship status for women as carers of children (1989). Whilst right to emphasise women as mothers, such a view inevitably perpetuates inequality and dependence and fails to identify families 'as families' (Donati, 1993). This needs to be looked at in the European context to see how an emphasis upon families may raise the economic, political and social significance of families (see following discussion on the Flemish Union, p. 68).

A more precise definition of Family Citizenship relates to the rights and duties held by individuals (only individuals can hold rights and duties) which are only held because of their location in families and participation in family practices. The notion of Family Citizenship provides an alternative means to categorise or assess family lives based on a more realistic and explicit recognition of the importance of families as families. Family Citizenship may be used as a means of recognising and enhancing individual citizenship, especially of vulnerable groups such as children, mothers with no paid work or the elderly.

Ask ten people if families are more important than individuals.

The apparent tension between individuals and families is a product of the way in which we conceptualise individuals. That is exactly the point about asserting the notion of Family Citizenship; we must refuse to accept that women as mothers must necessarily take a secondary role. Instead, we must build a form of citizenship that can be integrated into all civil, political and social debates to ensure that families as families are given much greater importance in all decision-making. The concept of Family Citizenship presents a way to locate and understand individual rights and obligations in the context of family living rather than in isolation. Recognising the role of all individuals *vis-à-vis* families is a significant step towards equality between all individuals. This offers the possibility of both recognising and supporting families and of generating real equality between individuals. If we are much clearer about rights, duties and obligations of all family members, this may well enhance the position and status of children by recognising their rights not in abstract isolation (to a decent childhood) but rather in relational location (the need for society to facilitate the provision of a decent childhood by parent(s)).

In looking at families as subjects, we confront the rights and duties (and the support to fulfil those duties) of all families, irrespective of wealth, status or type. We can all care better for our elders, our partners, our children and ourselves and have a duty to care better. We also have, however, a right to expect education, support and help in caring better. In contributing to a better society, we certainly can and do have obligations as individuals but society itself (through both state and influential organisations) has a prime obligation to facilitate that care.

Several feminists have explored the reasons why women behave as they do in the interiors of families. Much work has been done upon the nature of family 'obligations' (Finch, 1989) which place so many women in a situation of delivering care. What is of greatest importance here is to recognise that these distributive patterns are not solely a product of gender but rather conditional upon gender and location in 'families'.

> If society expects parents (mothers) to raise children, what can parents (mothers) expect from society?

An important refinement of the concept of Family Citizenship then involves recognising rights, duties and obligations that fall to individuals within families because of their status as members of families or their actions in family practices. We do not expect just any woman to care for any elderly or disabled person but we do expect a wife or daughter to take up the task if she is at all able to. Some European societies already go some way in recognising Family Citizenship in, for example, parental leave: leave to which individuals have a right as a result of their location in families.

New and better knowledge about family living may enable us to benefit and protect society. In establishing what families can and cannot do, we may be able to enhance and empower families in new and productive ways. We must enable families to deliver the good things and simultaneously educate and prepare families to avoid, prevent or resolve the bad things. If we worked towards enhancing Family Citizenship, we might directly and clearly move towards many of the goals that both the Left and Right seem to support. We may be able to encourage greater preparedness for marriage and parenting, greater family cohesion, higher quality childrearing, a narrowing of the gap between the generations and so on.

Family practices as distributive systems

We need to recognise that interactions are not simple, random and pointless events but rather involve some kind of exchange, of information, ideas, praise or criticism. Segal has typified images of family living as compromises between 'love, intimacy, stability, safety, security, privacy . . . [and] fears of abandonment, chaos, failure' (1983, p. 9).

Too often in modern societies, we seem to focus upon the 'easy to see' such as wealth, possessions and material goods. This has lead sociologists to focus on the most visible processes of industrialisation around production and distribution through economic exchange. What this view has done, however, is increasingly neglect the distributive role of families that predates industrialisation and has always involved both economic or material goods as well as non-economic or non-material goods.

> What does (or has) your family distribute(d): cash, time, energy, skill, knowledge? Make a list.

Families are the means whereby material goods (such as food, shelter, transport, money) are distributed to the majority of the population who are not economically active (children and the old, also some women). Much more than this, though, is the distribution of non-material goods centred around the caring relationship – the most obvious cases are in provision of care (usually by women) for men, children, the sick and elderly.

It is important to also note that whilst families distribute goods such as love, care, nurturance, there has always been significant evidence that they also distribute 'bads' such as anger, hate, despair, abuse or violence.

Thus the notion of Family Citizenship may provide an alternative means of understanding the location, occurrence and distribution of many 'bads' such as family abuse and associated beliefs or behaviours. This may go some way to clarifying what is sometimes called a 'transmission' of behaviours or circumstances such as poverty or abuse. These are not genetically inherited but rather are part of the distribution and exchange systems of family practices.

The notion of individual citizenship has always been flawed because some citizens are far more equal than others. Whilst the notion of Family Citizenship may not directly redress this imbalance, it at least recognises the inadequacy of a notion of citizenship that revolves only around individuals.

Do we want better parents in the future?

Child care or simply care?

Many 'family agendas' include a special appeal for the care or nurturance of children. At first sight this seems perfectly reasonable but it requires some critical thought. If taken too far, such an emphasis can generate inequalities between generations where one generation commands more resources than another. At present, for example, it is widely believed that more resources are commanded by the elderly meaning that fewer resources are available for children (Donati, 1993). Already there is a growing concern that the rapidly rising number of elderly people in Europe is diverting scarce resources from caring for our children. There is certainly some critical work around the potential individualism arising out of excessive child-centredness (Bjornberg, 1992b) as well as evidence emerging from nations such as China where there is the notion of 'child emperors' following the imposition of the 'one child' policy.

We need to focus not upon particular members but rather the family practices that we find so satisfying and important. This is perhaps best understood as the search for intimacy, care or comfort. For the present purposes, an effort will be made to recognise the needs of all categories of persons within families. In terms, then, of Family Citizenship, families have rights and duties concerning all members with no priorities.

Implicit in traditional views is the notion that all parents somehow know 'how to parent'; in modern societies there are good reasons to doubt this. If we think in terms of reciprocity and relationships, we should then begin to think about the skills and abilities necessary to engage in relationships. This is to say that in considering Family Citizenship, we should focus upon relationships between all parties rather than insist that one party (say, parents) has responsibilities towards others (children).

Family Associations

A final part of the jigsaw here relates to Family Associations. Family Associations, as described by Donati, are primary or secondary social networks with a degree of formal organisation that set out to address the needs of families as families (Bernardes, 1995a and 1995b, see Donati, 1994). These kinds of organisations are quite common in other European nations. This is a type of organisation quite distinct from those more familiar in the UK that tend to focus upon particular aspects of family life such as mothers, children, relationships or special disability groups.

European examples of such associations already possess a wealth of practical experience. The Union of Large and Young Families in the Flemish Community of Belgium boasts several million members out of a population of 7 million; activities include family life education, preparation for childbirth, loans and hire of baby equipment, self-help and mutual support groups for all types of families (single and dual parent), help for the disabled and elderly within families, advice on childrearing and dealing with teenagers. The Flemish Union of Families is constituted to promote solidarity between families, advance the interests of families, and advocate a family and child oriented society. The Flemish Union has developed a high-profile Five Year Agenda which aims to ensure that the family dimension is considered in every policy, that attention is paid to the financial capacity of families and that policy-makers recognise the changing nature of family living in terms of demography, social security, environment, paid work, education and caring.

Recent research reveals that there are very many small and short lived voluntary associations that address some part of family living in the UK (Bernardes, 1995b). The recent development of so many associations may be partly a result of welfare cutbacks and the increasing uncertainty of post-modernity. It seems unlikely that the UK will expand welfare provision in the coming years. It seems more likely that any support for families will come from voluntary associations. In this sense, the European models of Family Associations may provide valuable models of organisation and service delivery.

European Family Associations are often formed by ordinary families banding together to protect their interests. In lacking any such Family Associations, families in the UK are especially at risk. Indeed, this may be one explanation of why so many situations perceived as 'family problems' (divorce, single parenthood, family poverty) are so severe in the UK compared to other nations in the European Union. By substituting the idea of Family Citizenship for the assumed existence of 'the family', it may be possible to encourage the development of Family Associations in the UK and thereby make considerable progress in protecting the interests of all families.

A Family Studies perspective

Before moving on to look at experiences on a wide variety of family practices and family pathways in greater detail, it is appropriate to draw together the strategies adopted so far. At the outset, attention was paid to the power of the idea of 'the family' and a critique of the assumed existence of this stereotype or ideal type of family. In looking at theorising family lives, many practical and theoretical difficulties are to be encountered. One response to the range and extent of these difficulties is to develop a postmodern form of theorising which focuses upon family pathways. Family pathways are those situations in which individual life courses come together and some or all of the participants regard their shared lives as somehow being 'a family'.

In looking at why modernist accounts of 'the family' had ignored so much ordinary everyday family experience, for example, family abuse, attention focused on the responsibilities held by sociologists. This is a quite unusual view; it is more common for sociologists to believe they bear little or no responsibility and for the public at large to discount their work. In the power of family ideology, however, a clear issue of the responsibility of sociologists arises. Taking these responsibilities into account requires much more than simply a new theoretical approach, such as that of family pathways. What is required is a sensitivity to the political location and role of sociological concepts. Most important is the replacement of the idea of 'the family' by some other political entity. For the purposes of developing Family Studies in the UK, the notion of Family Citizenship was adopted.

Family Citizenship then is about how well families enable individuals to exercise rights and duties concerning resources that they possess or receive. Do parents know how to parent? How well can single parents provide for their children? How well do spouses relate to one another? Are parents enabled to distribute time, affection, care to children (born and unborn) in the recognition that this will benefit the child and parent and ultimately society (witness traditional calls for 'better parenting' and 'less delinquency').

In developing Family Studies, the most important developments are those of exploring family practices and expanding Family Citizenship. We should develop means by which families can express demands and wishes which command respect and action. At the same time, this must be done in a way that is sensitive to values and ethics. We already see that, given particular choices in particular circumstances, families will tend to shift towards extreme individualism and materialism. What families express as wishes can be 'wrong' in terms of being damaging and destructive, noticeably sacrificing short-term gratification for long-term stability. It is important, therefore, to remember the values and responsibilities with which sociologists need to work in the study of family lives.

Suggested reading

Bernardes, J. 1993: 'Responsibilities in Studying Postmodern Families'. *Journal of Family Issues*, 14, 1, 35–49.

Dallos, R. and McLaughlin, E. 1993: *Social Problems and the Family*. London: Sage.

Durham, M. 1991: *Sex and Politics: The Family and Morality in the Thatcher Years*. Basingstoke: Macmillan.

Gubrium, J. F. and Holstein, J. A. 1990: *What Is Family?* Mountain View, California: Mayfield.

Chapter 4

Families in society

Introduction

Most accounts of family living focus upon the presumed 'functions' of the family, especially mate selection and reproduction. This results in a major disservice to many millions of partners, parents and children in the way in which their routine survival through the bulk of family pathways is ignored in most textbooks.

When trying to understand complex and diverse family pathways, it is the ordinary and everyday aspects of family practices that provide some of the most valuable insights. In a wider sense, many aspects of ordinary everyday family practices revolve around the impact of the external material environment and its production processes upon the intimate interior of families. What follows is a selection of what are felt to be key issues: abuse, paid and unpaid work, environments beyond families, activities contributing to the construction of families and health issues.

Family abuse

Family abuse is a subject of popular discourse from Greek myths through Dickens to the present. There is no clear understanding of the link between wider forms of abuse (from public brawling and murder to civil and international warfare) and family abuse. It may be that family abuse is the origin of wider forms of abuse or, indeed, that wider abuse leads to family abuse.

There have been recent scandals around child deaths, child sexual abuse, physical abuse of women and family abuse of the elderly. More recently, discussion has raised the possibility of marital rape, female sexual abuse (see Allen, 1990; Elliott, 1992) and even the possibility of significant levels of females physically abusing males (see George, 1994), or men being forced into sexual contact with women by women (see Struckman-Johnson and Struckman-Johnson, 1994). Textbooks on family life give remarkably little attention to abuse except perhaps to mention families in which abuse occurs as 'deviant' or 'dysfunctional'.

The key problem, as Richards observes in connection with sexual abuse, is that of definitions. Richards argues that 'What counts as . . . abuse may differ from the points of view of children, adults, different professionals, researchers' (1988, Frontispiece). There is a real problem of 'defining' abuse; should it include neglect, intimidation, aggression, violence? Do we include self-abuse and addictions to cigarettes, alcohol, food, legal and illegal drugs? Given the often glamorised images of female children, how far do we go in defining sexual abuse: should it include 'sexy talk', voyeurism, child pornography, child prostitution?

It is also important to note that the subject is made extremely difficult because of cultural differences ranging from infanticide, male and female circumcision to whether babies are left to cry until some predetermined 'feeding time'. As estimates of the prevalence of abuse rise, it is increasingly likely that 'experts' and decision-makers have been abused themselves and that their own shame and secrecy may create problems.

Giddens has argued that:

> The home is, in fact, the most dangerous place in modern society. In statistical terms, a person of any age or of either sex is far more likely to be subject to physical attack in the home than on the street at night. One in four murders in the UK is committed by one family member against another.
>
> (1989, p. 408)

The 'discovery' of family abuse in the 1970s stimulated a very large literature. This ranged from the physical abuse of children to the physical abuse of women, the sexual abuse of children and recently the sexual abuse of women in marriage.

What is family abuse?

Within the term 'family abuse' are included family practices involving emotional, psychological, sexual and physical abuse of family member(s) by other family member(s). Levinson lists some forty distinct types of family violence (Levinson, 1989, p. 26). Included is child sexual abuse, marital rape, elder abuse, physical child abuse, physical violence towards and between partners. One of the clearest and broadest definitions was proposed in 1993 by Penhale in a review of elder abuse but is applicable elsewhere, 'Most definitions of abuse, however, include the following categories: physical abuse; sexual abuse; psychological and social abuse (e.g. emotional and verbal abuse and harassment; isolation or abandonment); and financial (or material) abuse and exploitation' (1993, p. 96).

> In what personal situations do you believe violence is acceptable? Would you act violently towards someone you know had abused your own parent, partner or child?

A great deal of the literature has adopted simplistic notions of essentially powerful males abusing less powerful females and children. Whilst this was an important step, it was only one step in the right direction. What the largely feminist revelation of family abuse has suggested is that 'ordinary families' may contain abuse. This is far from surprising; historically, the human species is clearly prone to engage in individual examples of violence right across to periods of mass violence during wars. Whilst there are some cases of female warriors, and women clearly play a part in modern warfare, it is tempting to believe that women 'follow' men and would not normally be so violent.

We should recognise that victims and perpetrators do not divide neatly into the abused and non-abused. As any observer of children playing will attest, children may abuse each other quite readily. There is a large area of sibling abuse, both physical and sexual, that remains to be explored. Given the high levels of violence by young people, especially males, it seems likely that 'teenage thugs' are just as violent at home towards siblings and parents. Agnew and Hugeley argue that researchers have 'largely ignored the third major type of family abuse: parent abuse' (1989, p. 699). This violence may reflect behaviour learnt as children and have some element of revenge in it. Similarly, the elderly may abuse both those in their own age group, most obviously their partners, and younger age groups by way of established tyranny or physical violence.

Whilst a great deal of value is placed upon intimacy in modern Western societies, there seems to be a widespread tendency to deny or ignore the 'other side of the coin'. In 1982, Alford made a simple but vital point, 'Many theorists of family conflict have suggested that the more intimate a relationship is,· the more intense the conflict will be within that relationship' (1982, p. 361). It is pertinent to recall that the mother/child and father/child relationships are encouraged to be among the most intense relationships a child experiences. Intimacy and love are portrayed in a wide range of folk mythology as the sources of some of the most violent of human emotions, especially jealousy, passion and rage. It is becoming clear that intimate relationships are potentially abusive in a wide range of ways, the most extreme of which is family murder.

> List the widest possible range of 'types' of abuse within families.

The landmark for the modern revelation of domestic violence in the UK remains with the work of Erin Pizzey who set up the first Women's Refuge in Chiswick in 1972 (see Pizzey, 1974). No one expected the very high levels of demand placed on the refuges that rapidly sprang up around the country. In the UK, Mooney's (1993) North London Domestic Violence Survey suggested that around 50 per cent of women had experienced threats or actual violence from partners. The same work explains why some previous estimates were so much lower by finding that 45 per cent of women who had experienced domestic violence in the previous twelve months had not told anyone. In 1994, Mooney revealed that only 14 per cent of experiences of abuse were reported to the police. In 1992, Dobash and Dobash felt they could argue that, 'In many countries it is now well known that violence in the home is commonplace, that women are its usual victims and men its usual perpetrators' (1992, pp. 1–2).

Historical work and common sense suggest that males are far more violent than females. This should not be taken to mean, however, that females are incapable of violence and abuse nor that such abuse does not exist. In 1992, DeMaris tested the assumption that female violence is a response to male violence and found that women often initiated violence. This may be an atypical finding or may indicate the tip of yet another iceberg of abuse by women. Flynn, for example, has suggested that 'women may use violence as often as men do' (1990, p. 194) and George has reviewed a wide range of studies that suggest relatively high levels of abuse of males by females, many of which had been previously discounted in the light of largely feminist arguments presenting females as victims of male power (1994). More recently, concern has begun to emerge in the US and UK about female gang violence; it seems that girls are perfectly capable of being just as violent and abusive as boys.

Oates discusses evidence that more than half of all mothers believed they had hit their children too hard and over 40 per cent feared that they might harm their children one day (1982, p. 4). Driver and Droisen (1989) review a great deal of evidence suggesting that child sexual abuse is more common than generally believed. Hadley finds evidence to suggest that 'four million adults in Britain have experienced some form of sexual abuse as children' (1987, p. 24). These estimates relate only to the more 'acceptable' dimension of the sexual abuse of girls by men and exclude what may be significant levels of abuse of children by children and of children by women. More to the point, it would seem likely that physical and emotional abuse is more common than sexual abuse.

Visit any supermarket and record the extent of yelling, scolding, slapping, punching, hitting and yanking perpetrated upon children of all ages. Ask yourself whether you felt that a particular behaviour 'deserved' physical punishment.

Whilst 'helpless children' can be readily accepted as victims, levels of conflict between parents and children are likely to rise in adolescent years when such young people are much more likely to be involved in violence. In exploring 'Violence towards Youth', Bybee (1979) identifies the paradox of a society that disapproves of violence towards children and youth and yet approves of punishment, smacking and aggressive sports. By far the majority of public violent crimes involve young males and the whole image of males maturing involves violence and aggression. This raises the possibility that young males are so violent because they have been, and still are, exposed to violence at home.

Do we want our young men to be competitive, aggressive and violent?

It also seems probable that youth is the period when both males and females experience, even revel in, high levels of physical and sexual abuse within peer groups. It is likely that young people are all too well aware of levels of emotional, physical and sexual abuse between their own parents. We know about teenage gangs, rising levels of teenage sexual activity, deep confusion about sexuality and the real possibility of 'confused messages' between males and females. In 1993 Wyatt *et al.* undertook a detailed exploration of the areas of sexual abuse and consensual sex, especially among children and adolescents. Distinguishing abusive childhood sexual behaviour from voluntary or consensual sexual behaviour is not only difficult for observers but, the authors argue, central for individuals in their later development. Hoghughi and Richardson

(1990) note that hundreds of rapes are committed annually in the UK by boys aged between 10 and 14 years of age. One of the recently recognised forms of abuse is that of 'date rape', when a young couple engages in intimacy of some form but the male coerces the female into full intercourse. It seems likely that such young people may have difficulty distinguishing between sexual experimentation and abuse.

The public recognition of what has become known as 'elder abuse' occurred in the US in the 1970s. In 1982, Eastman claimed that there had been no UK research on 'granny battering'. Eastman deliberately took a role in the national press in claiming that 'granny battering' did exist, using American material from 1979 and 1980 (see Eastman, 1982; Eastman and Sutton, 1982).

Recent discussions, such as Glendenning (1993) have expanded the range of 'types' of elder abuse. Current understandings now include physical abuse such as slapping, withholding care or medicine; psychological abuse such as threats, fear, isolation; drug abuse in encouraging the elderly to take sedative drugs; material abuses such as simple theft of property and money; violation of rights, such as forcing elderly people into a nursing home against their wishes.

In family settings, however, it is vital not to think in simplistic terms of defenceless old people abused by resentful bullies of sons or daughters. Neate (1991) has suggested that over 50 per cent of carers are themselves abused by those they care for. Old people have histories and may well have been (and continue to be) violent, aggressive and domineering. Several cases of child sexual abuse in the UK have implicated the role of grandparents (especially grandfathers). There is also no reason why an abusive partner should cease to be abusive in old age, indeed, it seems possible that the abuse of one partner by another might even increase.

Hidden social structure

In terms of sociological theory, emerging evidence about the range of types and extent of family abuse presents a major problem. Most sociological portrayals of social structure suggest clear 'rules', functioning systems, or, at worst, the use of largely economic power by some parties to control other parties. These kinds of accounts have been based upon observations of structure notably around social class, economic location, and more recently gender and ethnicity. What these accounts lack is an indication of the way in which intimidation, fear and abuse may be routine and common in ordinary family lives – from the dispute between siblings right through to child murder or spousal murder. Research and teaching in this area has led me to formulate the notion of a 'hidden social structure' of fear and intimidation based upon and reflecting widespread abuse within families.

This is not to displace or replace existing models of society and social structure but rather to add to these and assert, as elsewhere, the incredibly complex variation and diversity of modern family living. In work on families, then, clear allowance should be made for wide ranging accounts of abuse between all family members. This is to say that a focus upon explicit social structure is inadequate and almost certainly misleading. What must be added is a concern for the hidden structure of fear and intimidation that plays a role in determining where we are and where we go, and where we do not go, at what time and in what ways. This is just as true in the family home ('Don't go in there, he's in a real mood . . . ') as it is in the external world in avoiding the 'bad parts' of town.

Paid and unpaid work

Gender: unpaid and paid work

From the earliest possible moments of life, male and female are differentiated in all kinds of ways. In the Western nations, babies may be identified by colours and dress. Male destiny is centred on paid work, competition and aggression. Female destiny is centred on marriage, some paid work, and the unpaid work of childbearing and nurturing. Whilst there has been a great deal of talk about the 'new man' who shares housework and participates in the care of children, there is little evidence of such a dramatic shift in behaviours. It is easy to 'blame' men for this failure to 'do their share' but people do not generally change their lives in one respect unless something else changes to encourage that adaptation. It simply remains the case that men are expected to pursue lifelong paid work whilst women are expected to break their commitment to paid work for the unpaid work of mothering.

Housework

The 'sociology of work' usually ignores mothering and housework. Discussion of work in 'family textbooks' tends to focus upon paid work and treats this quite separately to the huge volume of unpaid domestic work that goes into housework, motherhood and other caring work.

In the UK, Oakley pioneered the study of housework with two books published in 1974. The physical labour involved in motherhood and housework almost certainly exceeds the physical labour involved in paid work. In short, all courses and articles on 'work' should be at least half about motherhood and housework.

We can grasp why people travel to a workplace and undertake specified tasks for limited periods, there is a clearly understood reward structure. What is much more difficult and interesting to explain is why very large numbers of women and mothers undertake a huge range of unspecified tasks for unlimited periods with no clear or obvious rewards at all. The answer to this question involves understanding the strength and power of widespread beliefs in the differences between men and women and the 'rightness' of their different roles within families. This in turn relates to the wider issues of power, ideology, belief systems and gender inequality.

> For non-mothers: how much would you want paying for undertaking child care, housework, shopping, cooking, cleaning for one month?

It bears repeating that most adult women and mothers face a 'dual burden' in that they may take up some level of paid work but, regardless of this, they remain the individual mostly responsible for unpaid domestic work which often includes what Duncombe and Marsden have suggested be seen as 'the "emotion work" necessary to maintain the couple relationship itself' (1995, p. 150).

Occasional studies, such as Nickols and Metzen (1982) have found that women's employment has very little impact upon men's contribution to housework. Fox and Nickols (1983), for example, noted how women did less housework when working full time but that their occupation had little impact upon the amount of time spent by men or children on housework. In 1985, Coverman found that most male involvement was by younger men, with children, employed wives and by men holding paid jobs that do not require long hours. Wheelock found that even when the husband was unemployed and the wife working, women still bore the main responsibility for housework. While men may 'do more about the house', role reversal was rare (Wheelock, 1990).

> For mothers: how much would you have to pay a man to do all the housework and mothering for one month?

In exploring the social standing of a housewife, Nilson (1978) made the general point that housework is a significant and onerous task that should be recognised and praised. Valadrez and Clignet (1984) conceptualise housework as an ordeal that binds women together just as ordeals in paid work or war bind men together. The point of this article is that of 'balancing' the way in which many professional women and feminists seem to condemn so many other women to a 'second class role'. Housework, like paid work, has real and positive meanings as well as being debasing. It is unlikely that women can or should 'escape' housework. What might help are systems to encourage men to 'do more' combined with a public recognition and esteem which might, in itself, encourage men to do more.

Caring work

One aspect of the assumed 'naturalness' of women engaging in the caring work of motherhood and housework is the extension of women's roles to 'care' in very many other situations. These may range from occupations (nursing, etc.) to looking after aged relatives, even to responsibility for household pets.

Ask five mothers which member of the family actually looks after the family pet(s).

With the dramatic rise in longevity in many Western nations, the role of many middle-aged women in caring not just for their children and partners but also for other kin, especially grandchildren and the elderly, has come to be more centrally recognised. This, in its turn, has helped reveal the extent to which such women also undertake considerable long-term care for the chronically sick, impaired and disabled whether they be close kin, distant kin or merely neighbours. In 1985, Parker argued that evidence demonstrated 'unequivocally that families do already care for their dependent relatives but that the major part of the burden of care falls on women' (1985, p. 40).

Marsden and Abrams studied the experiences of thirty-eight married daughters caring for elderly mothers who lived with them. What becomes clear is that simple models of caring for someone who previously cared for you are inadequate to describe the range of quite different experiences. The quality of relationships varies from love and companionship to hatred and resentment (Marsden and Abrams, 1987).

As with housework, it is probable that caregiving can have positive aspects such as a sense of satisfaction and fulfilment. In 1990, Aronson explored women's views on informal caregiving: 'While subjects subscribed to cultural assumptions about families, responsibility, gender and old age, they experienced awkwardness in translating them into their own lives. . . . Feelings of guilt and shame were associated with not living up to these expectations' (1990, p. 61).

Paid work roles

Despite a popular rhetoric about the importance of family life, it is clear that paid work roles are given higher social priority. Some time ago, Pleck identified the 'work family role system' in which there are strains and conflicts between male paid work roles and female family roles (1977). Clearly, paid work roles such as work scheduling, shift work patterns and commuting all influence families.

Identify ten ways in which paid work influences family practices.

Finch has demonstrated in *Married to the Job* (1983), that women's lives are influenced by their husband's paid work. In some cases, wives may be expected to attend business functions, in other cases stresses at work may spill over into the family home or, more routinely, many fathers may take work home from time to time. The simple absence of someone from the family home whilst engaged in paid work can have major results; Chandler looks at the way the husband's job may create, effectively, 'women without men' (1991). In the 1990s a popular television advertisement portrayed the workaholic father managing to regain some involvement in family life by way of telephoning his children.

For many families, the career of the main breadwinner, usually male, can have a significant impact upon even geographical location. Leslie and Richardson (1961) explore the issues of family life cycle, career pattern and the decision to move. Many employing companies seem to devise locational patterns that ensure that the interests of families are put second to the interests of the companies.

Paid work for what?

In most Western societies, paid work takes a pre-eminent place in politics, public discussions and many personal aspirations. The European Commission and associated bodies such as COFACE (The Confederation of Family Organisations in the European Community) have, for some time, been exploring the question of 'Paid Work for What?'

Debate within the European Union has centred on the simple issue of a 'Europe of Families' rather than a 'Europe of Economic Production'. This contrasts starkly with the UK of the 1980s and 1990s which places everything second to the importance of the economic marketplace. The issue is one of seeing economic production as the means to the end of underpinning family life rather than as an end in itself.

> Should paid work be a means to support families, or families be a means to support paid workers?

If the aim of work is to establish and maintain family life, it seems particularly strange that many of the difficulties facing contemporary families arise from paid work. Most notable is gender inequality in paid work. This is perhaps best expressed in the idea of female inequality in the paid work sphere and male inequality in the unpaid domestic sphere.

Dual career/dual work

More or less all the research undertaken since the pioneering work of the Rapoports has supported the early theme of 'task overload' for women who take up some kind of paid employment (see Rapoports, 1976; Lewis *et al.*, 1992). It is important to put this in perspective and observe that this is not a new situation in industrial nations, many of which used female and child labour in the heaviest of industrial workplaces in the nineteenth century and during national emergencies in the twentieth century.

The dual burden faced by women who take up paid work was identified in 1956 by Myrdal and Klein (see Myrdal and Klein, 1968). In 1986, Burris simply stated that reproduction and production conflict. For non-professional women the conflict is in 'inflexible scheduling, husband's resistance, and inability to buy support services'. For professional women, 'it is largely the absorptiveness [*sic*] of their careers, and incompatibilities between the nature of professional work and the nature of mothering' (1986, p. 18). In exploring a feminist sociology of motherhood, Ribbens opens by insisting that roles in paid work need to be recognised as constituting a 'second shift' for women in that they continue to be housewives and mothers (1994, p. 2). In an extensive study, *Two careers/One family*, Gilbert reminds us that women working in poorly paid 'second' jobs are far from new; what is new in Gilbert's view is 'men and women as equally able economic providers' (1993, p. xii). Despite detailing considerable evidence of continuing gender inequalities, even in situations with equal economic providers, Gilbert remains optimistic that such situations at least offer the promise of gender equality.

Unemployment

In societies where family lives are so decisively centred upon the wage system, it is hardly surprising that unemployment can have a dramatic and destructive effect upon families. It is also not surprising to find industrial interests, even governments, attempting to deny or downplay the significance of unemployment for families.

During the 1980s, as unemployment began to rise steeply in the UK and other European countries, some voices were raised in protest over the impact on families of economic policies creating unemployment. In 1984, Fagin and Little detailed the family life of the unemployed, noting especially that unemployment was so stressful for many fathers that their own health and family relationships were severely affected.

> List the differences unemployment would make to a family. Pay attention to income, locations of people in time and space, and relationships.

In 1985, Allan devoted an entire chapter in *Family Life* to the issue of 'Unemployment and Family Life'. Allan observed that studies of, usually male, unemployment 'treat the unemployed as individuals and pay relatively little attention to the domestic and family relationships of the unemployed' (1985, p. 149). Noting the long history of unemployment, Allan assembled evidence that unemployment inevitably affects people unevenly, being most likely to happen to 'those who are already disadvantaged – those without marketable skills, those in low paid jobs, the old and the young in the labour force, those from ethnic minorities, the handicapped and disabled' (1985, p. 147). More than this, Jackson and Walsh argue that unemployment is 'a family experience rather than a solitary event' (1987, p. 195). The same authors make clear that:

> Unemployment cannot be understood without recourse to the social context of the families within which most people live. Moreover, a family approach to unemployment research can avoid the narrow assumptions implicit in much research that both employment and unemployment are more important to men than women.
>
> (1987, p. 194)

Unemployment has a marked impact upon marital dissolution; Gallie reviews a range of evidence to conclude that, 'The marriage of an unemployed person was 2.3 times as likely to end in divorce in the following year as the marriage of a person who has never been unemployed' (1994, p. 128).

In her chapter exploring 'Economic Restructuring and Unemployment', Elliot details 'the consequences of unemployment and sub-employment for (i) men, (ii) women, and (iii) young people' (1996, p. 83). Elliot later links the impacts of unemployment to what has become known as 'the underclass debate' in which the media often portrays a lawless underclass of families thus:

> In Britain and elsewhere in Europe, the term is used . . . to refer to groups of people – 'Black' or 'White' and living on run-down council estates or in inner city areas – who are disadvantaged in a number of ways and who have lost touch with the official world.
>
> (1996, p. 104)

Whilst there are a very wide range of diverging views about the 'underclass', even whether it exists, a frequent theme is that underclass families are typically single parent, poor, often from minority ethnic groups and often labelled as 'deviant'.

Workplace family policies

Whilst it is still rare to find material in the UK which draws links between paid work and family pathways, such research does exist in the USA. For example, Friedman explores 'Corporate Response to Family Needs' (1990) in which he examines American work on 'family friendly' atmospheres in the workplace and notes that 40 per cent of the workforce are now dual earners. Most of the employers surveyed made some kind of provision for recognising the demands of child care and elder care by way of allowing time off, permitting flexitime work schedules, agreeing career breaks or allowing leave for new fathers. Aldous has looked at Workplace Family Policies in American companies, and argues that development cannot be left to a few progressive companies because 'The business of America is families, and especially the children they nurture' (1990, p. 365).

More interesting and exciting for the UK, however, are recent initiatives in the European Commission that generated conferences in 1992 (Commission of the European Communities, 1992, 1993a). If the logic of the observation that we put paid work rather than families first is taken seriously, we need to begin to think about the consequences of the reverse. In the context of the UK and Europe, it seems obvious that a great deal of work remains to be done in identifying the conflicts between family lives and paid work lives and developing strategies to resolve these.

Paid work, retirement and gender

The relationship of individuals to paid work is the key to understanding the plight and status of later life families. Modern societies place paid work and earning wages above everything else. When families do not contain a wage earning member, they risk a fall into obscurity and poverty. This can most clearly be seen in later life families, especially in the United Kingdom. Various studies have suggested that, when adjusting for standard of living, UK pensioners have something like 40 per cent less buying power at their disposal than German pensioners.

> Ask ten pensioners to identify the most difficult things about retirement.

The nature of the paid work careers of both partners may have significant impacts upon later life. The value of pensions generated during paid working life is one obvious impact as is health. The value that people place upon paid work *vis-à-vis* family life is of crucial importance. For many people, especially men, the ability to earn an income is a vital element of their own identity.

One area that has received some attention is that of the impacts of the retirement of the breadwinner (usually male) upon the homemaker (usually female). At a general level, it would seem likely that couples may become less gender differentiated in old age, with men becoming more expressive while women become more powerful in the household.

Brubaker noted that, 'Several studies indicate that there may not be a great deal of change after retirement in the way older couples divided the responsibility for household tasks' (1985, p. 33). Keating and Cole encapsulated the changes in the housewife role after retirement in the title of 'What Do I Do With Him 24 Hours a Day?' (1980). In exploring the experiences of dual paid working couples on retirement, Szinovacz (1980) found both negative and positive effects. On the one hand, there was a reduction of tension from dual paid work; on the other hand, there arose the need to invest more effort in achieving marital adjustment. A wide range of factors in later life marriages contain the possibility of changing gender responsibilities: retirement, unemployment or redundancy, departure of offspring, birth of grandchildren and death of relatives. Mason, however, is clear that: 'a fundamental renegotiation of gendered responsibilities . . . does not occur in later life' (1986, p. 2).

Environments beyond families

Reading many textbooks, it would be easy to believe that 'the family' as 'an institution' is somehow timeless and without real form. Families, however, exist in a real material world in which the quality of the environment has a real impact. This is true from the squalor of 'shanty towns' in developing nations, through the punishment of placing homeless families in inadequate 'bed and breakfast' hotels in the UK, to the splendour of Hollywood mansions.

Gender: private and public space

In following pathways through external environments, families are, in many ways, pursuing pathways through what is essentially a White man's world. Family pathways not only exist in a material environment but are heavily influenced by the primarily 'male' nature of that environment. It is tempting to perceive sexual inequality in the limited terms of men taking particular roles and denying these roles to women, especially in continuous paid work. This approach is inadequate because it seems to imply that women could be 'more equal' if only they take up paid work and somehow assert themselves. This model also presupposes the superiority of, or even 'naturalness' of, paid work and the inferiority of unpaid work, especially housework and mothering.

One of the more rarely acknowledged and yet crucial points about family lives is the 'gender' of the private domestic spaces of households and the public spaces in which many activities take place. Roberts (1991) has explored the gender assumptions in housing design, most obvious are assumptions about the primarily female nature of kitchen design and the sale of cooking and laundry equipment.

> Borrow a baby buggy, make the trip on foot or on public transport to shops a couple of miles away, then to municipal buildings (say the Town Hall), and then to the local school at the end of the school day and then home.

It is fascinating how our material environment reinforces notions of the centrality of male paid work and notions of traditional images of 'the family'. The Matrix authors argue that 'no amount of mechanistic plans for communities or villages or social interaction can prevent men from dominating the space outside the home – and keeping women in from fear' (1984, p. 49). These concerns relate to sexuality, fear of violence; these concerns are linked to the presumption of mothering taking place inside the home. It will not be until men have much wider and routine experiences of the way physical design influences family pathways that such design will change.

Culture and ethnicity

In the UK, and indeed most Western societies, the presumptions made in all kinds of areas are those of dominant White culture. This cultural dominance is usually allied to one or other form of Christianity and the kinds of civil law associated with Christian countries. Not only is gender important in the external environment, but the cultural context of any family pathway is of course crucial. It is important to realise that there are real variations within White groups (Christian, Jews, etc.) just as there are within African-Caribbean or Asian groups (see Stones, 1994, pp. 4–5). Amongst these, Asian family pathways are but one range of diverse forms. In criticising the stereotype of 'the Asian family', Westwood and Bhachu pointed out that 'Even the term, "Asian" is misleading. It was a colonial invention used to describe people of Indian descent . . . few "Asians" in Britain identify with this term in any meaningful way' (1988, p. 30). Many such people prefer to 'see themselves as peoples of Indian, Pakistani or Bangladeshi origin or identify themselves as Black people and as Punjabis or Patels' (1988, p. 20).

With more than a million Asian people in the UK, almost half of whom were born in the UK, there is considerable ethnic diversity: Punjabis, Tamils, Gujaratis, Goans and Bengalis who practise a wide range of religions including Sikhs, Muslims (Sunni and Shia), Hindus (including many subgroups), and many Christian groups. Within any one group, there may be a very wide range of diversity according, for example, to traditional notions of 'caste' amongst Hindus and more modern interpretations of caste and marriage within UK Hindu populations (see Searle-Chatterjee and Sharma, 1994). There is some evidence that caste is now treated as one of many factors taken into account in selecting appropriate marriage partners. The point is simply that of considerable variation and cultural diversity which White researchers may not even be able to access let alone understand.

The basic assumption that we tend to make is that other people have the same kinds of feelings as we do. This is plainly not true. Hanson (1991) has explored what is labelled as 'contextual emotion', that is, the way in which emotions are different in different settings. Hanson makes the point that Japanese people experience filial obligation, an emotion for which there is no equivalent term in the West. In the same way, I am sure that a White, middle-class male or female cannot experience the emotions involved in a variety of Asian parental situations in the UK.

Can a White Christian researcher understand Hindu 'caste'? Can a Hindu 'low caste' researcher understand White upper-class mate selection processes?

Outside family members or extended kin

As Ribbens has recently made clear, the experiences of the external world are importantly influenced by outside family members, that is, kin not resident in the immediate 'family household' and yet regarded as 'part of the family', such as grandparents, uncles, aunts or children who have left home (1994, Chapter 4). In many cultures, ancient and modern, outside family members are given a vital role in the everyday lives of families. In many Eastern societies, such as China or Korea, deceased ancestors are regarded as available for advice and able to exert influences upon family members. Particular individuals are often given clear culturally prescribed roles; in many Eastern societies, it was 'traditional' for a newly married couple to move into the groom's home and the bride's mother-in-law would take charge of all domestic affairs.

Relationships with outside family members are not always harmonious; folk mythology in many cultures records struggles not only between parents and natural children but also between partners and 'parents-in-law', uncles, cousins or grandparents. In modern Western societies, ties of blood and marriage often generate senses of reciprocity, obligation and responsibility. A mother-in-law may feel 'entitled' to comment on the way her grandchildren are brought up, just as a wife and mother may feel 'obligated' to visit aged relatives, even delivering care.

Survey ten married people and establish how much influence, positive or negative, 'in-laws' have upon them.

In allowing children to have contacts and activities 'beyond home and family', mothers continue to play a key role in child care by continually paying attention to knowing where children are (see Ribbens, 1994, p. 83). This also relates to an important part of the childrearing process of worries about letting children go out of the home and, ultimately, decisions about when and how to allow children greater freedom.

Shopping

Families in modern Western societies clearly have shifted from a degree of self-sufficiency and production to being largely consumers. One of the key means of consumption is shopping, usually undertaken outside the home but also possible by way of catalogues and television based 'shopping channels'. Shopping may appear to be a simple 'neutral' process; looked at critically, the activity is undertaken largely by women in locations and ways largely determined by men. Shopping represents a major form of unpaid work, often undertaken by women, but also it is one of the occasions when families may venture out into the external world together.

> Visit any supermarket or shopping centre and record the way in which retail outlets appeal to families and/or family members in both design and products.

Whilst mentioned in some accounts of housework, shopping is a much neglected area. Shopping is a vital topic because it is the means by which family consumption is possible and because it is the means by which the values embodied in material production 'get into' so many millions of family homes. This often involves clear expressions of family ideology on product labelling, which end up in cupboards, on tables or work surfaces in family homes.

Alcohol, tobacco and other drugs

One of the important dimensions of family pathways is that of drugs such as alcohol and tobacco. First, it must be realised that these are huge industries in most Western nations which exploit people's propensities and addictions to generate very large profits. Second, all Western governments depend very much upon taxation on these products to conduct government business. Third, whilst such drug use may appear at first sight to relate to individuals (smokers and drinkers) in public places (for example, pubs and bars), this is far from the case. The drug producing industries have direct and critical impacts upon a wide range of family practices and pathways as well as employing a large number of family members. Finally, there are significant degrees of gendering associated with such drug consumption. 'Fighting between drunks' is not usually associated with mothers of the new-born just as smoking has been seen as a primarily male pastime until recent times when young female smoking rates began to rise.

One of the most popular recreational drugs in most Western nations is alcohol. In 1982, Orford and Harwin pinpointed the link between alcoholism and family life:

> We are persuaded that the family is among the principal settings in which the consumption of alcohol is both enjoyed and restrained, and that it constitutes a most important natural resource for the prevention and control of excessive consumption. As the family is our society's main source of social support, and alcohol its chief recreational drug, the field of overlap between the two is bound to be of the utmost practical and theoretical importance.
>
> (1982, Preface)

Sketch out an account of the damage done by alcoholism to any family.

Whilst not generally identified in 'family texts', alcohol is a significant 'family issue' across Europe and the USA. Against the separation of pubs and homes must be weighed what Wilson called the 'hidden tragedy' of children whose lives are blighted by an alcoholic parent (1982). Whilst there are debates about disentangling biological inheritance and social learning in families of alcoholics, clearly a significant number of alcohol problems may be transmitted in families (see Davies, 1982). In the USA, Steinglass developed a 'Life History Model of the Alcoholic Family' (1980). The point of this work was to demonstrate that alcoholism needs to be seen in the context of a family's developmental past, present and future.

Another popular drug in most Western societies is tobacco, often in the form of cigarettes. Tobacco consumption is rarely as destructive as alcohol in the sense of the behaviour of the addict. It is important to realise, however, that tobacco use may be just as damaging to families and shape family practices and pathways, primarily by way of health impacts.

Sketch out an account of the damage done by tobacco to any family.

It is now clear that smoking brings about higher levels of short-term illnesses, is causal in many long-term illnesses such as lung cancer, and is one of the major causes of premature death among adults. More recently, the dangers of 'secondary smoking' have been extensively debated; it seems likely that smoking by adult family members seriously affects the health of non-smoking children.

Giving up smoking is very far from easy. Doherty and Whitehead (1986) explore how family relationships may come under stress and even change when one (or more) member(s) attempts to give up smoking or other members of the family attempt to persuade one member to stop smoking. As with most addictions, there are real behavioural changes resulting from withdrawal (such as anxiety, frustration and bad temper) which will clearly spill over to affect other family members.

Other forms of drugs, whether legal or illegal, medically prescribed or otherwise obtained, may have similarly devastating effects upon families (see Dorn *et al.*, 1987). Various forms of drug abuse seem to be associated with youth culture or taken up in teenage years. In many ways, both legal and illegal drugs symbolise the transition from childhood to maturity and the 'unattaching' of children from families.

Identify drugs, legal and illegal, and how they affect families.

Young drug addicts may live with their addiction for many years, having a variety of intimate partnerships and parenting situations. Drug addiction may endanger unborn babies by way of the poor health of the mother and the dangers of disease transmission such as HIV or AIDS. Recent discussions suggest that 'drug experimentation' is a common childhood experience, perhaps even a modern 'rite of passage' which may present many challenges for parents. Foxcroft and Lowe's (1995) study of adolescent drinking, smoking and stimulant/sedative abuse makes clear that there are links, albeit more complex than expected, between such abuse and perceived family environment. Young males who experienced their families as 'authoritarian' or 'neglecting' tended to have higher levels of abuse of alcohol, tobacco and 'hard' drugs; in the case of females, there was less abuse and the relationship was less clear.

Family practices: constructing families

Modernist accounts of family life have always focused upon marriage and parenthood as the key ways in which families are created. Whilst these elements are important, we know very little indeed about ordinary everyday family practices. There are, however, some indicators of the sorts of things that serve to construct and reinforce a sense of 'being family' for some or all of the participants.

Mealtimes

Whilst modern families are changing, and 'time together' may be declining, one of the important remaining areas of family practices is mealtimes. Burgoyne and Clark have argued that 'The mundane tasks of cooking, eating and clearing up – such central activities within any domestic regime – are curiously absent from existing sociological descriptions of family life' (1985, p. 152). Some recent work suggests that many families now eat in stages with different family members eating different things at different times.

Ask six mothers of school-age children about how many different meals are prepared, how well their children eat, and whether mealtimes are battlegrounds or not.

Mealtimes seem to involve all sorts of issues around gender (women do most of the food preparation), power (parents attempt to control the situation), and commercial power (many parents buy advertised foods because of children's expressed wishes). DeVault's study, *Feeding the Family*, points out that this is not only about shopping, planning and cooking but also about 'constructing the family' as a social group. DeVault argues that one of the keys means by which to highlight gendered roles both within families and the wider society is to use the study of feeding families as a means to 'bring the work of daily maintenance and sociability into view' (1991, p. 242).

Careful consideration of television advertising around food reveals that industry is ready to exploit parental concern about what children eat and how they eat it. As a father, I still reflect upon the prophetic words of various baby manuals that warned against allowing 'mealtimes to become battlegrounds'.

Contrary to what might be expected, children have very definite 'likes' and 'dislikes' when it comes to food. It seems likely that these are the cause of a great deal of conflict and even abuse. It seems clear that parents adopt all kinds of different strategies – from allowing children to snack on anything at anytime to strict mealtimes where only 'wholesome' are foods offered with no substitutes. It also seems clear that many meal preparers, mainly women, go to great lengths to find foods that their children will eat.

Photographs and albums

In exploring 'what are families like?' at every opportunity in every possible location for many years, one recurrent response from people has been to show me photographs or other images of their parents, partners, children and other family members. Inside many family homes, pride of place is given to photographs of immediate and more distant family members. I have been fascinated to find such displays not only in the UK and Europe but also in South America and China.

> Ask people to show you their family albums and provide a commentary. Pay attention to explanations of family relationships and events.

Spence and Holland (1991) explore the meanings of 'domestic photography' in a number of ways. What becomes clear is that family photography is both part of a process of family construction as well as an attempt to define and maintain what may be fragmented realities. In some ways, family photographs may be used by one or more members to create a 'sense of family' that may be rather different to the experiences of other family members. In an unpublished paper presented at the 'British Sociological Association Family Studies Group', Cotterill and Letherby (1993) are frank enough to admit destroying unflattering photographs of themselves. Decisions about whose photographs are displayed and whose are included in family albums are an important means by which members define 'their family' both at a moment in time and over time.

Toys, games and play

Play for contemporary children often revolves around material objects produced by profitable industries (see Kline, 1993). In the mid-1980s, Margaret Thatcher argued that, 'The people who give everything to their children because they don't like to exercise family discipline don't get it right' (Fitzgerald, 1983, p. 51). This contrasted starkly with the trend throughout the 1980s and 1990s where parents faced ever greater demands from children, often stimulated by television, for the 'latest' toys. Whilst the educational aspect of toys, games and play is often identified, the stress of parent–child disputes over their purchase seems to be ignored.

> Visit a toy shop 'as an alien', what conclusions would you reach about the users of the toys?

Modern play tends to involve the intrusion of large industrial concerns into the intimate private centres of families. More than this, the way in which toys are advertised on television has created a very powerful means by which particular ideas and images are imported into families; Kline identifies this process as 'Playing with Culture' (1993, see Chapter 10). Despite all my best efforts as a parent, many of my daughter's toys involve clear 'gender images', even if we have managed to avoid too many dolls and images of mothering. My son's toys nearly all have weapons attached and seem to revolve around killing and winning, from 'Cowboys and Indians' to 'Stars Wars'.

Toys, games and play, then, seem to regularly involve sex-typing, clear themes of war and aggression and other values reflecting modern industrial behaviour, such as competition and material wealth. There is clearly room to ask whether specific toys are harmful to children, or even addictive, as in the case of video games. From both television and video games, some children will mimic the kinds of aggressive fight scenes portrayed and, perhaps just as serious, will adopt all kinds of anti-social attitudes towards siblings and parents that may create enormous stress and disputes.

Television and video

Modern societies are changing very rapidly and one aspect of technology, the television, is gaining more and more attention. By way of television, children are exposed to all kinds of images and information (broadcast, satellite, cable and recorded media).

Winn characterises television as *The Plug-in Drug* and it is important to remember that children probably spend more time watching television than in the school classroom or in interaction with their parents. In greater detail, Winn argues that, 'By it's domination of the time families spend together, it [the television] destroys the special qualities that distinguishes one family from another' and later that 'yet parents have accepted the television dominated life so completely, that they cannot see how the medium is involved in whatever problems they might be having' (Winn, 1985, p. 141). Rogge takes this idea further to argue that, 'The media form part of the family system, a part many can no longer imagine living without' (1989, p. 169).

The debate about the impact of television upon children has a long and chequered history with one party assigning maturity and discrimination to children and another party assigning children almost as 'empty vessels' filled with violence and sexuality by television. The relationships between children and parents are significantly changed and children's television viewing perme-ates family life from shopping decisions to bedtimes. In exploring television watching and family tensions, Rosenblatt and Cunningham (1976) found that higher levels of tension were found in families with high levels of television watching and suggested that television watching is used by some families as a means of avoiding rather than resolving emerging tensions.

> Ask any parent for their feelings about children and television advertising.

It seems obvious to me that television does have a significant impact upon myself and my own children. Children can experience a huge and incredible range of views and experiences that should enrich their lives and intellects. Television media have the potential to make us all less ignorant and less intolerant. They also have the reverse potential and can be used to enormous propaganda effect. The main current propaganda effect seems to continually extol major social values around violence and power, ethnocentricity, sexuality, materialism, and the easy trivialisation of 'tradition' and 'history'.

Home computing

Information technology has recently invaded family homes in all kinds of ways, perhaps the most significant is the home computer which is rapidly becoming more powerful. It is extremely difficult to predict what precise impacts home computing will have upon families but it is important to realise that such technology does and will have major impacts.

> Survey the positive and negative aspects of home computers.

The best way to think of this potential is to remember that family practices and pathways represent the way in which individuals come together and interact. Information technology can significantly influence those practices in all kinds of ways. Most obvious is the reduction in overall interaction because children are 'always playing games on the computer' or perhaps because 'Dad is hooked on the computer' or 'Mum is working from home using the computer'.

Information technology can also influence the nature of interactions, the obvious example comes from concerns about the high levels of violence portrayed in some computer games. This is likely to be overshadowed in the future as the nature of software and links between home computers and other computers become more common.

Bedtimes

Notwithstanding any tendency for being 'night people' or 'day people' (see Adams and Cromwell, 1978), most commentators seem to believe that children need more sleep than adults and that children should 'be in bed' somewhat earlier than adults. This may also reflect a wish by parents to have some time to themselves before retiring to bed.

Bedtimes are a key issue in some households and may sometimes be an issue over which conflict and abuse emerge, especially as children grow older. We know little about bedtimes and sleeping patterns and very little about children's views of bedtimes.

> Ask six parents about the 'bedtimes' of their children and whether these are matters of dispute.

In the UK, major television companies operate a 'watershed' hour of 9.00 p.m. after which they feel less restrained in showing programmes containing sexuality and violence. The assumption is that most 'impressionable children' will, by that time, be in bed. It is unfortunate that social science cannot at the moment be more helpful in presenting evidence about bedtimes for children.

Nagging

There are very many areas in which parents attempt to erect and impose rules that children ignore, challenge or resist. The struggle around imposing control is not conducted with clear, rational argument but with a range of techniques and strategies among which are simple bribery (we'll go to the cinema if you're good) and nagging.

> Ask ten parents to identify the areas in which most disputes emerge with children.

It is important to note at the outset that folk tales, modern cartoons, and 'children's stories' are often based upon worlds in which usual 'adult rules' do not apply. In playing, we encourage our children to 'use their imagination'. In view of this, it should come as no surprise (and probably is no surprise to any parent) that children may not immediately recognise the necessity of good communication, let alone agree to 'follow the rules' of conversation.

The one feature of communication patterns with children that deserves a great deal more attention is that of the way in which carers, usually mothers and sometimes fathers, resort to nagging children. Nagging is to find fault with, to urge to do something, to cause pain to, or continually annoy. In popular discourse, it is usually women who nag men and children. Whilst men may be more familiar with more formal and public forms of communication, it seems to me to be likely that men can and do nag just as much as women. Children tend not to recognise more formal 'rules' of communication and, in an increasingly anti-violence and anti-physical punishment climate, it seems quite possible that nagging of children is on the increase.

> Visit any supermarket after school or at a weekend and record the incidence of nagging, who nags who, and why?

The occasion to nag probably relates to areas in which children and parents disagree for a variety of reasons. There are, in modern families, obvious interventions by commercial interests that can be seen clearly on television. Other areas in which nagging occurs are those relating to mealtimes, bedtimes, the use of toys and play. As children mature, it is likely that such nagging will move to other topics such as sex, smoking, alcohol and drugs (see Brannen *et al.*, 1994, pp. 165–79).

Nagging is about exerting influence and control when other means, such as physical force or material reward, are either not available or not recognised by the nagged. Thus the toddler who wants to throw a toy into the road is not amenable to rational discussion. The man who refuses to visit the in-laws or dig the garden cannot be beaten into submission or find his 'housekeeping' withheld.

As many feminists have observed, women have less material and physical power, so nagging is probably the only form of effective communication left. Mason has suggested that, 'The main point is that nagging is only nagging as opposed to monitoring, interfering or talking over in so far as it is to be considered to be talk about something inconsequential' (Mason, 1987, p. 104). The point is that an individual, whether a child or male partner, defines the talk as nagging as a way of asserting that it is of no great consequence.

Nagging, then, is probably one of the main forms of adult–child communication and reflects the very different worlds the two inhabit. It is surprising that feminist work has not looked more at the issue of nagging and explored the different power systems underlying communication. Nagging may be a manifestation of gender and age structuring. It seems clear that men, women and children possess quite different levels of power in terms of physical force and control of material rewards. This is not to say that the 'weakest' do not resort to physical force at times. Ask parents (usually mothers) at play groups or school gates whether a child's tantrums have ever physically hurt them.

> Compare and contrast the way in which men and women may each 'get what they want' in the workplace, at home in front of the children, and in complete privacy.

Family lives and health

Few, if any, family textbooks discuss health issues in any detail. Consider for a moment that the bulk of the burden of ill health for children and adults will fall upon carers who are likely to be involved in partnerships, including marriage. By mid-life, families will usually have had considerable experience of health problems from the short lived 'childhood diseases' through to long-term chronic sickness and disability. It is vital to grasp that illness and disability do not simply mean shifts in caring tasks, or 'looking after' the ill or disabled, but rather represent major influences on family practices. Lyons *et al.* assert that, 'There is increasing evidence that illness and disability change social networks and relationships. Illness intrudes on the roles and pleasures that originally constituted close relationships with family and friends' (1995, p. 125). Clearly, there are a wide variety of family health pathways, some of which are predictable, some of which are not. Among the more predictable issues in family health pathways is the inevitable decline of health of parents in mid-life and the inevitable feature of the death of family members such as grandparents or kin.

Health and marriage

Whilst there is some significant work on family life and health in the USA, there is very little such work in the UK. In an early work, Anne Oakley examined 'The Family, Marriage, and its Relationship to Illness' (1976). In this detailed study, Oakley locates family life as the major context in which ill people find themselves. It is within families that the bulk of care of the sick is undertaken, especially of chronic or long-term conditions.

Plainly, a wide range of health-related conditions will affect family pathways. Some sense of the enormous range of health conditions can be seen in Elliott's work in 1993 which includes brief reviews of trends and programmatic issues for family health in America, many of which apply equally well to the UK and Europe. These issues include debates about public health, health promotion, disease prevention, minority health experiences, ageing, hospice care, mental illness, substance abuse, AIDS, disability, chronic illness, and long-term care. These impacts can perhaps be best understood as additional 'burdens', as suggested by Gubman and Tessler in the case of mental illness (1987, p. 226).

Oakley is also one of the pioneers exploring the issue of gender and illness, noting how women tend to care for men who are ill and yet have to care for themselves when ill because of the unavailability of men (who may put paid work first). As the roles of diet, housing, psychological development and stress in contributing to illness become clearer, so it becomes clear that family pathways are involved in the origins as well as the treatment of many diseases. In all of this, again, women take an important role as the primary carers.

> Ask middle-aged parents (especially mothers) about family health over the previous twenty years.

Bernard (1982) demonstrated the health dimension of the 'two marriages', that is 'his' marriage and 'her' marriage. Married men are significantly healthier than single men; married women, on the other hand, are significantly less healthy than their single counterparts. There is no reason to suspect that this inequality does not apply equally to cohabitation. The health of one's partner can be crucial in personal experience. Fletcher discusses male death rates by occupation and notes how women's death rates match these 'Thus the males' job risks affect the life expectancy of both partners' (1983, p. 123). Peterson found that spouses of the disabled 'become encased by the disability, altering appreciably the context of these marriages' (1979, p. 47). In exploring weight, obesity and dieting, Sobal (1984) makes the point that weight and diet, especially feelings and disputes about these, are all part of the dynamic of family interaction and influence family relationships.

Mid-life and menopause

Textbooks on family life rarely refer to issues concerning the well-being of women during menstruation or monthly 'periods' during which a natural clearing of blood and debris from the womb occurs. A related and similarly neglected area is that of menstrual disorders and menopause in middle-age. The female menopause involves 'the change' from regular menstruation and potential child-bearing. This phase is often associated with a range of medical and emotional changes, many of which may be distressing. In her wide ranging popular study, *The Change – Women, Ageing and the Menopause*, Greer demonstrates how changes and distress are made more difficult because of essentially 'male' views in medicine and popular beliefs (Greer, 1991, see Introduction).

In mid-life, especially in relation to the menopause, male views within medicine combined with physiological and emotional changes as well as dramatic shifts in the nature of unpaid work responsibilities, mark female path-ways as distinct. If men were deprived of a lifelong identity in paid work, experienced wide ranging changes in unpaid work roles and underwent major physiological and emotional changes, it seems probable that some more extensive research and support would have been developed long ago.

Speculate on the changes in society if men experienced 'periods' and the menopause.

This is not to suggest that men do not undergo some changes in mid-life although these tend to be far less dramatic than those experienced by women. It is quite common nowadays to come across debates about the existence of the 'male menopause'. Whilst there is no evidence of major physiological changes associated with the male reproductive system, a range of physiological and other changes that occur around middle-age may coincide with what is often called a 'mid-life crisis'. Men at this time may be losing their vigour and youthfulness and may have difficulties 'coming to terms' with a declining work horizon and facing old age. This period is, of course, heightened for some by the youthfulness of their children.

Family pathways and disability

Ours is a society that discriminates against the sick and disabled. Whilst something like 1 in 10 persons in the UK are disabled, less than 1 per cent of those in employment or higher education are disabled. There are probably more than 200,000 families in the UK caring for disabled children with what NCH Action for Children (1994) describes as inadequate support services and benefits. Such families struggle to care for their children in a confused atmosphere that often involves pity, fear and insensitivity.

Kazak (1986) has argued that families with a physically handicapped child face considerable additional stress. In the face of 'public images' of families which do not contain disabled persons, it is likely that the burden of stress is doubled. Booth and Booth have recently explored, *Parenting under Pressure*, that is, the experiences of mothers and fathers with learning difficulties (1994).

Bernier (1990) reviews the various discussions of how parents adjust to the birth of a disabled child and emphasises that this cannot be understood as a single event but rather requires a wide range of different approaches. Parents continually need to readjust to the disability of the child over time and often find themselves facing 'recurrent grief'. This in itself suggests the need for continually changing systems of support and help as children with disabilities grow and mature.

Recently recognised diseases, such as AIDS, are relevant here. In the American context, Cates *et al.* argue that, 'With the increasing longevity of persons with AIDS, the family has begun to assume greater long-term respon-sibility for care of family members' (1990, p. 195). In looking at the family care of adults with chronic mental and physical illnesses, Biegel *et al.* suggest that, 'Informal service providers, like the family, have always been the primary source of human service care to individuals in need' (1991, p. 7). In the UK, Elliot devotes a chapter in *Gender, Family and Society* to the exploration of 'AIDS: Battleground of Competing Moralities' and presents the various positions in some detail. Overall, however, Elliot makes clear that the debates about AIDS have consequences in terms of epitomising 'the ambivalences, anxieties and problems of post-permissive Western Societies' (1996, p. 212); in this sense, AIDS may well have impacts upon sexual behaviour which, in turn, will impact upon heterosexual partnering and ultimately marriage.

Child health

Whilst the childhood diseases are no longer such widespread killers, they are still a common experience for most children and require periods of care. Such care may also be required as a result of everyday viruses, colds and 'flu and the serious but common causes of ill health such as appendicitis, asthma, hearing or sight impairments. To these should be added a range of factors from alcoholism or childhood substance abuse to the effects of smoking.

Graham has done much work in the UK on the special role women and mothers play in the maintenance of family health, even to the detriment of their own health. Unlike most of the European Union, the care of sick children (our 'future generations' which we publicly claim to cherish) and other family members is not catered for in employment protection (see Ditch, 1996a, pp. 41–61) and is one of the main reasons for difficulties women face in obtaining and keeping paid work. When you begin to consider how often people are afflicted by illness and the number of people whose lives are impaired in some way, it is inevitable that very large numbers of families, if not all families, are significantly influenced by health factors.

> When did you, your partner, parents or children last experience any impairment of health or fitness? Who cared for the sick person?

A study by Graham (1993) concentrates on *Hardship and Health in Women's Lives*. Graham documents the roles of six million extremely diverse mothers caring for children and the health dimensions of women's roles in housing, motherhood, child care, paid employment, managing budgets and their own health patterns. As elsewhere, the picture is a very clear one of women and mothers experiencing considerable physical and emotional stress in their caring roles; whilst some men do undertake such roles, clearly the main burden is carried by women.

Brannen *et al.* (1994) explore health issues such as diet, drugs, alcohol and smoking. As children encounter the transition to adulthood, so they begin to take on control and responsibility for these health dimensions of their lives. These transitions can involve conflict, negotiation and stress and can, in some cases, lead to harmful risk-taking. Young people may take up smoking or drug-taking as a symbol of moving out of the control of their parents. Sweeting and West have explored evidence concerning what they claim to be the largely ignored influence of families upon the health of adolescents, especially referring to family structure, culture and family conflict. This work helps explain the means by which different families produce different sorts of outcomes for adolescent health and Sweeting and West go as far as arguing that 'in adolescence family life may have more direct effects on family health than material factors and, through social mobility, may be indirectly linked to health inequalities in adulthood' (1995, p. 163).

> Should we allow any adults to be poor? Should we allow the children of poor adults to suffer deprivation and ill health?

One of the major factors related to ill health is that of family poverty. This was the central theme of the report chaired by Sir Douglas Black and published in 1980 (known as the Black Report). The report made a number of wide ranging recommendations to address issues of ill health as a matter of urgency that the government of the day explicitly refused to endorse. This report was updated in 1987 by the Health Education Council and appeared as the *Health Divide* (see Townsend *et al.*, 1988).

Ill health in later life

One of the key events of later life families is the decline of health of one or both marital partners. Brubaker has noted that, 'As a couple ages, there is an increased probability that one of the spouses will become a caregiver for the other' (1985, p. 45). This is, of course, especially true in couples over 75 years of age. The majority of wives find themselves providing care for their husband before becoming widows. When a spouse becomes ill, the nature of inter-dependence between husband and wife may be altered dramatically.

> List the consequences of ill health in later life families.

Rossiter and Wicks (1982) explored the circumstances of the elderly. As age increases so the occurrence of health problems is likely to rise, what are minor illnesses become serious and disabling. Related to increasing old age is the decline of housing quality: many old people living alone can no longer maintain their accommodation nor call upon others to help. One of the key reasons for the relatively poor housing situation of many elderly people is their low incomes. Rates of income support in the UK (in real terms) in old age have declined in recent years as the numbers of elderly and the overall cost of income support has risen. It is a matter of some considerable shame that the United Kingdom shares with other countries in Europe the problem of hypothermia deaths of elderly people. Each winter, hundreds, even thousands, of poor elderly people fail to be able to adequately heat themselves (see Wicks, 1978 and 1987).

Death and bereavement

Death and bereavement are two of the certainties of family pathways. Whilst many traditional societies have clear sets of rules and procedures to cope with these events, modern societies have increasingly destroyed such rules.

The processes of death and dying have been removed from the family sphere into the hands of medical and funereal professions. Whilst medical intervention has clearly been of great importance in lengthening life for individuals, this does have consequences. At the simplest level, many people now survive what were once life threatening illnesses and this tends to create the expectation that all our illness can be cured. Partners and relatives often find the death of a loved one much more of a shock because of a belief that the illness can be treated. This means that, for many, the process of bereavement and readjustment is not only extremely distressing but also a period of enormous uncertainty about how to behave.

This uncertainty can be increased by the rapid secularisation of society, or the decline of the importance of religion, especially the decline of Christianity among the dominant White culture. Christianity, like many religions, emphasises continuity in death and suggests at least some kind of future for the dead by way of the spirit or soul. In an increasingly individualistic and materialistic society, such spiritual values are shunned in favour of the pursuit of wealth and consumption. This materialism leaves the bereaved with little sense of how to understand their loss. This, of course, may have dramatic and clear consequences within families.

Widowhood

In all but the rarest of cases, one partner will die before the other, meaning that widowhood and widowerhood are common experiences which many of us will face. There are diverse paths into widowhood ranging from long-term sickness to sudden and unexpected death. Wedemeyer (1986) argues that the effects of a death in a family can vary from welcomed relief to painful paralysis of family functioning (also see *Journal of Family Issues* – Special issue, 1986). Long-term carers of a dependent partner face not only bereavement but also dramatic change in domestic work.

How many widows and widowers are there in the UK?

Preceding widowhood, there is likely to be a short or long period of ill health and increasing dependency of one partner. With the better longevity of females, it tends to be women who care for their dependent husbands and then have to achieve the transition from wife to widow. Beyond widowhood, the survivor may live for a short or long period in good or declining health that may or may not require support and care from other people.

The lack of preparation for widowhood combined with the lack of clear rules or social locations for widows make the process of grieving even more intense and difficult. Upon being widowed, individuals may experience a whole range of emotions including chaos, anger, resentment, denial and disbelief. This may be followed by intense grief and a search for the lost person. Eventual acceptance of the death of one's partner can lead to depression and apathy. To successfully survive, the widow has to reorganise his or her life in an entirely new and unexpected way.

Upon bereavement in a gendered society, both sexes face the task of 'substituting' their own labour for that of their partner. Men may have to learn how to cook, clean and do the laundry. Women may have to learn how to drive and undertake household maintenance. Whilst couples who no longer have a breadwinner tend to be neglected by societies which value productivity, it is widows who experience some of the worst objective conditions in our societies. Many widows fall into deep poverty from which the only escape is their own death.

> Could you be (or have been) better prepared for the loss of your partner? How?

The gendering of death not only has biological elements but also clear social elements, which may or may not be part of the explanation of female longevity. Women tend to have developed social networks beyond paid work throughout their lives of childrearing and homemaking; these may often survive into old age. Men, on the other hand, tend to build social networks around paid work and social activities such as sport that may decline in old age. In this way, women may have at hand far more extensive and supportive social networks in widowhood whereas men may have far less support.

Suggested reading

DeVault, M. L. 1991: *Feeding the Family: The Social Organisation of Caring as Gendered Work*. Chicago: University of Chicago Press.

Dobash, R. E. and Dobash, R. P. 1992: *Women, Violence and Social Change*. London: Routledge.

Elliot, F. R. 1996: *Gender, Family and Society*. Basingstoke: Macmillan.

Graham, H. 1993: *Hardship and Health in Women's Lives*. Hemel Hempstead: Harvester Wheatsheaf.

La Fontaine, J. 1990: *Child Sexual Abuse*. Cambridge: Polity.

Lewis, S., Dafna, N., Izraeli, N. and Hootsman, H. 1992: *Dual-Earner Families: International Perspectives*. London: Sage.

Matrix Book Group 1984: *Making Space: Women and the Man Made Environment*. London: Pluto.

Chapter 5

Children in
families

Introduction

Across Europe millions of children are born each year: some are rich, some poor, some Black, some White; together, they are born into dozens of different languages and cultures. The vast majority, however, are born into families and spend a considerable number of years more or less exclusively in the care of family members, usually parents.

Whilst children are often seen as distinguishing families from non-families, it is interesting to see how differently children are treated throughout the world. In modern Western societies, children and childhood are visible in television, media, shops and education. This reflects not only how much we claim to care about children but also that children and childhood are very big business.

Despite the prominence of children and childhood in our societies, Morrow argued in 1993 that children are rarely seen and never heard in sociological analyses of family life. This chapter reflects adult views of children and childhood but will attempt, where possible, to alert the reader to the need to seek the views and feelings of children.

> Imagine yourself as a dependent individual who cannot vote, drive or legally take up full-time paid work. How would you (do you) feel?

It is only very recently that researchers have begun to look systematically at 'Children's Accounts and Accounts of Childhood', drawing upon the views and feelings of children involved in family pathways (see Brannen and O'Brien, 1995, Section IV) and even then there is a major problem of adults interpreting the statements of children. In the context of social work, Williamson and Butler have argued that 'What is of greatest concern is that children are sceptical that responses by adults will be appropriate in their terms; they have no faith in the capacity of adults to listen to and hear their side of the story' (1995, p. 294). We also have very little material that seeks to emphasise the wide variation and diversity of childhood experiences on family pathways.

Just as much traditional family sociology has taken 'the family' as a central stereotypical image, so much sociology and psychology have taken the idea of 'the child' and 'childhood' as stereotypes. Many accounts of childhood focus upon a simplistic model of socialisation in which parents facilitate their children in learning the skills and abilities required to be a mature adult. Socialisation is much more complex than this; it is a two way process that is as enormously rich and varied as the circumstances in which children find themselves.

The sociology of childhood

Most sociological textbooks do not even mention childhood except as the period of 'primary socialisation'. Whilst psychological textbooks tend to contain more discussions, these are often in terms of models of child development. Brim and Ryff discuss the interaction of biological, social and psychological events and the way in which researchers focus upon the normal, predictable and expected and therefore ignore and even deny the 'unexpected' (1980, p. 367). It is, of course, the unexpected, the variable and changeable that makes life interesting. Most American 'Family Studies' textbooks do include a full chapter on children or 'the child' but this is usually from an adult point of view.

In 1982, Jenks proposed the development of a Sociology of Childhood. Jenks begins from the point that we create children and childhood and is critical of the assumption of unidirectional socialisation, that is, parents rearing children to become mature, rational adults. In looking at children almost as aliens, Jenks asks 'Just what, after all, are we to make of children?' We work with a host of images and typifications of childhood ranging from unsocialised beasts to untainted angels. Jenks concludes that, 'Simply stated the child is familiar to us and yet strange' (1982, p. 9). This is perhaps the clearest and yet most astonishing indictment of contemporary sociology. How can we all have 'passed through' childhood and yet, as adults, be so deeply ignorant and disinterested in childhood?

Children are largely absent from grand theorising, when they are present they tend to be located as passive receivers of adult rearing practices. In attempting to further develop a sociology of childhood, Alanen argued that we need to deconstruct 'the family'. We need to change our approach to childhood quite dramatically and begin to move from child as victim to recognise children as 'participants and constructors in the very processes that make their – and our – world' (Alanen, 1988, p. 65). This theme is echoed by Qvortrup who welcomes the shift to "'children in families' rather than . . . 'families with children'" in Brannen and O'Brien's edited collection (1996, pp. xii–xiii).

Images of childhood

Perhaps the clearest sense of the enormous amount of work that remains to be done in developing a Sociology of Childhood comes from Holland's attempt to portray *What is a Child?* (1992). This is a valuable insight into popular images of children and childhood that explores the differences, ambiguities and contradictions in our images of children and childhood. Holland develops a detailed commentary on a wide range of popular images including cuddly babies, temper tantrums, superbrats, pupils, the fantasy of children's rights, youth, sex and sexuality, damaged children.

Collect six 'images of children' from the popular press. What sorts of things do these images suggest?

Implicit in the wide range of popular images of children is the oppression of children in many ways including gender, ethnicity, sexuality, power, material wealth. In concluding her book, Holland comments that children 'respond to the imagery that surrounds us all, making use of it to define themselves and their experiences. Yet of all social groups, children are the least able to explore their view of themselves in the public domain' (1992, p. 174). This in turn suggests a complex interaction between parents' views of their children, their own children's views and the way in which children 'receive' images and messages about 'being a child' from the media. Holland presents a general argument for us to readjust our concept of childhood and give more voice to children themselves (ibid.). This issue is parallel in many ways to recent debates in sociology about the place and role of subjects. It seems clear and obvious that we should begin to devote a great deal more effort to children's own accounts of family pathways.

This argument is not without a major difficulty. Modern societies have constructed children to have different understandings, interests and preoccupations to adults. This means that adult researchers may well face considerable problems in understanding children's own accounts just as parents often find themselves unable to understand a child's anger, sadness or tantrum.

Ask ten children what they think is the 'most important thing' in their lives.

The experiences of childhood have a very clear effect on adult life. Whilst it is plainly not as easy as saying that abused children will become abusers or that children of poorly educated parents will themselves do poorly at school, clearly a child's experiences are vital for the rest of his or her life. It is astonishing that complex modern societies do very little in the way of systematic preparation or education to ensure that parents or carers are aware of 'good' and 'bad' practice.

The concept of childhood

It is vital, at the outset, to clarify the point that the very idea of childhood is located in history and culture; different cultures have treated children rather differently in various historical periods. One major theory derives from the work of Phillipe Aries who argued in 1960 that childhood as we understand it in the West emerged after the medieval period when children were portrayed primarily as 'little adults' (see Aries, 1986). Childhood as understood in contemporary Western societies developed in the late nineteenth and early twentieth centuries with legislation removing children from the paid work place and legislation making available universal compulsory education (see Jenks, 1996, Chapter 5).

Pollock has developed a fierce criticism of the work of Aries and others to ague that the idea of children and childhood has changed remarkably little over the recorded centuries. Pollock is critical of the lack of solid evidence, 'The evidence presented for the thesis that there was no concept of childhood and that parents were, at best, indifferent to their offspring and, at worst, cruel to them, is varied' (1983, p. 23). What Pollock believes to have happened is that there have been major changes in public attitudes towards children but that these have not been reflected in the realities of parental behaviour. In some periods children have been relatively absent from public debate but this did not mean that the concept of childhood was missing. In the modern period, children are seen as important but, as many other authors have noted, this does not mean that children are particularly well treated.

Not all other contemporary cultures treat children as we do. What are in the West regarded as 'dependent young children' are to be found engaged in hard physical labour, sold into virtual slavery or prostitution in many countries around the world. Taken a step further, however, this points to the way in which children in different cultures within a Western society, like the UK, may be regarded in rather different ways according to culture, religion or ethnicity. Within a UK school there may be very wide ranges of childhood experience with regard to parental discipline, freedom to play, freedom to associate across religion and culture, material wealth and degree of parental interest.

In exploring conceptions of childhood in the UK, Ribbens draws upon the accounts of mothers to support three current typifications of children: as natural innocents, as little devils, and as small people (1994, p. 148). Whilst it seems unlikely that we could easily uncover all the available typifications, the point is that our public images may bear little relationship to everyday family practices. What is clear is that children in Western societies are treated as 'being different' to adults. This is such a deeply taken-for-granted attitude that it may require a moment's reflection.

Whilst there was a flurry of concern about the 'liberation of children' in the 1970s (see Holt, 1974), there has been remarkably little change over past decades in the way in which we view children as immature and inferior. I was somewhat taken aback at a conference in which a participant simply asked why children cannot vote. The immediate response centres around notions of maturity and responsibility. In the simple response that 'obviously children should not vote', the arguments are the same as those once used to justify not giving the vote to poor people, women or, until recently in some countries, particular racial groups.

We should reflect for a moment upon the way in which children as a social grouping are powerless and subject to all kinds of control and oppression. Archard has explored the 'rights' of children, including discussions of the issues of voting and sexuality (1993, pp. 7–81).

Sketch out the nature of the oppression of children by listing the sorts of things we refuse to allow children to do.

This is not to suggest that we allow children complete freedom, I am sure my own children would spend our weekly family budget rather differently if they were in control! The point to understand is the way in which we expect parents to control the lives of children.

Nature or nurture?

One perennial question for parents, philosophers, psychologists and sociologists is the degree to which a child's character and ability is determined by biological inheritance or social learning within families and formal education. This question is debated in many textbooks in terms of the Nature (biological inheritance) versus Nurture (social learning) debate. This debate is at the very centre of the split between those who see human beings largely in biological terms and those who see human beings largely in social terms.

On the biological side (Nature), 'the family' is seen as universal, as is 'female inferiority' and the 'natural' role of women in caregiving. On this side of the debate, many have argued that children are genetically programmed in certain ways; the most notable area of this debate is in the study of gender and race. Whilst the ideas about gender and race surface from time to time, most informed commentators now doubt that females or Black people are somehow genetically 'inferior' to men or White people.

On the social side (Nurture), 'the family' is seen as a human social construction that varies by culture and history and gender roles are seen as socially constructed and therefore changeable. On the nurture side of the debate, many have argued that children are largely products of the type and quality of nurturing or childrearing, usually focusing upon the childrearing aspects of families.

> Ask any mother of more than one child to describe how different her children are.

What is missing in both arguments is a simple recognition of human uniqueness and spontaneity. All human beings, from birth onwards, play an active part in determining 'who they are'. In doing this, human beings certainly are influenced by nature and nurture but the real point to grasp is the way in which human individuality operates in social contexts.

Socialisation

The key issue in virtually every discussion of childhood centres around a process called socialisation. Socialisation refers to the many and varied processes of 'learning' by which a helpless infant becomes a mature adult member of society. When one looks at the new-born infant in the arms of an adult, the sheer difference between the two in terms of skills and abilities is astonishing.

List the key differences between the new-born child and the mature adult.

Analysis usually emphasises the issue of child development, that is, a progressive learning of new skills and abilities. After developing facial responses, babies begin to gain more deliberate control of their limbs and begin a rapid learning curve that includes the development of mobility (crawling, 'toddling' and walking) and speech. It is important to note that most accounts of child development emphasise apparently universal or widely shared skills and abilities and usually completely ignore variation in these abilities or the environment in which they occur. In this way, differences due to material wealth or ethnic background or religious practices are often given very low priority.

Also ignored are the deep confusions about how exactly we want our children to grow up. There is a popular rhetoric that emphasises conflicting behaviours such as obedience and educational success yet also aggressiveness and competition. We want people to 'respect' both property and authority and yet clearly deny many the opportunity to obtain property or wealth. Whilst we have a broad idea of equal citizenship in adulthood, we plainly do not care that children may be born into very unequal circumstances. Whilst we are critical of the poor, although perhaps seeing the disabled as 'deserving poor', and may even 'blame' the poor for their own plight, we do not seem concerned to prevent future poverty. In this way, we conspire to punish the children of the poor, the disabled or the imprisoned. We seem entirely happy for the children of the poor, disabled or chronically ill to share the experience of poverty rather than attempting to compensate those children.

Imagine yourself in the position of a young child growing up in what are often labelled as 'deprived families'. What lessons do you think you would learn about the attitude of society to families and their children? It seems clear that the child would soon realise that he or she is less valued than other children simply because of the situation of his or her parent.

More to the point, in the lack of any preparation or advice about 'how to parent', clearly our societies are happy to see large numbers of children made to suffer for the characteristics of their parents. Socialisation, then, is not only about how a helpless infant becomes a mature adult but rather how helpless new-born infants are channelled into becoming a wide range of very unequal mature adults.

Who socialises who?

A very great deal of literature around socialisation focuses upon what adult parents do to babies, children and young adults. It is clearly the case that children learn a great deal from their carers. It must be remembered that the child may be largely cared for, and learn mobility and language, from a range of people including grandparents (especially grandmothers), childminders and baby sitters, siblings, neighbours who act as 'aunts' or other 'fictive kin'. To this must be added the huge and rapidly expanding range of other influences, the most obvious examples being television, video and computer games as well as more traditional media such as comics or storybooks.

> To observe children socialising their parents, look in any toy store before Christmas or similar gift giving occasion, or a supermarket at any time of the year.

What must be added is that children 'make sense' of and respond to what they experience and decide for themselves how to react, even if they themselves do not understand why they behave as they do. This is true in the case of a toddler who has tantrums for no apparent reason right through to the sulky teenager and the anti-social adult. Ambert (1992) also argues that the effect of children upon parents is neglected, as is the way in which children may contribute to parents feeling that they have lost control of their own lives. Ambert details numerous areas of parental lives upon which children have an impact: health, work, physical space, finance, personal relationships, values, beliefs and attitudes.

Early human life involves an avalanche of rapid and 'developmental' changes. A child is not simply born but is rather born into society and social structure and has a location in that structure *vis-à-vis* parents, education, the law. Like all human beings, children do not merely exist as passive slaves or machines but rather interact with their physical and social environment. Clearly, children create dramatic changes in patterns of family pathways. The experiences of children in their own families have significant and lasting effects for the rest of their lives.

Childrearing

In terms of sex-role development, popular belief is that there should be two partners, one of each sex. Following the work of Bowlby (1965), it seems to be widely accepted that intense mother love in infancy is as important to a child's development as adequate nutrition and shelter. Popular culture goes much further in locating the blame for 'bad behaviour' or delinquency with socialisation within families. These discussions often relate delinquency to inadequate mothering, either the absence of the mother or perhaps her poor performance.

In societies that emphasise the need to train people for paid work roles and simultaneously set extremely high standards for childrearing, it is striking how much childrearing is left to the judgement of untrained parents. There is a sense in which parents can never win; for example, no matter how hard parents strive to supervise their children they may be criticised for being 'over-protective' whilst those who seek to encourage independence and self-exploration may also be criticised for neglect and putting their children at risk.

> Ask ten people for suggestions about what parents should and should not do in parenting.

The issue of 'good' or 'good enough' parenting is fraught with dilemmas. Plainly, different age groups, historical periods, religions and cultures all have clearly different prescriptions about what a child should and should not be 'allowed to do'. Similarly, in that parents receive a great deal of exhortation but little practical training, it is likely that a great many of the 'faults' of previous generations will be passed on to new generations. Further, in all of this, there is little systematic work on the views and responses of children although every parent will be all too aware that children do have views and may protest in all kinds of ways.

A very great deal has been written about the working patterns of women and the way in which mothers have to arrange 'child care'. What is less clear is how children feel about the presence of either or both parents. Taking child development theories for granted means that we tend to assume that a child is better off with his or her mother for most of his or her early years. This plainly does not reflect the experiences of many children and it remains to enquire of children themselves who they prefer to be with at what times of their lives.

In recent years, a great deal of attention has been focused upon the idea that children reared by single mothers are believed to be especially prone to delinquency; this is usually seen in terms of the absence of a father (Dennis and Erdos, 1993). Many researchers have suggested that it is not the gender of the parent(s) that is so important as the quality and determination with which they undertake their roles. Despite a popular belief that single mothers are somehow rearing children in 'inferior' settings, there is clear evidence from a wide range of sources that the absence of a man does not damage sex-role development for male or female children (Cashion, 1984).

There is also growing evidence from a variety of sources that parental sexuality or sexual preferences do not distort a child's development. Bigner and Bozett go as far as to argue, 'There is no evidence of any kind that demonstrates that living with a homosexual parent has any significant negative effects on children' (1989, p. 163). Gottman (1989) found that adult daughters of lesbian mothers showed little or no difference to daughters of heterosexual mothers in terms of gender identification or sexual orientation. Miller argues that the 'coming out' of gay fathers can relieve tensions rather than create harm (1979, p. 544). Lewin goes further than many in exploring lesbian motherhood as a means by which 'success at motherhood (as measured by how well one's child turned out) would demonstrate that children did not need the structure of a heterosexual family' (Lewin, 1994, p. 335).

Modern parents have to somehow negotiate a balance between the moral high ground that requires them to rear children 'properly' (so as not to be delinquents, under-achievers, unemployed, homeless, etc.) and the marketplace that requires them to underwrite ever growing consumption by children. This balancing act is often expressed in open disputes on a variety of 'battlefronts'.

Feminist scholars have done a very great deal to place many 'family issues' (childbirth, motherhood, housework) 'on the agenda'. One issue that commands a central location in the USA, UK and Europe is that of child care provisions outside 'the home'. In comparing child care elsewhere, several authors have observed that the UK is particularly poorly placed (see Cohen and Fraser, 1991, pp. 43–56; Ditch 1996a, 1996b).

Ask ten mothers of pre-school and school-age children what sorts of ideal child care arrangements they would like.

A serious question that needs to be asked is child care for whom? There is some evidence that pre-school child care aids a child's sociability and readiness for formal schooling. This tends to reflect properly run play schools that operate for only short periods of the day. This is not to say that the use of registered childminding or other services for long periods is good for children. In some cases, for example, a child may utter his or her first words to the childminder, indeed may even call the childminder 'Mum' rather than his or her own mother. Cohen and Fraser argue that child care should be seen as a key component of modern welfare, designed to serve the interests of parents, children, communities and the wider society (1991, pp. 57–92).

Experiences of children

Childhood is tremendously varied from the sheltered pre-schooler of Western nations to the maimed street beggar or gun-carrying 'freedom fighter' of less industrialised nations. There is surprisingly little material on the nature of childhood among different cultures within Western nations.

Khan (1979) gives a brief glimpse in *Minority Families in Britain* and there is rather more work on 'Black Families' in the USA. With regard to Asian childhood in the UK, there is a potential conflict of values or emphases. Dominant White culture tends to emphasise individualism and 'detachment' from parents upon marriage whilst Asian cultures often emphasise obligation, obedience and loyalty to one's own family over individual self-interest.

List the range of 'occupations' children may engage in. How old should a boy or girl be before they have the 'right' to 'work' or sell themselves for sexual purposes? Do we have child prostitutes in Europe? (In Britain?)

Recent evidence in the UK has suggested that there are a significant number of children who do not experience the popular image of 'childhood' at all. Children may grow up in a wide variety of different and potentially damaging situations. There are occasional alarming reports of child prostitution linked to runaway children and drug use; there is a growing recognition that children are used in the making of pornography. We also know from recent studies that many children of less than 10 years old may be the main carer in family situations where their parent is chronically ill or disabled.

For many children, then, childhood may be very far from a pleasant time and may involve the direct experience of oppression, abuse, exploitation, not to mention parental divorce, poor health and poverty. The apparently simple developmental models of childhood fail to capture the enormous diversity of childhood experience. Childhood experience is extremely diverse by way of region, social class, housing quality, income, culture and ethnicity, prejudice, diet, disease and abuse.

Children and fun

It is important to point out that Western ideas of family life are very much about enjoyment, pleasure or fun. In Western societies, we have removed children from the paid workplace and given them considerable amounts of time to engage in play of one kind or another. Play is quite different to paid or unpaid work or adult leisure pursuits. Many textbooks seem to ignore the fun, the giggles, the cuddles, the games, the laughter.

It is also easy to assume that a child engaged in some form of play is enjoying that activity. Families can be abusive towards children in all kinds of ways and insisting that they 'go out and play' may be abusive in some situations. It seems possible that many children we see as non-abused might, if asked, reveal that they feel abused. There are clear issues here of how much love, time, effort and material wealth are expended on children. There is a popular view that it is possible to 'give too much' to children and 'spoil' them. At the same time, insisting they pursue certain activities at certain times might be something they would resist if they felt they could do so successfully.

> Explore the sorts of things children enjoy about family living. Holidays? Days out? Chatting? Goodnight Hugs?

In preparing this chapter, I searched in vain for the detailed and rigorously itemised lists of childhood activities, fun and pleasure that you might expect. There are enormous tracts of paper devoted to the nature of the nuclear family, child development or abuse within families but remarkably little about the simple point that family practices and pathways may be pleasurable.

The secret worlds of children

The neglect of childhood experiences reflects the assumption of adult values and the way in which childhood experiences do not revolve around those values. Observation of parent–child interaction reveals that parents seem to spend much time persuading children to do things that they initially resist. We simply do not know what 'goes on' in the heads of children and whether they use the same kinds of concepts and beliefs that adults use. It seems that children may well take part in family practices and pathways with rather different interests and ambitions in mind.

It remains to be discovered what issues preoccupy most children in their daily experiences and their roles in family pathways. In modern Western nations, some children will spend a portion of their lives ensuring they obtain sufficient shelter and food but these are, for most, simply taken for granted. It does seem likely that most children are essentially hedonistic or pleasure seeking in many of their activities but it remains to be seen whether this form of hedonism is similar to adult behaviours. Whether this hedonism is somehow essential to Western childhood or imposed through models of play and toys also remains to be seen.

Read any children's comics or storybooks. What do the themes of these tell us about children and childhood?

In the UK, O'Brien has recently explored the perspectives of children in the allocation of household resources. O'Brien makes the point that 'most thinking about family inequality has been rather adult-centred' (1995, p. 514) and demonstrates that children have a wide variety of forms of access to and roles in the allocation of, money, food, space and time. In all of these areas there will be wide variation across class, culture, ethnicity and gender, to name but a few variables. It is, as O'Brien observes, important that children are added into the understanding of the workings of family households. All too often, children are 'forgotten or considered by proxy in sociological research on the distribution of resources' (1995, p. 501).

Celebrations and gifts

Another notable omission from most family textbooks is that of celebrations, especially those involving gift giving to children. It seems to be common practice to give gifts to children on their birthdays and perhaps have some kind of party. Cheal suggests that gift giving has a vital function to play in the 'structuration of intimacy' (1987, p. 150). Gift giving, then, speaks of the intimacies inside families and the kinds of relationships with people outside families. The way in which gifts are nowadays centred upon children reflects their increasing importance in modern societies.

Similar comments about gift giving apply to national holidays. Modern nations grind to a halt for Christmas celebrations that often seem to centre upon 'Christmas is for Children' (see Wolin and Bennett, 1984). Again, there is considerable gift giving as well as clear ritual celebrations of which Cheal argues, 'ritual consists of repetitive stylised acts that are directed towards persons and things that are highly valued. The repetition of family rituals is facilitated by the existence of festive occasions, such as Christmas, that recur every year' (1988, p. 642).

Celebrations and gift giving maintain family structures but also change in themselves. It is important to note that the headlong dash of developing nations into modernisation and even postmodernity is often characterised by abandoning previous family rituals (such as ancestor worship) and adopting more 'Western' festivals (such as Christmas).

Children and child care

In Western societies, children spend a great deal of their lives 'in the care' of other people be they natural parents, foster or adoptive parents, grandparents, relatives or kin, paid baby carers, childminders and nursery schools or play schools. Longfield found that 25 per cent of under 5 year olds were looked after for major parts of the working day by grandmothers (1984, p. 4).

Whilst the key relationships of children are generally assumed to be with parents, it is important to realise that many others may be involved. Although fertility is declining in Western societies, most children will experience a relationship with a brother or sister, at some time. The potential for co-operation, play and enjoyment has to be balanced against the potential for competition, intimidation and abuse. More to the point, the significance of a non-parental carer may be far in excess of the amount of time spent with that person. A few hours or a day with a different carer may create all kinds of different perspectives or behaviour. Again, there is a parental dilemma: if the child is unhappy with the carer, the parents may be made to feel guilty for neglecting the child, whilst if the child is happy with the carer, the parents may feel that this reflects upon their inadequacies as parents.

Children will also form relationships with the children of neighbours, school friends and so on. Whilst this widening of social contacts may be a valuable development, it also holds the potential for the child experiencing different views of the world. There are clearly situations in which children refer to outside friends in defending behaviour ('my friend's parents don't make him go to bed so early') or seeking to obtain goods ('everyone at school has a computer').

As a parent (or imagine yourself to be a parent), what sort of child would you refuse to let your own children play with?

There has also been work in psychology that seeks to distinguish first born children from middle and latest born. Mott and Haurin (1982) discuss the need to understand the child's perception of being an 'only child'. In modern times, more and more children will find themselves relating to step-siblings who may be much older, of similar age or much younger. There are many other factors in a child's experiences including siblings, friends, frequent visitors, 'special' objects (such as cuddly toys or blankets), or pets (see *Marriage and Family Review*, 1985).

Childhood, family and education

Modern societies have moved education out of family homes into schools. Schools are often studied as settings in which some kind of formal learning may (or may not) take place. Literature in the UK and USA focuses upon issues around educational achievement; curiously, whilst 'family' is certainly a key variable in these debates, the assumption is usually that of the role of the 'family environment' in determining educational outcomes. Of at least equal, if not greater importance, should be a consideration of the informal learning that goes on in schools and the impact of both formal and informal learning upon family practices and pathways.

A child's experience of education may be quite different from adult perspectives. Many children are distressed on starting school, this may be the first time they have been separated from their mother or carer for whole days. Within the school environment, children may encounter other children and other forms of behaviour that are completely unfamiliar. In this clash of different backgrounds, some level of conflict is inevitable but many schools appear to contain significant numbers of bullies. In the mid-1990s, the issue of disruptive school pupils came to national attention in several ways. It seems likely that most children will either experience, or engage in, bullying in one form or another during their school career from primary through to school leaving. Such experiences inevitably leave their mark on children and perhaps predispose them to the later role of abuser or survivor.

Linked to abuse at school and abuse at home, another area of concern is the increasing number of children who run away from home, now estimated at nearly 100,000 per year in the UK. What both abuse within schools and family abuse reveal is the secret intimate worlds of children. It seems clear that many, even most, children 'experiment' with all kinds of things including sexual behaviour, smoking, drugs and other substances (i.e. solvent abuse, alcohol), violence and theft. Nearly all of these 'secrets' have their later equivalent 'social problems' (teenage pregnancy, addictions, delinquencies) and yet we seem, as societies, more or less completely disinterested in how children have their 'first experiences'.

Divorce

In many discussions of divorce, attention is given first and foremost to the break-up of the marital partnership. In recent years, however, more and more concerns have been expressed about the impact of parental divorce upon children. It seems clear that parental divorce results in significant disruption in the lives of children; this may or may not be damaging. It is often assumed that it is better for children if parents separate rather than continue in a marriage marked by disputes and violence. In 1985, Mitchell argued that this is not always the case in the UK where children may prefer their parents to remain together despite marital difficulties. Where there are high levels of violence between partners and towards children, divorce may present solutions to many problems for children but divorce also carries with it a wide range of new problems for children as well as for the divorcing couple. Wallerstein and Kelly's longitudinal study identified three phases of divorce: the initial period after separation when effects were acute, a transition period of making adaptations of between 2 and 5 years, and sometime after 5 years a completed adaptation (1980).

Generally, though, studies in the US and UK confirm that it is not divorce itself that is so damaging but how the process of divorce is managed by all concerned. Several studies have suggested that it is the continuation of conflict between divorced parents that can be most damaging to children. Mitchell characterises the situation as *Children in the Middle* and argues very clearly that all parties to divorce, including professionals and family friends:

> should be fully conscious of the unhappiness and bewilderment children may be experiencing, especially if they do not show their feelings. . . . The more time lost in establishing satisfactory post-separation relationships between children and both of their parents, the harder it is to restore such links.

(1985, p. 190)

In the UK, Cockett and Tripp's study of the impact of family breakdown on children has proven to be controversial, suggesting that family breakdown is now such a common experience that 'it must be considered to be a normal part of family experience' (1994, p. 61). As other researchers have done, Cockett and Tripp argue that 'there is no disagreement that children involved in . . . family reorganisation are disadvantaged in a number of ways' (ibid.), including having lower self-esteem, difficulties in daily living and eventually obtaining poorer jobs and less stable relationships than children who do not experience such family reorganisation. Having said this, the authors do argue that 'these adverse outcomes are not universal, but apply to groups of children whose experiences are very varied' (ibid.). In common with other authors, Cockett and Tripp identify issues of debate about what increases or decreases the likelihood of children being disadvantaged by the separation of their parents. It does seem obvious that separation and divorce are likely to be disruptive for children.

However, it must also be recognised that separation and divorce should not automatically be seen as 'failure' or a 'problem'. For many of those involved, perhaps including children, separation and divorce may be 'success' and 'solution': think about finally escaping an abusive parent.

White *et al.* (1985) found that divorce does not affect attachment to the custodial parent but does reduce attachment to the non-custodial parent. In some countries, such as the UK, where custody is not automatically awarded jointly, children can become 'bargaining counters' in adversarial legal processes. In the early 1980s this led to the emergence of child snatching in the USA (see Palmer and Noble, 1984) and later in the UK. Debates about 'what to do with the children' in situations of divorce really do come rather too late. I am sure that most children would prefer that parents were better prepared to modify and sustain their relationships. De'Ath has gone as far as to suggest that the widespread debate about divorce and re-marriage should be re-cast, 'Understanding how families manage change and supporting all families to provide good enough parenting is likely to be a better investment for children than cataloguing disadvantages and difficulties and denigrating different family structures' (De'Ath, 1996, p. 82).

Children: paid and unpaid work

One key aspect of Western societies is the way in which we have removed children from the paid workplace and appear to be requiring less and less unpaid work from children in the home. It should be clearly remembered that today children all over the world may engage in hard physical labour, sometimes having been effectively sold into slavery by their parents. It seems likely that such experiences are much rarer for Western children but both paid and unpaid work will have an enormous impact upon their lives. Some children work long hours in family businesses, or have a variety of part-time jobs beyond the commonly assumed newspaper rounds. Many of these jobs, like work in the family business, are effectively invisible. Allen and Wolkowitz (1987) document the role of children in home working and suggest that a small but significant number of children still undertake such work with their mothers. We also know that children may take a wide range of part-time work (probably far more than officially known) or undertake arduous care for disabled relatives or kin.

In societies in which men have continuous work careers and women often work whilst children are young, clearly the nature of paid work will influence the nature, quality and even presence of parents. Hood and Golden have noted how the working patterns of men have real consequences for their relationships with children (1979). Shift work and workaholism can all eat into the time available to spend with children. More than this, the nature of parental work is likely to impact upon children; a 'bad day at work' is often a cause of bad temper, arguments or even abuse. The stresses and strains of 'task overload' in dual-work families may limit interaction with children and plainly influence the quality of that interaction.

> As a father who has laboured long nights and weekends on this book, I offer my abject apologies to my daughter, Eleanor, and my son, Jacob. My own sense of guilt is all the greater because of the topic of this book!

There is some evidence that the extent of unpaid work by children in the form of housework and related caring tasks is generally declining. Within this context, Morrow has explored the issue of children and housework to find quite extensive work in the UK (1992); Cogle and Tasker, on the other hand, suggested that the input of children to housework was quite limited in the USA (1982). How much housework children undertake seems to depend upon age and sex and whether the mother works.

Delinquency

One continual theme throughout history has been the 'bad behaviour' of children, by this is usually implied children who do not conform to their parents' wishes or wider social regulation. When you combine the indifference towards the secret worlds of family childhoods with the heavy emphases upon children becoming independent teenagers, it is hardly surprising that so many 'problem' behaviours are established in childhood and teenage years.

> List what you would consider to be 'bad behaviour' by children. Why do children behave in this way?

The view of the behaviour of children depends upon class, locality and visibility. What may be delinquency in a large public housing estate may be perceived as 'high spirits' in a public school or perhaps a sign of a 'Hyperactive Child' in middle-class settings (see Douglas, 1991). Whilst accepting some major methodological problems, Wilson found evidence that delinquency is related to degree and nature of parental supervision (1987). This is a popular theme for those from the right of politics, and those who claim to be 'ethical socialists', such work tends to explore *Families without Fathers* (Dennis and Erdos, 1993) or defend *The Family* (Davies, 1993).

In exploring *Crime and the Family*, Utting *et al.* (1993) explored the common premise that delinquency is partly or largely the result of poor parenting. This study lays out a comprehensive and detailed family-based strategy for preventing delinquency. What marks this study out is the implicit theme of the need to work with all families from all kinds of backgrounds rather than target specific 'problem families'.

Poverty and wealth

It is easy to assume that whilst there may be 'temporary setbacks', the UK is still somehow an 'advanced society'. Recent work by UNICEF shows Britain to be 27th in the world in childhood immunisation against measles, behind China and Chile. Much more shocking was the note that whilst child poverty is declining world-wide, the number of families living below the poverty line (40 per cent of national median disposable income) had risen by some 40 per cent in the UK during the 1980s (see Adamson, 1993). Whilst Britain does have a relatively high disposable income, this still reflects that more and more of our children are receiving less and less of our national wealth.

Whilst we often talk about children as 'innocent' and 'blameless', most societies are organised in such a way that the 'sins of the parents' are visited upon the children in the clearest and most direct of ways. We have clear evidence that the majority of children of single parents (especially lone mothers) are likely to live in poverty and similar evidence about the lives of chronically sick and disabled children.

Do the children of poor parents 'deserve' all they get?

This seems to me the clearest possible evidence for a dramatic and radical rethink about how money is distributed in our society. At present, most money is distributed primarily through wages and then redistributed within families. If the original wages are insufficient, it is inevitable that children will suffer no matter how valiant the efforts of parents. There is a clear case here to distribute sufficient goods and services to compensate for parental poverty.

Whilst family poverty can be potentially damaging for children's development and health, it should not be thought that extreme wealth is necessarily a 'good thing'. Pittman observes that, 'Great wealth has undoubted benefits, but it is not good for children. It distorts their functional relationship with the world, belittles their own accomplishments, and it grotesquely amplifies their sense of what is good enough' (1985, p. 461).

Childhood health

There is a very large range of health conditions which affect children, some of which are specific to childhood, some of which carry through to adulthood. Woodroffe *et al.* report that, 'UK infant mortality is higher than in several comparable Western European countries, such as France, Germany and the Netherlands' (1993, p. 38). Most shocking is to find that well over 5 per cent of 5–15 year olds experience limiting long-term illness whilst 15 per cent experience some form of long-standing illness. This represents many millions of children and families across the UK. It is shocking to find that few, if any, traditional textbooks even mention illness and an alien reader would be forgiven for thinking that families never experience any sickness.

Childhood illness can be extremely stressful. It is common in the rest of Europe for the jobs of working women to be protected in the case of having to care for sick children; it remains a mark of shame that this is not the case in the UK. Another important point to note is that much disability, impairment and chronic sickness goes practically unseen because such children have limited access to public places for a variety of reasons.

Burton (1975) and Blaxter (1981) have both explored the family lives of sick children. Whilst American in orientation, the work of Hobbs *et al.* provides one of the few comprehensive accounts of the very many aspects of the very many diseases and conditions which influence *Chronically Ill Children and Their Families* (1985).

Make a list of all health conditions which may affect family pathways, noting the implications this may have for carers or parents.

In addressing the issue of how parents 'cope with the daily hassles and long term strains of caring for a disabled child' (1994, p. 1), Beresford adopts a more recent model of caring which emphasises how parents cope with stress rather than simply the effects of those stresses. At the heart of this work is the focus on coping resources and coping strategies by which parents actively manage the care of disabled children rather than being 'passive recipients of an onslaught of stress' (1994, p. 111). Within this positive picture of caring for disabled children, the author argues that, 'Special attention should be paid to groups who are vulnerable to lack of support. This includes ethnic minority groups, lone parents, parents with low incomes, parents of children with difficult temperaments or unusual appearance or behaviour' (1994, p. 116).

Wikler (1983) explored the chronic stresses of families with 'mentally retarded' children. There is a general view that once a family has adjusted to the birth of an impaired child, some kind of equilibrium is established. Wikler suggests the regular re-emergence of problems with development, notably relating to parental expectations and child performance. Greengross (1980) has highlighted our attitudes to the handicapped in exploring the way in which we deny the sexuality of handicapped children even more clearly than we deny the sexuality of 'healthy' children.

Also important, from a child's point of view, is the fact of death. The death of family members, such as siblings, parents, or more likely grandparents, may be very traumatic for a child. The relative rarity of death and isolation of modern families may make the trauma all the worse. We see many death reports but rarely encounter death directly. We have handed over the whole business of death and dying to professionals and away from family systems. A recent study, the *Sociology of Death* by Clark (1993), is quite striking in that it pays very little attention to the 'family dimension' of death and dying and it has to be said that virtually all UK sociology and family texts completely ignore the issue. Also ignored is the way in which funerals and inheritance issues often generate or bring to the surface long-simmering family disputes.

The future of childhood

It bears repeating that the 'way people are' in any society is partly, if not largely, the result of the experiences people had as children. It is something of a paradox, then, that whilst modern societies are often called 'child centred', we have no clear idea of what most childhoods are like nor how to deliver 'better childhoods'.

Sketch out your view of what childhood should be like. Remember abuse, sexuality, delinquency, future partnering and parenting. What policies would be relevant?

As the pace of technology accelerates, so the pressures and demands placed on children rise. We expect our children to somehow cope with a world of technology that our grandparents hardly dreamt of. It seems to me obvious that we must discover what being a child is like from children themselves. We know something of the obvious and measurable, educational attainment, the extent of child abuse, the number of runaway children and the extent of parental unemployment. We know very little of what underlies these features. We must seek to uncover the secret and hidden worlds of childhood (as my son Jacob just said to me, 'Parents don't understand children').

It is important to explore our modern Western societies critically, a useful way to do this is to make use of the United Nations Declaration of Rights of the Child. Included in the Declaration are the rights of children to: healthy mental and physical development; sufficient food, housing and medical care; love, understanding and care; free education, play and recreation; protection from cruelty; and protection from persecution. Whilst we tend to believe that children in modern Western societies are somehow 'well off', it remains to be seen how many of them will express themselves satisfied with the UN Declaration.

Suggested reading

Archard, D. 1993: *Children: Rights and Childhood*. London: Routledge.
Holland, P. 1992: *What is a Child? Popular Images of Childhood*. London: Virago.
Jenks, C. 1996: *Childhood*. London: Routledge.

Chapter 6

Partnering

Introduction

Whilst many regard having children as synonymous with 'starting a family', most Western societies prefer children to be born into stable intimate partnerships. Whilst there are societies in which men and women live separately, most Western societies favour men and women marrying at some point and then living together as couples. One of the keys to understanding family living then is 'partnering'. Partnering involves the creation of exclusive intimate partnerships between small numbers of people, sometimes two (monogamy), sometimes more (polygamy). These relationships are extremely varied and diverse, may be short- or long-term and may be culturally or socially sanctioned as 'marriages'.

This chapter focuses upon the way in which society invests heavily in the transition from dependency and 'childhood', through increasingly early puberty, to independence and 'partnering'. This may move through friendships, dating, 'going steady', singlehood, to cohabiting, engagement and marriage.

In one sense most adults have been or currently are in partnerships and may therefore be tempted to believe that they 'know about' the nature of such partnerships. This is similar to the point that most of us grow up in families and therefore believe we know about families. Our own individual knowledge is almost certainly limited and partial and is likely to be biased. In the wider scientific sense, it is remarkable how little we know about what goes on inside intimate partnerships. On the one hand, there is popular wisdom about love and harmony but, on the other hand, equally popular wisdom about disputes, abuse and the breakdown of relationships. There are rather few detailed systematic studies of the ordinary interiors of intimate partnerships. Whilst there are some accounts of the inside of marriages, there are few accounts of the kinds of processes involved in divorce and, beyond public statements about the reasons for seeking divorce, remarkably few theories about why intimate partnerships break up. In view of our ignorance, there is an urgent need to extend and develop our knowledge of intimate partnering and do all we can to prepare individuals for these partnerships.

Towards partnering

In more traditional societies, family members, often parents, make decisions about marriage partners. In societies with free mate selection, arrangements have developed where young individuals leave the state of 'childhood' behind for an intermediate phase in which they spend a considerable portion of their time engaged in a variety of activities that may offer the opportunity for meeting potential marital partners. This is most clearly seen in the relatively recent creation in Western societies of 'teenagerhood'. This period relates to the transition from childhood to adulthood and mirrors many of the value changes that modern societies require. It is no accident that teenagers have acquired a wide range of visible displays of 'difference' from both children and adults.

The most obvious point about teenagers is the often discussed 'generation gap' between children and their parents. Whilst many commentators regret this, many profitable industries thrive on this gap. Dating, courtship and marriage are big business involving high levels of consumption. The two clearest symbols of the generation gap are music and fashion. It is no accident that every high street has many profitable retail outlets selling high volumes of music and fashion goods.

The 1950s and the 1960s saw a remarkable rise in youth culture. In a period of rising affluence, young people commanded more wealth and prominence in society. This central position of young people has recently declined, especially in the United Kingdom. In the face of rapidly rising unemployment amongst the school-leaving group, the UK government cut access to welfare benefits. This coincided with increasing diversity in family life as a result of divorce, single parenthood and housing problems. Between 1991 and 1993, the unemployment of 16- and 17-year-olds rose by 43 per cent. These kinds of stresses may have contributed to an apparent increase in the abuse of teenagers by their parents. One consequence of this is that we have begun to see more teenage beggars on the streets of UK cities.

> Visit any large shopping centre and estimate the percentage of space given over to fashion and music. Then consider who makes and takes the profits.

Teenagerhood tends to conjure up the image of 'summer holiday', 'foot-loose and fancy free'. This image omits poverty, homelessness, violence and abuse, the experience of conflicts with parental values, substance abuse, furtive sexuality, bulimia and anorexia. The NCH (formerly the National Children's Home) characterised vulnerable young people living apart from their families as *A Lost Generation* and described in detail how modern societies have no place for such 'unattached' children (1993). Whilst most teenagers survive the tempestuous years within families it is worth noting that this may be far more difficult than it need be because of the lack of preparation and support for both parents and teenagers.

Singlehood

In exploring the strong tendency to create intimate partnerships, one key area is the image and reality of singlehood. It is informative to see that singlehood is seen as normal only at certain stages of life. Predominant ideologies emphasise the 'normality' of forming intimate partnerships and the 'abnormality' of remaining single for too long (see Gordon, 1994).

Many years of gender differentiation in childhood, with boys oriented to paid work and girls oriented to marriage and motherhood, come to fruition in singlehood. The nature or extent of the difference in gender can be seen in teenage literature. Roman *et al.* argue that in teenage romance novels 'feminine power becomes confined to that informal system of persuasion, fragility and seeming helpless' (1988, p. 85); these magazines have a heavy heterosexual emphasis. On the other hand, 'the phrase "men's magazine" has become a euphemism for pornography, instead of a name for a publication dealing with clothes, relationships, health and social questions as "women's magazines" do' (Root, 1984, p. 38).

Once unattached from parents, society exerts social pressures towards marriage in the form of 'pushes' out of singlehood and 'pulls' into the more attractive status of marriage. In 1981, Anne Oakley noted that, 'Spinsters, divorcees and lesbians are suspect because they appear to deny the truth of the cultural dogma that men and women unite to form a whole' (1981, p. 236). It remains true that the majority of young people, especially those with no access to higher education, move from their parents home to a cohabitation or marriage.

> Ask six people to 'characterise' a single man and a single woman of 40 years of age.

Dating

The whole business of dating or partner selection is subject to all kinds of explicit and implicit controls. Most cultures contain some clear rule about when children 'come of age'. In the West, there has been a general decline from 21 years to 18 years corresponding to the legal age of majority and voting age.

For singles and the recently de-married (divorced and widowed), a major life preoccupation is presumed to be that of dating. Children's television and other media seem to suggest experimentation with intimate partnerships quite early in life. At young ages this is not seen as anything 'serious' but even pre-teen relationships may imitate the search for a long-term partnership. There are, of course, cultural groups where the selection of appropriate partners is undertaken by other people such as 'match-makers', parents or family advisors. For such groups, a major concern is the clash between a 'traditional culture' and the values transmitted by the dominant culture.

> List the range of social events where single people can meet prospective partners.

Most Western societies permit or encourage young single people to meet socially in a variety of ways ranging from religious and cultural groups to commercial enterprises such as popular entertainment. Class and culture have clear impacts upon the kinds of events attended and the opportunities for meeting people of the opposite sex. Wealthy upper-class groups tend to organise exclusive social events for their children to meet potential mates whilst some cultures do not allow dating at all.

One of the consequences of very lengthy gender differentiation is that the two sexes come to dating with quite different perspectives. Root argues that when the two sexes meet it is almost like two alien species meeting, so different are their ideals and expectations (1984, p. 25). Lees (1986) identified the processes within UK schools which lead to the assessment of a girl's reputation on the basis of her sexuality and sexual availability; a great deal of pain can be inflicted on a girl with terms like 'cow', 'slag', 'slut' that have no male equivalents. In this way, gendered language and discourse leads to major gender differences that are routinely taken for granted. Whilst females are encouraged to concern themselves with fashion, physical appearance and romance, males are encouraged to engage in sport and aggression and tend to regard sexuality as far more important than romance. It is remarkable that whilst their ideals and expectations may be so different, there is immense pressure to make this unlikely union into a lasting one.

The dating period involves breaking as well as making relationships. The de-partnering or unbonding of partnerships is likely to involve a variety of phases each of which involves challenges and tasks. A review of female teenage magazines reveals all kinds of perspectives on 'breaking up' involving, amongst other things, ideas of success and failure in the 'competition' of the dating game. Whilst this may be thought of as useful preparation to eventually selecting the 'right' partner it might also suggest to young people that relationships may be treated as temporary.

> Identify the 'stages' of 'breaking up' in female teenage magazines.

Partnering and intimacy

People of all ages do seem to have a very strong wish to establish and maintain intimate partnerships. There is in virtually every culture a very strong folk tradition around relationships that explores issues of love, passion, duty, honour, shame, property inheritance, incest, wealth, propriety, impropriety and racial purity. These are the topics of contemporary television 'soap operas' just as they are of ancient Greek mythology and folk tales from across the world. To realise this point, one need merely observe the enormous effort all known societies put into encouraging people to enter particular kinds of relationships rather than others (for example, the general disapproval of partnerships across class, ethnic or religious groups).

Sexuality

Sexuality is a tremendously powerful force, shaped and controlled by society. Many personal relationships lack a sexual base and many sexual relationships lack any personal dimension. It is no accident that prostitution is often regarded as 'the oldest profession' and clearly signals 'another way' of dealing with sexuality. Having said this, sexuality is one of the keys to intimate partnerships.

Most studies have suggested that there has been an increasing focus upon the importance of privacy and sex lives. Whilst this is true for married people, it has been particularly significant for the unmarried. There is much material which demonstrates that rates of sexual behaviour outside marriage have risen dramatically for all adult age groups and social classes.

> Count the number and type of sexual images in popular newspapers and television.

The widespread publication of scientific research findings, especially those of Kinsey and colleagues in 1948 and 1953 (see Reinisch with Beasley, 1991) has done a great deal to change attitudes, especially towards the part played by women in sexual behaviour. Most often discussed is the arrival of the female contraceptive pill which meant that women could, for the first time in history, be sexually active without fear of pregnancy.

Teenagers are now open to all kinds of influences beyond the home, especially by way of the media, which include challenges to authority, sexual propriety, tradition and so on. Also part of the media is the creation of an erotic environment in which all kinds of 'possibilities' are portrayed before our eyes. Giddens (1992) has identified this as the development of a 'plastic sexuality', that is, a separation of sexuality from reproduction which has encouraged very real changes in social order.

Despite a widespread concern about youthful sexual activity, there is a popular morality in the UK that opposes such activity rather than attempts to educate and prepare young people to deal with their own sexualities. This may have contributed to dramatically increasing the spread of sexually transmitted diseases including the modern diseases of HIV and AIDS.

A very great deal of commercial activity revolves around sexuality, not only in the pornography industry but also in the popular media. In a study, *Sexuality and its Discontents*, Weeks (1991) explains the process by which sex has become a commercial commodity that is important in modern industrial production. Rather than sexuality being about reproduction, it is also used both as a means to sell goods (for example, in advertising) and as the basis upon which production is based (for example, in the fashion and cosmetics industries, not to mention the contraceptive and pornography industries). It is significant that one of the richest men in the UK made a great deal of his wealth from various commercial concerns involving sex.

How many sexually transmitted diseases can you list? Aim for ten or more.

Brock and Jennings provide a graphic account of 'What Daughters in the 30s wish their mothers had told them' and found that, 'What most wished for was not so much specific facts as a particular approach to sexuality education, an approach that presents sexuality positively as "a normal, natural thing"' (1993, p. 64). There is a fundamental conflict of public attitudes by which sexuality is an issue of major public concern and yet sexual behaviour is regarded as rightly private.

The public confusion over sexuality is illustrated by Durham (1985) who concisely teases out the relationship between sex and politics in *Sex and Politics: The Family and Morality in the Thatcher Years*. The abortion debate, for example, demonstrates how many groups are deeply hostile to abortion yet deeply hostile to children 'knowing too much' about sex, pregnancy and contraception. Another example is that in which Mrs Gillick challenged the Department of Health's ruling that contraceptive advice should be available to her daughter regardless of age or parental consent. The debate brought to the surface many concerns about parental control versus promiscuity; the view of many of those on the Right seems to be that making contraceptives available will encourage promiscuity whilst many of those opposing this view argue that such behaviour is inevitable and that contraceptives will at least prevent unwanted pregnancies. Durham argues that, 'The Gillick campaign's argument that it is defending the family against the state, morality against promiscuity and young girls against exploitation is a powerful one which enabled it to tap a significant reservoir of support' (1991, pp. 55–6).

Intimacy

Whilst biology, nurturance, sexuality and so forth are important in many relationships they are not definitive. Understanding personal relationships depends on recognising what people do when they establish relationships, whether they be among a large work unit or an intense heterosexual pair. The key to defining any relationship is the exclusion of others. In the case of intimate partnerships, this exclusion is combined with the creation of intimacy, closeness or privacy. Zinn and Eitzen identify intimacy as a process 'by which a couple – in expression of thought, emotion and behaviour – attempts to move toward more complete communication on all levels' (1990, p. 221).

Intimate partnering does not necessarily imply 'romantic love', warmth, affection or even non-violence. Intimate partnering implies exclusivity in some aspects of life between individuals. There is a considerable literature around the abuse of both women and children that suggests that 'survivors' still 'love' or 'feel close to' their abuser. It is the very intimacy and privacy that we value that can also mean that outsiders are excluded from seeing what is really going on in abusive situations.

One of the other key features of intimacy is that it tends to be anti-solidaristic; the emphasis upon personal intimacy runs counter to attempts to create solidarity across class, gender or other social groups. This is why some social movements, such as the early kibbutzim in Israel or the Western commune movement were hostile to intimate partnerships.

Love and ethnicity

One of the most common claims in Western societies is that people marry because they are 'in love'. Callan and Noller explore definitions of love, 'Love has been linked with attachment, care, responsibility and respect for others' (1987, p. 80). The authors cite Pope's very Western idea of love as:

> A preoccupation with another person. A deeply felt desire to be with the loved one. A feeling of incompleteness without him or her. Thinking of the loved one often, whether together or part. Separation frequently evokes feelings of genuine despair or else tantalising anticipation of reunion.
>
> (Ibid.)

Is 'love' enough in itself to sustain fifty years of partnership?

Many texts on family life contain an almost exclusively Western, White, middle-class, heterosexual image. The whole point of such widespread and powerful sets of ideas is to reinforce notions of what is obvious and natural in a particular culture. This point is clearly illustrated in Skynner and Cleese's *Families: And How To Survive Them* in which the authors assert that people marry, 'Because they're in love' (1983, p. 13). Many White British couples find themselves 'having to marry', even today, because of premarital pregnancy. Many Asian British couples marry for quite different reasons and with different expectations; such reasons and expectations are part of British Asian cultural norms.

> For 'White' people: how many different 'kinds' of Black family lives are you aware of? For Asian and African-Caribbean people: how many different kinds of 'White' family lives are you aware of?

There is a tradition of studying 'Black family life' in the US and mentions of Asian and African-Caribbean families are sometimes found in UK discussions. Whilst this may be progress, there are dangers too: just as it is easy to stereotype the White 'nuclear family', so it is just as easy to stereotype Asian or African-Caribbean families. Despite stereotypes around 'arranged marriages', what little work there is suggests that young Asian women are no more or less alienated from their parents than females of other cultures. It has always been easy for White researchers, journalists and others to identify different values as 'problematic' but this is not to say that the individuals concerned view their lives in this way. Many Asian women, both before and after marriage, are considerably more 'independent' than their White counterparts. There is a high value placed upon education and Muslim Asian women are more likely to be in full-time work than White counterparts.

Westwood and Bhachu conclude that:

> British society, through the images of Asian families that are constructed and reproduced, especially in the popular press, amplifies the role of the state by ignoring the diversity of British society and working with a view of 'them' and 'us'. It is a redundant view, redolent with racism and long overdue for revision.

> (1988, p. 22)

One of the clearest forms of institutional racism is the way in which British immigration laws do not recognise Asian 'arranged marriages' and hence often prevent Asian families in the UK from bringing brides or grooms into the country to marry their sons or daughters.

Cohabitation

Living together unmarried, or cohabitation, has always existed in history and has at various times been more or less common. It seems clear that cohabitation is already as popular as marriage in Denmark (Manniche, 1991) and is rapidly assuming similar importance in other European nations. There are important variations between countries, many of which are related to the degree of formal recognition of cohabitation.

> Ask ten people what is wrong with cohabitation.

According to Kiernan and Estaugh (1993), whilst in 1979 only 3 per cent of single women were cohabiting in the UK this had risen to 26 per cent by 1989. At the same time, births outside marriage stood at 30 per cent in 1990 compared to 12 per cent in 1980 (1993, p. 5). The same report found that the majority of cohabitants were between 20 and 35 years old and that most cohabitations lasted less than five years, often ending in marriage. The socio-economic conditions of childless marriages and childless cohabitations were similar whilst cohabitants with children tended to be worse off than married couples with children.

Cohabitation is far from a single type of relationship or arrangement. Macklin identified five types: temporary casual convenience; affectionate dating/going together; trial marriage; temporary alternative to marriage; permanent alternative to marriage (1980, p. 290).

There have been many discussions of cohabitation as a 'new relationship' in which partners will establish 'new' patterns of equality and sharing. Shelton and John (1993) discuss evidence that cohabiting women do less housework than married women whilst men do much the same. This suggests that it is not merely the presence of a man that raises female housework, but rather that a husband increases the amount of housework undertaken by a woman. A decade or more of high levels of cohabitation do not seem to have contributed to the phenomena of the 'new man'.

One feature of the rise of cohabitation is that homosexual cohabitation has become more tolerated; many groups have called for lesbian and gay couples to be recognised in public (see Meyer, 1989). It is probably much more difficult for gay and lesbian couples from ethnic minorities; they face not only general prejudice but prejudice from within their own cultural group combined with wider discrimination (see Morales, 1989). Rothblum and Cole (1989) suggest that homosexual relationships are perhaps more loving than heterosexual relationships and Pearce has argued that domestic tasks and other aspects of intimate partnerships may be more equal in lesbian couples (1993). Along with the progressive 'uncovering' of abuse in family settings, there is now some evidence that both gay and lesbian relationships may be no more or less equal, no more or less abusive than heterosexual relationships (see Coleman, 1994; and Letellier, 1994).

Marriages

Most known societies have some form of legal, religious or cultural recognition of intimate partnerships that equates with the term of 'marriage'. This is most clearly seen in wedding ceremonies, common to most religions, in which partners make public statements about their agreement to marry. Weddings have enormous personal significance, many brides keep their wedding dress for the rest of their lives. Also important here is the question of the legality of marriage; in the West, bigamy or taking multiple spouses is illegal and inter-racial marriage was, until recently, illegal in South Africa. It is tempting to believe that Western notions of monogamous romantic love and free mate selection are gaining ground. Murdock found that 80 per cent of the World Ethnographic Sample permitted polygamy where a husband (polygyny) or wife (polyandry) is permitted more than one spouse (Giddens, 1989, p. 386). In most societies world-wide, marriage is arranged by kin rather than the bride and groom. This is not to say that romantic love does not exist in such societies but that it has a different role and importance.

It is important to realise that around 90 per cent of all women marry in the UK today compared to 70 per cent in the Victorian era. Britain has one of the highest rates of marriage in the European Union. By the age of 40 years, 95 per cent of women and 91 per cent of men have married. This very large number of marriages represents a multi-million pound business.

List all the costs involved in getting married; survey friends, magazines and other sources to estimate the total cost.

Feminists have critically examined marriage as both unequal and oppressive. Gittins observed that:

> Heterosexuality, marriage and having children are . . . all part of the Western patriarchal parcel of rules for appropriate sexual relations and behaviour between men and women. Indulging in one without accepting the rest of the 'parcel' has been, and still is, widely condemned.
>
> (1993, p. 92)

For individuals from dominant White culture, marriage is seen very much as a matter of choice. Mansfield and Collard noted that, 'Unlike their ancestors, today's young lovers are said to be free to marry whoever they choose, when-ever they choose' (1988, p. 51). Leonard and Speakman point out that in Western societies, marriages are not so very different from arranged marriages in that the 'chosen' partners are usually from 'the same class and ethnic back-ground and live within five miles of each other when they meet, and the man is taller and around two years older than the women' (1986, p. 12).

Whilst it is common to live with parents in some cultures, dominant White culture emphasises the married couple moving away from parents. Recent work by Pickvance and Pickvance (1995) has revealed that the help given by parents to their adult children in 'setting up home' is far less than generally believed, particularly in the South East of England where housing costs are highest and the population is generally affluent.

Teenage marriages

Whilst early betrothal and even marriage is common in some cultures, Western nations have been concerned for some time with what is seen as the 'problem' of early or teenage marriage. The reason for this was summarised by Kiernan in 1986: 'In virtually every study of marital breakdown it has been found that marriage at young ages is the most powerful discrimination between marriages which survive and those that do not' (1986, p. 43).

There is some evidence that teenage marriages are often the result of pre-marital conception and hence perhaps not the union of two people who have decided they are compatible. Haskey (1987) has explored divorce in the early years of marriage and found that couples who apparently cohabited had a lower chance of divorce, whereas those who lived close to each other had a higher chance. Several studies have explored the complex links between premarital pregnancy, teenage marriage and divorce. Ineichen conceptualised early marriages as exposed to a 'vortex of disadvantage' in education, jobs, income and housing (1977). Related to premarital conception are, of course, the factors of class, education and contraceptive use. Kiernan also argues that teenage brides can be distinguished by having the 'least advantaged family backgrounds, education and occupational careers' (1986, p. 53).

Types of marriages

Many commentators speak of marriage 'as an institution' and implicitly behave as if marriages are of one single type in modern societies. There may be a distinction made between intact (successful) marriages and divorced (failed) marriages and the distinction between different cultural groups. This kind of view is seriously flawed because it fails to address the very wide variation and diversity of marriages.

One of the key issues in looking at types of marriages is that of gender. In her analysis of the *Future of Marriage* first published in 1972, Jessie Bernard argued that there is not one marriage but two marriages, 'His' and 'Hers', that are quite distinct and unequal (see Bernard, 1982). These marriages reflect quite different expectations, experiences and outcomes. Bernard characterised the inequality by observing that men rarely marry 'socially superior' women leaving two groups unmarried: the female 'cream of the crop' and the male 'bottom of the barrel' (1982, p. 33). Bernard went further to demonstrate that whilst married men are much better off than single men as a result of marriage in terms of mental health and other measures, married women are generally worse off than their single counterparts in terms of mental and physical health. This observation remains a matter of debate but underlies much subsequent feminist work on the nature of male oppression of women in marriage.

List all possible differences between 'his' and 'her' partnerships.

The list of things that might influence the quality of marriages is potentially endless but some of the factors discussed at various times include the legality of marriage ('informal' homosexual 'marriage' or very youthful 'child marriages'); the cultural location of marriage (cultures other than White, middle-class Christian; marriages across class, culture and religions). There may be heterogeneity of personal backgrounds (age discrepancy, handicap and impairment) or variation by work (dual career, commuter marriage, corporate marriage and women as senior partners). There may be considerable variation in sexuality (secret and consensual adultery, married homosexual men and women). Among the remaining host of variations, there are many possible variations in the names taken after marriage depending on law and culture.

All of these kinds of factors can lead to quite different qualitative outcomes. Perhaps the best known qualitative typology of marriage came from Cuber and Haroff who identified five types of enduring marriages (see Cuber and Haroff, 1974) ranging from those in which conflict is accepted, through to those where partners remain intensely involved. These types of marriages are probably recognisable to most people. Heaton and Albrecht (1991) have explored the varied circumstances of 'Stable Unhappy Marriages'. It is probably a mistake to seek out clusters of behaviours or characteristics that define any particular types of marriage. The point to take is that marriages are extremely complex.

Later life marriage

With increased longevity, most later life families involve a married couple. The need for intimacy and affection continues into old age. Connidis makes the point

139

about later life marriages that, 'Marital status is a central variable in structuring social life, and is related to living arrangements, loneliness, suicide, psychological well-being and health' (Connidis, 1989, p. 15). In this vein, we have very little idea about what goes on within later life marriages but it seems likely that stress, conflict and abuse present in earlier phases may continue. In one of the rare UK studies of later life families, Mason has explored the range of transitions and consequent re-negotiations faced by couples. This work confirmed a general finding that the home remains in later life 'a contested domain of meaning and experience between men and women' (1990, p. 121); this suggests that later life does not necessarily mean an end to potential strife or stress.

We have virtually no work at all on poor quality marriages in later life. One of the areas in which we do have some knowledge is that of marital quality over the family life course. This work has usually been conducted with an interest in marriage and childrearing and only includes later life families to give an overall picture. With a wide variety of measures such as marital satisfaction and marital adjustment a range of patterns in later life have been found. By far the most common finding, however, is the curvilinear relationship in which there is a decrease in marital satisfaction with the birth of children, a low period during middle-age and then a marked increase in marital satisfaction upon the launching of children. The significance of this is that, as Connidis observes, 'Marital satisfaction is a major contributor to overall well-being and ranks in importance with good health in the lives of adults' (1989, p. 17). Connidis suggests that older people are more likely to be very satisfied in their marriages. This may be 'reflected in intense activity and interaction between the husband and wife' (1989, pp. 21–2).

Inside partnerships

It is easy for those married to think of their marriages as intensely personal affairs concerning only themselves. This is very far from the case, society and culture define appropriate forms of behaviours from childhood onwards. The nature of any given marriage is shaped by the 'external world' which has an important role to play in determining expectations and ambitions. The role of the wider society is seen in family ideology which defines the nature of partnering and reproduction. It is also important to see how most societies go to great lengths to celebrate marriages with both formal ceremonies and more informal and personal processions, receptions, parties and sharing of meals.

Locate five images of the 'inside' of intimate partnerships.

It remains to explain why on earth people should want to engage in exclusive intimate relationships. Gittins points out that people give rather vague answers when asked why they marry such as 'it just happened' or 'everyone does' (1993, p. 73). Plainly, both social expectations and the availability or attractiveness of alternatives are important.

Most people remain in relationships, even if unpleasant or abusive, because the very act of having a relationship is the basic and fundamental 'social event'. The creation of societies rests upon the ability and willingness of most individuals to engage in and sustain personal relationships. Most important are those with children and partners; 'non-family' relationships beyond these are crucial but properly explored elsewhere.

Communication in partnerships

The classic work on the nature of intimate partnerships is that of Berger and Kellner (1971) who explored the social construction of reality within marriage. In essence, this model portrays marriage as an ongoing conversation by which partners develop a shared understanding of the world. Applicable to all intimate partnerships, this approach emphasises the way in which we all need and seek reassurance. Our partners are one of the main ways in which we find confirmation of our own role and value in the world. This is not a simple relationship, however; partners need to compromise and come to common agreements. In doing this, partners build a shared view of the world.

Whilst Berger and Kellner's work is rather conservative and presupposes a Western view of marriage, it does highlight the centrality of communication. Communication between partners helps to define a relationship by sharing information, attitudes and opinions. It seems likely that many people decide to hide things from one another. What they hide from one another may be of crucial importance to those interested in families. For example, people can and do hide private sexual activities, other relationships (adultery) and even private feelings.

Communication certainly seems to be about establishing and reaffirming the rules of the relationship and the respective roles of the partners, enabling people to express feelings, co-operate in making plans and decisions and, hopefully, resolve problems and conflicts. This is all very well and good and begins to present human communication as a smooth, well-ordered affair.

The truth, of course, is rather different. Casual observation of any human encounter, be it in a shop, between adult and child or between intimate partners, suggests that people do an awful lot of communicating for remarkably little outcome.

> Analyse any ordinary everyday conversation.

The main problem with communication is that it is very often not about two parties reaching some kind of 'agreement' but rather about two or more parties trying to achieve rather different things.

It is easy, as some psychologically inclined analysts have suggested, to identify 'communication problems' in intimate partnerships. Callan and Noller, for example, suggest that these include: lack of listening, lack of expressivity, vague or contradictory messages, wandering off the topic, over generalising and even negativity and coercion (1987, pp. 141–51). You may be able to adopt good listening skills, seek clarification, take responsibility for misunderstandings, stay on the topic and avoid negativity. In the end, however, if you want to stay in and watch television together and your partner wants to go to the pub together, someone is going to 'lose'.

Preparation for partnering?

Clearly, the creation of intimate partnerships is something that the vast majority of our population wish to take part in. This alone suggests that the topic should be one about which we have the best possible research material. This is simply not the case. In a similar vein, given the extent and costs of divorce, it might be reasonable to expect major government supported projects exploring the interior of marriage and marital breakdown. At a basic level, we do not really know if most current partners even like each other, let alone what kinds of strategies they use to 'get along' together. There is surprisingly little detailed work on what happens inside ordinary everyday intimate partnerships. What work does exist tends to be psychologically oriented and emphasises the inter-action between two personalities. A common theme, especially in the USA, is reference to measurement of marital satisfaction, marital happiness or marital adjustment.

Modern technological societies do not seem to believe that we need preparation for intimate partnerships despite engaging in education for most aspects of paid work. When you look at the anguish, social costs, health costs and economic costs of failed intimate partnerships, it seems only sensible that society engages in some widespread preparation for intimate partnerships.

Perhaps the most obvious and reasonable preparation would be an educational programme designed to generate realistic expectations and deliberately set out to modify or destroy the more unrealistic expectations in love, sexuality and personal fulfilment.

Should we prepare people for the breakdown of intimate relationships including marriage breakdown?

De-partnering

Whilst many would claim that divorce is somehow a 'modern problem', it is important to realise that this is a result of the legal regulation of both marriage and divorce. We really have no idea how many people formed intimate partnerships in the past nor how common were processes of de-partnering. With rising levels of premarital cohabitation, divorce and subsequent cohabitation, perhaps before re-marriage, it is very difficult to tell how many contemporary non-marital intimate partnerships break up. It seems safe to assume that divorce rates, nowadays suggested to be between 1 in 3 and 1 in 2 of marrying couples, apply to cohabitation. Since we know that divorce can lead to poverty, homelessness, addictions and even suicide, it seems reasonable to suggest that non-marital de-partnering can be just as damaging.

Divorce

Whilst there is a very great deal of rhetoric and debate about divorce, it must be remembered that remaining married does not necessarily indicate that all is well. Divorce in the UK has risen with each liberalisation of the law. By 1991 there was one divorce in the UK for every two weddings. In the 1980s, the majority of all petitions were granted to wives, over half on the grounds of 'unreasonable behaviour'. This may not be significant where divorce is unopposed by husbands but may be very revealing in opposed divorces. Male petitions are usually based on the wife's adultery.

The largest proportion of divorces occur somewhere between 5 and 9 years after the marriage; there is a steady decline thereafter but large numbers of people still divorce after 15 or 20 years of marriage. In all cases, the distinction between the actual marital breakdown (*de facto* divorce) and the legal sanction of divorce (*de jure* divorce) is important (see Chester, 1971). Around a quarter of divorces involve one partner who had previously divorced; this is likely to rise in the future.

In general terms, Gibson has argued that the level of divorce is reasonably stable and we can expect only relatively minor rises and falls over the coming years. This apparent stability reflects a range of changes:

Some of these changing features are rising unemployment with its strong association towards divorce; childhood assimilation of, and socialisation towards, parental separation as an increasingly standard life event; the ethos of individualism; and growing community acceptance of divorce and single parenting. Those that divorce will do so at an earlier age and this helps to explain the fewer children per divorcing couple. The majority of parents will marry again, while an increasing proportion will be cohabitors.

(Gibson, 1994, pp. 216–17)

Attitudes towards divorce vary significantly by culture and religion within the UK. We know very little, for example, about the position of separated or divorcing couples from Black or Asian backgrounds although popular culture suggests that this is a common experience in African-Caribbean families whilst much rarer and a cause of 'shame' in Asian families.

Robinson (1991) argues that divorce indicates a transformation of family living towards 'the Post Nuclear Family'. This notion relates to the increasingly common cycle of marriage, divorce and re-marriage; around 35 per cent of marriages in 1987 were re-marriages, the majority of partners were previously divorced. Families 'arrive' at divorce by way of many different routes and will undergo the experiences associated with divorce in many different ways. Many people ask why divorce is rising and often suggest that this implies that families are somehow 'declining' in importance. This is simply not reflected in the popularity of intimate partnerships and marriage. Whilst there has never been one particular type of family, it seems equally clear that what we are witnessing is not the emergence of a single 'new family type' but rather an increasingly common family pathway.

Divorce, whilst frequently seen as 'the only course of action', often leaves adults and children with a sense of grief, hostility and loss. Certainly, more and more adults and children are likely to share these experiences in Western nations. Callan and Noller suggest that there is no one explanation for divorce but adopt Scanzoni's emphasis upon individualism as 'a demand for personal autonomy and a corresponding respect for the . . . right to privacy, to self-expression, and to the free exercise of . . . will within limits set by the need for social cohesion' (1987, p. 279). Individualism is placing new pressures, and indeed greater expectations, upon marriage. This combines with the rising expectations of married women and social pressures that appear to permit divorce.

Most work has focused upon divorce as an example of a 'social problem', usually because it is taken to indicate something about the 'collapse of marriage'. In popular discussions, divorce is usually taken to be something that we should seek to discourage, usually by making divorce less attractive for those involved.

> Ask ten people to identify situations in which we should see divorce as a solution rather than a problem.

There is another way of looking at divorce that pays a little more respect to the wishes and intentions of those divorcing. Divorce might be seen not as a failure but as a successful strategy, a solution to particular problems faced by one or both partners in the marriage. If you take some feminist critiques of inequality in marriage combined with work on the extent of abuse in families, it is clearly possible that divorce is a means of resolving a wide range of problems. Divorce, especially when initiated by mothers, may indicate a clear trend to seek solutions to male violence and sexual abuse.

Ahrons argues that divorce is not a simple end to family stress but rather a series of five transitions 'Within each of these transitions, stresses associated with major role transitions and common family coping strategies are identified. Rather than dissolving the family, divorce culminates in its redefinition from a nuclear to a binuclear system' (1983, p. 222). Ahrons goes on to argue that maintaining meaningful relationships between adults can reduce stresses. On the other hand, Berman discusses the need for 'Psychological Divorce', that is, 'detachment from the ex-spouse and the formation of a new life with new emotional bonds and commitments' (1985, p. 375). In Berman's view, at least 25 per cent of divorced people have trouble completing this.

Much work suggests that those divorced experience 'physical and psychological disturbance, including higher rates of alcoholism, suicide, poorer mental health and lower levels of life satisfaction than married people' (Callan and Noller, 1987, p. 283). Dominian *et al.* (1991) present a wealth of detailed evidence linking marital breakdown to a wide range of health indices. Again, it seems clear that whilst women experience slightly poorer health after divorce, men experience significantly poorer health as a result of divorce.

In 1987, Goldthorpe observed that, 'Our kinship system permits divorce, but does not provide for its consequences' (1987, p. 229). Divorce creates enormous diversity within families in terms of income, housing, employment and child care arrangements. One major adjustment to divorce for children is adjustment to poverty when in single mother families. Franks has suggested that in the UK in 1990 only 10–15 per cent of fathers were awarded custody of one or more children (1990, p. 3).

Adultery and sexuality

One very common theme in popular literature and folk mythology is that of adultery. Lawson's (1988) study of adultery in the UK suggests that well over half of all men and women engage in adulterous affairs at some time. Plainly, adulteries can be short- or long-lived and have a wide range of outcomes, may be declared or secret, may lead to stress or even revenge and are often cited in divorce cases. Whilst classic sex studies, such as Kinsey *et al.* (1948, 1953), revealed far higher levels of extra-marital sex than previously suspected, it seems unlikely that we have reliable research even now. What this hints at, however, is the hidden structure of sexuality.

> Find out how many 'soft porn' magazines are sold each month. What does this suggest about public beliefs about sexual behaviour.

Sexuality is a key aspect of all our lives, and a vital component of family practices and pathways, ranging from loving intimate partnerships through to rape and sexual abuse. Sexuality is often treated in a very narrow sense, perhaps included in discussions of 'mate selection' and 'reproduction' but often absent from discussions of routine everyday family pathways. In this way the enormous fun and satisfaction derived from sexuality is ignored, as is the potential power of sexually based emotions. Contemporary family practices and pathways plainly will all involve, at times, passion, desire and jealousy. These powerful forces need to be integrated into appreciations of relationships between adults, and even between adults and children.

There is a current debate within feminism both 'for' and 'against' a range of types of pornography. There are some workers who consider all sexualised images as exploitative and therefore argue for their censorship whilst others discuss the dangers of censorship, especially regarding 'normal' sexual orientations and behaviours. It seems clear that many societies world-wide have traditions of sexualised images and 'approved' means of sexually stimulating couples. A great deal of work remains to be done to incorporate the hidden structures of sexuality into our understanding of family practices and family pathways.

Re-marriage

In many countries, especially the UK, there is a very high chance that divorced people will re-marry. It seems clear that this is a product of the overwhelming unattractiveness of the 'single option' combined with a very strong ideology emphasising marriage as demonstrating personal success. Burgoyne and Clark noted the importance of material considerations in re-marriage: single parents, especially mothers, often find they need help with income, child care and domestic work. The same authors suggested that people marry in the 'optimistic desire to reconstitute family life afresh through remarriage' (Burgoyne and Clark, 1981, p. 346). It remains a great irony that people whose marriages ended in divorce tend to re-marry; in the re-marriages, rates of divorce are even higher than for first marriages.

Re-marriages tend to be extremely varied ranging from childless partners in their twenties right through to late middle-aged couples with grown up children. There is also a clear trend to greater age discrepancy in re-marriage meaning that children from previous marriages may be of very different age groups. This can create a situation of mature children from one marriage, school-age children from the other marriage, and new-borns from the re-marriage itself. Robinson (1991) found that divorce contributes to a situation in which 1 in 7 households is likely to contain a single parent and 1 in 8 is probably a stepfamily. In 1987, around 35 per cent of marriages were re-marriages for one or both partners, the majority of which were divorced. Re-marriage is not the end of one partnership and the beginning of another but rather involves the, often painful, redrawing of family boundaries. All manner of friends, relatives and kin may be involved in redefining relationships; some who were previously 'close' may find themselves kept at a 'distance'.

The future of partnering

In her classic study, *The Future of Marriage*, Jessie Bernard asserted very strongly that the future of marriage was certain:

> The future of marriage is, I believe, as assured as any human social form can be. . . . For men and women will continue to want intimacy. They will continue to want to celebrate their mutuality, to experience the mystic unity which once led the church to consider marriage a sacrament. . . . There is hardly any probability that such commitments will disappear or that all relationships between them will become merely casual and transient.
>
> (Bernard, 1982, pp. 269–70)

I believe that Jessie Bernard was substantially correct except in the detail of marriage itself. We have already seen marriage transforming itself in Northern Europe (especially Scandinavian countries such as Denmark) where cohabitation is recognised in law and partners have clearly protected rights. As our awareness of racism develops, so we have begun to recognise and respect the very different bases of marriages in different cultural groups. We are also aware of the rising tide of divorce, and increasingly recognise abuse between partners and the enormous stresses placed on individuals by intimate partnering. At the same time, intimate partnerships are one of the more attractive and enduring objectives for most individuals in modern societies.

The future of intimate partnering is assured but it may be one of rising abuse, divorce, individualism and materialism. It remains puzzling as to why a feature of human social life that the majority appear to favour is so little understood.

Whilst many have agonised over the costs of failed intimate relationships, few have commented upon the need to better prepare people for relationships. Society can decide to take positive steps to improve those relationships. A policy programme should clearly involve education for partnering aimed at providing realistic expectations and encouraging individuals to sustain relationships once established. We should also develop strategies to minimise the cost and pain of de-partnering.

Suggested reading

Bernard, J. 1982 (Revised edition): *The Future of Marriage*. London: Yale University Press.

Kiernan, K. E. and Estaugh, V. 1993: *Cohabitation: Extra-Marital Childbearing and Social Policy*. London: Family Policy Studies Centre.

Lawson, A. 1988: *Adultery: An Analysis of Love and Betrayal*. Oxford: Blackwell.

Mansfield, P. and Collard, J. 1988: *The Beginning of the Rest of Your Life? A Portrait of Newly-Wed Marriage*. Basingstoke: Macmillan.

Chapter 7

Parenting

Introduction

Without the remarkable commitment of most adults to some form of parenting, any society would inevitably decline. It is easy to assume that this commitment is 'natural' and that parents voluntarily choose to undertake parenting. Many scholars assume, as Skolnick notes, that the 'needs' of parents and children somehow harmoniously interlock to facilitate good childrearing (1978, pp. 275–6). These kinds of views neglect the enormous effort which most societies devote to the remarkable achievement of ensuring that adults bear and raise children. This is all the more remarkable when you realise that the UK, like most societies, lacks any systematic preparation for parenthood.

The majority of what social science currently 'knows' about parenting is actually an ideal type portrayal of married heterosexual parents doing socialisation to their children. The children follow neat developmental sequences to become well-adjusted mature adults. Where children do not turn out to be mature well-adjusted adults, we can safely 'blame the parents'.

149

Parenting is not at all like this: we know very little about ordinary day-to-day parenting. Parenting is extremely varied and diverse. The practice of parenting is one of great joy and pleasure for many but also involves many costs and challenges, especially for women. The presumption of motherhood and interrupted work patterns is one of the main bases for gender discrimination in the paid work place; this, in turn, is one of the keys to wider gender inequality in modern societies. In a similar way, the presumption of female mothering reflects the presumption of continuity in male work patterns through parenthood which is one of the means by which men are prevented from greater participation in parenting. In the pursuit of better parenting and greater equality, the question of whether men can or should mother needs to be addressed.

Diversity in parenting

Whilst there is still a widespread belief in 'the family', it is important to note that diversity in parenting was recognised in the early 1970s. Among the early work was the recognition of variation by the timing, number and spacing of births. Another classic concern was the heterogeneity or mixing of marital partners across classes, religious faiths and racial groups. In the UK, this recognition was marked by Rapoport *et al.* (1977) who included a chapter on 'Diversity in Parenting Situations'. This study also includes sections on: divorce, childlessness, single parenthood, adoption and fostering, communes, dual-worker families, stepfamilies and families with a handicapped child. There are, of course, innumerable other forms of diversity including, for example, social class, sickness, culture and religion, income, sexual orientation of partners, presence of abuse or parenting by grandparents. More recently Glenn *et al.* have used their study of mothering as a means to challenge universalism and demonstrate diversity in mothering (Glenn *et al.*, 1994).

List all possible forms of diversity in parenting.

Diversity in parenting is recognised not as signalling the complexity of parenting itself but rather as indicating some kind of 'problem'. In regarding or labelling a diverse form of parenting as indicating a 'problem', popular culture has managed to retain and protect a central image of parenting within the 'nuclear family'. Such arguments are often interwoven with justifications of discrimination and inequality, especially around social class and race or ethnicity. This is seen in popular concerns about single parenthood and especially Black single parenthood (usually stereotyping single African-Caribbean mothers).

Single parenthood

Popular ideology presents parenting alone as 'less desirable' than dual parenthood. There are, however, a wide range of situations when one parent is absent due to working away, imprisonment, separation, divorce, widowhood or refusal to acknowledge parenthood (see Chandler, 1991). As Ferraro *et al.* (1983) note, the imprisoning of a parent generates real punishment for the remaining parent and children as well as for the offender.

Whilst Queen Victoria was a single parent for many years, she is not thought of as a 'problem parent'. Most concerns about the 'problem' of single parenthood are really concerns about poor single parents, usually single mothers, who are seen as both 'burdens' on the state and as producing children more prone to low educational attainment, delinquency, unemployment and crime (see Dennis and Erdos, 1993).

Parenting demands both a decent income, usually derived from paid work, and a high level of interaction with children. It is often difficult for dual-working parents to manage both paid work and time with their children, for many single parents it is a continual struggle. Added to this, the bulk of single parents are mothers whose incomes from paid work tend to be lower than those of men. Marsden's *Mothers Alone: Poverty and the Fatherless Family*, published in 1969, began to indicate the multiple disadvantages faced by single mothers in terms of paid work or reliance upon benefits, housing, child care and many other aspects. Haskey (1991) has estimated that, in 1989, there were around one and a half million single parent families in the UK containing very nearly two million dependent children. Around 1 in 6 families with dependent children were single parent families, with the biggest growth in numbers among the never married rather than the divorced.

> Explore the media for characterisations of single parenthood. Compare the negative and positive characterisations.

Burghes notes how, 'In 1991, public anxiety and debate was rekindled . . . [as to] . . . whether children of lone parents were doing less well in school and were more likely to engage in delinquent behaviour' (1994, p. 7). Burghes concentrates upon the outcomes for children of what he terms *Lone Parenthood and Family Disruption*; whilst recognising some positive outcomes for single parenthood and even negative outcomes for dual parenthood, Burghes ends with a call for more research.

In thinking of family practices and pathways, it is probable that single parenting may often be a solution to problems. It seems likely that much single parenthood is a result of escaping relationships that were abusive or destructive for partners or children. More to the point, it seems clear that if this is the case, we should positively support those parents who are seeking to bring up their children in non-abusive and non-destructive environments. Seen in this light, it is important to understand single parenthood as a particular family pathway. Rather than blaming those involved, it may be more productive to consider how to ensure that people are less likely to find themselves having to adopt this solution to their problems.

Black single motherhood

The way in which popular prejudice against poorer sections of society and ethnic minorities is combined is seen most clearly in the stereotyping of Black single motherhood. There is a widespread belief that African-Caribbean women are over-represented as single mothers. Single mothers account for 14 per cent of births in the general population and 51 per cent in the African-Caribbean population. Also, the 1991 Census found that 42 per cent of African-Caribbean families were headed by a single mother.

> Locate evidence about the 'problem' of Black single mothers.

This kind of evidence must be handled with a great deal of care. If single motherhood among the dominant White population is a solution to a variety of wider social problems, then single motherhood in a particular ethnic group might pinpoint even greater problems.

Within all ethnic groups there are distinctive traditions of family patterns. There is also inevitable widespread variation and diversity. African-Caribbean men are discriminated against in harsh ways in the UK, most clearly seen in poverty, unemployment and education. Whereas 38 per cent of single mothers in the general population earn an income, 59 per cent of Black single mothers do. This suggests that Black single mothers are vigorous and economically active rather than passive victims of Black men. It is likely that Black single motherhood is far from being a 'problem' when taking account of employment, income and social class. Perhaps the plight of Black single motherhood should suggest the need for supportive social policies. Such policies might be designed to lessen the disproportionate chances of unemployment, poverty and parenting under enormous pressure for Black citizens.

The practice of parenting

Many popular sources portray parenting as a task of joy, pleasure and satisfaction. There are positive aspects, pleasures and benefits from parenting. There is certainly a widespread rhetoric of respect and reward for parenting which conveys maturity and respectability. Whilst this is muted in the case of parenting alone, there is some evidence that parenting together provides a central axis around which communication revolves and perhaps maintains relationships that might otherwise decline or decay.

Whilst there are those who choose to remain childless, having children is a life ambition for many. In the case of infertility, couples sometimes go to extreme lengths to bear children. For the fertile, children are one of the main positive aspects of their existence and a source of considerable pride and satisfaction. Whilst much is written about parents rearing children successfully, there is much less work on the benefits of children for adults. Clearly, popular rhetoric places relationships between parents and children on a comparable footing to relationships between intimate partners. It remains, however, to explore exactly how parents find pleasure, joy and love in their relationships with children.

The costs of parenting

Many authors assume what Zinn and Eitzen label as an 'Omnipotent Parents Model' (1990, p. 305) of confident and powerful parents socialising their children. In this model the flow is very much from parents to children who tend to be seen as 'empty vessels' awaiting being 'filled' with social learning. More recent work suggests that parenting is very much a 'two way street'. Whilst parents certainly do influence children, children also influence and change parents and all of this happens within a context of widespread social influences such as advertising, video violence and gender imaging.

Feminist work has identified the high emotional costs paid by women in mothering and related tasks. To this should be added the role of children in adding to stress and a range of related mental illness. Umberson made the clear statement that 'living with children is associated with psychological distress' (1989, p. 427); the causes of such distress may be sleeplessness with young infants, continual temper tantrums from toddlers right through to disputes with teenagers about times to return home. There are considerable, ongoing and very direct economic costs to all parents in clothing, heating, housing, feeding and so on. It really is deceitful to argue that parents 'should' bear these costs because 'they chose to have children'. The investment of such parents is of very little direct economic benefit to parents whilst it may be of great benefit to society in creating healthy and fit citizens.

> Make a rough calculation of the cost of housing, clothing, feeding and otherwise supporting a child from birth to 16 years of age, including toys and leisure goods (see Roll, 1986, for the costs of babies).

Ventura (1987) identifies four stress areas of parenthood:

1   Competing and conflicting demands between the roles of parent, spouse and paid worker.
2   The demands placed upon parents by infant care.
3   The changed nature of interactions with spouse.
4   The nature of interactions with other family members.

There is a considerable body of evidence to show that a variety of measures around marital quality (such as adjustment or satisfaction) decline in the parenting years. With rising expectations of both intimate relationships and parenting there is a clear conflict, primarily for mothers, between being a parent and being a partner.

> Develop a list of the non-economic costs of parenting.

Preparation for parenthood

Most parents seem to suffer a double disadvantage in modern materialistic societies. Not only are they given remarkably little support for their role but they are also victims of commercial interests by way of advertising and merchandising. Paid workers receive wages regardless of their family status; such parents are also the targets of demands from children created by widespread advertising. In exploring the very wide range of forms of stress on modern families, McKenry and Price (1994, pp. 303–10) develop an argument for supporting materially poor families in periods of stress and in engaging in broad preparation and education for family life as a way of alleviating some of the worst effects of such routine family stress events (such as children leaving home, divorce, unemployment, chronic illness or bereavement).

There are many concerns about the 'collapse of the family' and the 'problems' of family practices and pathways such as divorce and single parenthood. Many of these concerns involve a wish that somehow people behaved differently. If you want to drive a car, you must attain a certain age, learn how to drive and take a driving test. Even the simplest popular rhetoric suggests that parenting requires a wide range of skills.

List some of the skills and abilities needed to be a parent.

Many commentators who wish us to become 'better societies', have suggested that we need to improve the nature and quality of parenting. Whilst relatively unusual in the UK, preparation for parenthood is common in many industrial societies, especially the USA, Scandinavia and some European Union countries.

The Community Education Development Centre (CEDC) recognises that there does exist some preparation for parenthood in the UK but finds this confused and uncoordinated. The CEDC argues:

> What is needed is a wider conception of preparation for parenthood which recognises much of the good work in education about relationships that already takes place within schools, colleges and the youth service. At the same time we need to promote increased public awareness of the needs of children and their carers.
>
> (1992, p. 9)

The notion of 'Preparation for Parenthood' has also been a continuous theme of the work of the National Children's Bureau. As part of a 1979 initiative to 'raise the standards of parenting in this country', Pugh explored preparation for parenthood in schools, antenatal preparation, and support for families with young children (1980, see Foreword).

Many of these ideas were developed in the UK by Whitfield who laid out a clear argument for 'Family Life Education':

> A central concern of 'family life education' is one of primary prevention – the process of developing and supplying family members with personal resources which will enable them to fulfil their reasonable expectations and so keep them clear of serious trouble in such things as child growth and development problems, family conflict, divorce and family breakdown. Preventive processes require teaching and learning and are therefore essentially education processes. Family life education, if properly resourced, organised and evaluated, having regard to life cycle development within families prompting different needs over time, could therefore contribute greatly to reshaping our social fabric.
>
> (Whitfield, 1983, p. 20, also see 1980)

155

Where then is the investment in researching parenting, where is the commitment to improving parenting? Whilst the UK is certainly one of the most backward nations in studying family life and in 'parenthood education', no modern societies contain levels of activity in this area that might reflect real commitment.

In exploring the nature of 'parenting activities' for those in step-relationships, De'Ath and Slater provide a rare and coherent sense of what is involved in ordinary everyday parenting:

> WANTED: a responsible person, male or female, to undertake a life-time project. Candidates should be totally committed, willing to work up to 24 hours daily, including weekends. Occasional holidays possible after 5 years service. Knowledge of health care, nutrition, psychology, child development, and the education system essential. Necessary qualities: energy, tolerance, patience and a sense of humour. No training or experience needed. No salary, but very rewarding work for the right person.
>
> (De'Ath and Slater, 1992, p. 10)

In developing the case of confident parenting, Pugh *et al.* make 40 general recommendations, the first of which is, 'A coherent national family policy should be developed, creating a framework within which parent education and support can be provided locally, but also ensuring that social, employment, health, housing and economic policies support families in bringing up their children' (1994, p. 225). In 1996, Smith undertook a detailed review of current forms of parenting programmes, noting a 'considerable growth and interest in the more formal type of group-based parenting programme during the last five to ten years' (1996, p. 114). As a means to resolving the isolation of current parenting programmes, Smith recommends that, 'Dissemination, networking and discussion must become more widespread to avoid too much reinvention of the wheel' (ibid. p. 120).

Parenting practices and pathways

Whilst parenting does not follow an orderly sequence of events, there are changes over time and some kinds of events precede others on parenting pathways. Looking at parenting pathways should not be taken to imply that any particular area is necessary to be a good enough parent. Adoptive parents, for example, do not undergo many of the stages associated with childbirth that are often assumed to be essential for creating a 'loving relationship'. Similarly, parents who abuse and even murder their children appear to have followed quite ordinary parenting practices and pathways.

Childlessness and pronatalism

Those who believe that pregnancy and childbirth are ultimately natural, should examine their own attitudes and general social responses to the childless. Badinter (1981) has provided one of the more thorough critiques of the 'myth of the maternal instinct' in bearing and raising children. Clearly, there is a biological basis to sexual behaviour and conception but this should not be seen as predominant. If reproduction were biologically based, all women with partners would be continually bearing and rearing children from their early years until menopause, this is far from the case in most societies world-wide. Rather than simple biological drives, there are clear social pressures at work here. The negative evaluation of childlessness combined with the positive evaluation of having children is known as 'pronatalism'. It is difficult to underestimate the power and effectiveness of pronatalism. Those who cannot conform, such as infertile couples, will undergo arduous and expensive treatments, including the risk of multiple births, to conceive.

Gather a dozen pronatalist images from the popular press.

The study of the lives of the deliberately childless was pioneered in Canada. Veevers researched those who had decided to 'buck the trend' and remain childless (1974). What emerges is the way in which young couples are subject to a considerable range of pressures that encourage them to have children. Pressures come from simple observation ('Everyone else has kids'), through parental comments ('When are we going to be Grandparents?'), through to some careers that assume a 'normal family life'. Veevers encapsulated this in describing the way in which childless couples had to respond to the publicly understood 'social meanings of parenthood'. Parenthood is seen as moral, fulfilling religious obligations, demonstrating responsibility, proof of sexuality and maturity, improving marriage and being good for stability and mental health.

Busfield argues that reproduction is subject to culture and ideology: 'Ideologies play an important part in social control; they constrain individuals by presenting them with a set of expectations for their behaviour and appropriate rationales that support the expectations' (1986, p. 33). Married heterosexual couples do not generally have to justify why they have children, on the contrary, they need to be ready to explain why they have not yet done so. To defend themselves, the childless must build for themselves an alternative world view in which they justify not having children.

Society performs a complete somersault when it comes to 'non-approved' couples, such as lesbian or gay couples, who wish to have children. There have been numerous debates about whether the mentally or physically handicapped should be allowed or encouraged to engage in sexual activity and parenting. Suddenly, the 'naturalness' of having children is reversed, just as such impairments or sexual preferences are often labelled as 'not natural'.

Contraception, abortion, miscarriage, stillbirth and Sudden Infant Death

There is a widespread belief that modern contraception has brought about major changes in sexual behaviour and fertility. Whilst it does seem that young people now engage in more sexual behaviour than previously, Estaugh and Wheatley observe that many still become pregnant by failing to use contraceptives (1990). Estaugh and Wheatley argue that teenage and other unwanted pregnancies are a major cause of concern in a modern society. It is ironic that public concern about teenage pregnancies in the UK goes hand-in-hand with a limited programme of sex education in schools.

List six advantages and six disadvantages of far greater preparation for sexuality in schools.

One ___ me of pregnancy is abortion. Abortion is far from being a new phenon ___ the moral and legal aspects of abortion are extremely contentic ___ st European countries now permit abortion under particular circumstances. What is often neglected is the impact of abortion upon a woman's later feelings about pregnancy.

The maternal mortality rate in the UK is four times that of Ireland, twice that of Italy and less than two-thirds of the average of 27 industrialised countries (Adamson, 1993, p. 39). Even with improved health, the vast majority of women are likely to experience a miscarriage or perhaps a stillbirth or Sudden Infant Death (see Lovell, 1983). The impact of such loss is very personal; Rosenblatt and Burns describe how the impact of perinatal loss lasted for at least forty-four years in one case (1986, p. 237).

In looking at Sudden Infant Death, Smlalek (1978) discussed a range of reactions including: shock, disbelief, denial; negativism and hostility; self-reproach and guilt; identification of former unresolved guilt; previous fears of loss; relief. In a feminist analysis of miscarriage and ectopic pregnancy, Hey et al. (1989) echo similar feelings but identify one of the key problems as the way in which such events are labelled as 'pregnancy failures' and 'hidden' from view. It is this hiddenness that contributes to both confusion on the part of women and a denial of the emotional importance of such 'hidden loss' for women. In looking at the meaning of miscarriage, Letherby is highly critical of the very common reaction of 'never mind – better luck next time' which denies the emotional impact and fact of bereavement (1993, p. 165).

Pregnancy and childbirth

As an experience many women share, it is striking that the social sciences have undertaken so little serious research on pregnancy and childbirth beyond recent feminist work. The major figure here is undoubtedly Oakley with her work on childbirth and motherhood in 1979 and 1980. It is worth noting that, until that date, there was little work on the social processes of pregnancy and childbirth with a dominant medical view focusing upon physiology. In reviewing antenatal and postnatal health education, Combes and Schonveld argue that 'opportunities for parent education are being missed, and parent education is therefore falling short of the expectations and needs of parents' (1992, p. 101).

Oakley (1979 and 1980) focused on the gap between image and reality in childbirth. She described the way modern medicine labels pregnancy and childbirth as an 'illness' to be treated in hospitals by doctors where the woman's own preferences are ignored in favour of 'expert opinion'. This theme echoed work by Rothman who explored the history of medical men moving in and taking over at the birthplace (1982).

> Ask a range of mothers about 'their pregnancies'; be ready to listen for some time, this is not a trivial matter.

Pregnancy is a protracted period that most women will experience once. This can be an extremely varied process which women may enjoy, manage to cope with, or find deeply distressing. Macintyre (1985) explores the management of food and suggests we should take this much more seriously since such eating behaviours can disrupt everyday life in the short and long term. Murcott suggests that food cravings and aversions in pregnancy are part of popular beliefs about a period 'which is characterised as odd, peculiar and potentially dangerous' (1988, p. 761).

At childbirth, a woman may find herself experiencing multiple births. Such births become matters of public interest when five or six children survive but lesser numbers tend to be ignored. The experiences of families of twin or multiple births are markedly different to those of single births. The demands, strains and pressures of parenthood can effectively isolate new parents from the rest of society.

One of the major consequences for new mothers after childbirth is the experience of postnatal depression, 'baby blues' or, in a significant number of cases, post-partum psychosis (see Oakley, 1980, pp. 114–18). Several authors have claimed that more than half of all new mothers experience significant mental health impacts. Again, it is remarkable that little work has been done in this area and that little preventative work is undertaken. Several studies have found that many mothers experience panic reactions after birth and that this level of post-partum stress is related to lack of preparation. One wonders whether there would be similar disinterest if men experienced these symptoms following childbirth.

Whilst men generally used to be excluded from the birthplace, it seems that most modern societies now encourage them to attend. Presence at the birth should not be confused, however, with active involvement in childbirth or any commitment to participate in caring for the new-born.

Breast feeding

An interesting indicator of popular attitudes towards babies and children is the debate about breast feeding. There seem to be at least two strands to this debate. First, there is the issue of the way in which breast feeding 'ties' the mother to the child and prevents her from continuing paid work or spending time outside the home. Related to this is the debate about whether breast feeding should be allowed in public places in the UK. This is, in turn, part of the debate about whether we should allow children in public places (like pubs and restaurants) at all.

> Sample ten people and ask whether women should breast feed in public.

The production of baby feeds is a highly profitable industry and there is little doubt that advertising by the industry has contributed to public attitudes favouring bottle feeding. On the other side of the coin, the general dislike of public breast feeding may reflect not only male sexualisation of breasts but also the way in which females have internalised this view of their own sexuality. It does seem that there is a great deal to be learnt from what are often believed to be 'less developed' societies where breast feeding is much more acceptable, even praiseworthy.

The transition to parenting

Having a child, especially a first child, marks a period of dramatic change for all concerned. The birth of a baby, or perhaps the adoption of a child, tends to be a cause for celebration by the parents, relatives and other interested parties. On the other hand, there have been several studies that characterise the transition to parenthood as a period of challenges or even crises where a wide range of new situations and roles have to be accommodated very rapidly (see LaRossa and LaRossa, 1981). If partners are not able or willing to adapt to the new situations, this may create serious stress within the partnership, perhaps even contributing to divorce.

The birth of a baby is an ideal opportunity to observe the nature of divisions in society and our own reactions and feelings about those divisions. The classic concerns on the birth of a baby are for its health (we divide the healthy from the sick) and its sex (we divide male from female). It is ironic that a society that claims to be 'child oriented' (and plainly is, as long as it represents commercial advantage) refuses to recognise any links between the birth of a child and the role of the father in paid work. Many other European societies have forms of paternity leave but the UK Government still resists this in virtually all sectors of the economy.

In 1985 Cowan *et al.* developed a detailed review of the elements involved in the transition accompanying the birth of the first child. Whilst it might be expected that the transition to a second child was easier in some respects, Knox and Wilson (1978) have demonstrated that the second child means even less time for self, more noise, more work and decreased marital happiness. LeMasters spent considerable effort in the early 1970s exploring the transition to parenthood, including fascinating detail of the way parents encounter a wide range of myths about parenting (see LeMasters, 1978).

Ask six parents to identify 'myths' about parenting.

It should be obvious that the transition to parenthood is distinctly gendered. Just as there are 'his' and 'her' marriages, so there are 'his' and 'her' transitions to parenthood. Zinn and Eitzen discuss the way in which structural changes associated with the transition to parenthood may encourage couples to adopt more traditional, patriarchal roles (1990, p. 303). Cowan *et al.* (1985) identified negative changes; compared to non-parents, parental partners grew apart, there was a development of conflict and a lowering of marital satisfaction. Some researchers have suggested that it is in the childbearing phase that many of the seeds of later divorce are first sown. The transition to parenthood should not be seen as an experience of the parental pair alone, Power and Parke (1984) have made the general point that adaptation is much easier if there are extensive social networks, that is, links between friends, relatives, paid work mates and/or neighbours.

Howe *et al.* (1992) recently estimated that around half a million mothers in the UK had given up their children for adoption at birth. This is a difficult and painful process in which both the mothers and the children seem to be poorly treated. Birth parents in the UK do not have to satisfy any authority about their 'fitness' or 'suitability' to be a parent. Parenting is one of the few remaining activities that does not require training, tests or licences. Prospective foster or adoptive parents, on the other hand, are subject to all kinds of tests of suitability including items such as assessments of their intellectual understanding of racism. This seems to be drawn from recent social work practice focused upon the point that in growing up in a White family and a White environment, a Black child will not be taught appropriate 'coping mechanisms' for racism which will lead to serious identity confusion in later life.

Whilst it is possible to see why such tests have been developed, it does seem odd that we do not require birth parents to subject themselves to such assessments. It remains an interesting question how many adults would be deemed 'suitable parents' using the assessment criteria used in adoption procedures. This is not to suggest that adoption should be made more or less easy but rather that there are real differences in the way birth and adoptive families are treated.

Parents and adolescents

Most textbooks focus upon the 'key role' of socialising children in the earlier years of infanthood. Once the 'dramatic' events of language acquisition and establishing behaviour patterns are accomplished, most textbooks fall silent about the ordinary everyday business of parents in their 30–50s dealing with school-age children. This reflects both the lack of any clear 'function' of parenting adolescents and the widespread emphasis upon enabling children to prepare for paid work by schooling.

> Ask six parents of older children whether parenting became easier as the children got older?

Most studies of adolescents tend to be studies of 'youth', treating adolescents and young people as a distinct group, often labelled as 'alienated' or separated from the rest of society. One of the few studies of adolescents in families comes from Australia. In 1991, Noller and Callan introduced their study as follows: 'Adolescence can be a difficult time for all concerned. Issues such as youth employment, sexual behaviour and drug abuse have made it a matter of great concern to the community at large' (1991, Frontispiece). The main issue is that of children growing up and changing in ways that parents may find strange or threatening.

Noller and Callan detail the way in which family environment is central in enabling adolescents to cope during this transition. By means of conflict and negotiation, adolescents reformulate their relationships with parents and others. In exploring family environments, the authors argue that if families spend time together, this can be a vital place in which individuals grow. On the other hand, parents may attempt to control and restrict their children in ways that generate great hostility. Various studies demonstrate the importance of family life itself rather than particular rules or guidelines. In ensuring the successful development of adolescents, Noller and Callan emphasise family closeness, and adaptability (1991, p. 69).

De-parenting

One significant aspect of de-partnering is the way in which it leads, in parental situations, to some degree of de-parenting – that is, one or other parent becoming less involved in the parenting of a child. Jackson has explored what she terms the 'myth' of 'An absent mother equals a bad one, and probably a woman with loose morals' (1994, p. 15). Jackson's study makes it clear that de-parenting for women, or de-mothering, is not only enormously complex and varied but is also far from unnatural or deviant. The most obvious example of de-parenting is where one partner moves out of the family home and is effectively cut off from both previous partner and children. There are many factors involved in whether this happens or not but the significant ones do seem to be the adversarial nature of divorce in many nations and whether there are legal rules about custody and access.

Find someone whose parents divorced when they were still a child. Ask them how this affected their life.

Wallerstein and Kelly (1980) confirmed what many long believed – parental divorce generates intense emotional confusion for children. This is often used by moralists to support a call to make divorce more difficult to obtain. This argument needs handling with care; whilst children may suffer in divorce situations, it may be that they would suffer much more had their parents not divorced. What this suggests, of course, is not that divorce should be more difficult but that society should seek to make marriages less likely to end in divorce.

Some modern societies insist upon joint custody of children following divorce. Trost and Hultaker (1986) have argued that joint custody in Sweden has generally improved the quality of resident and non-resident fathering. The UK still maintains practices in which custody of children is subject to intense legal wrangles. Eaton demonstrates how the law tends to uphold traditional gender roles in decisions around family life (1986, pp. 87–98); the UK Children Act clearly states that the mother shall have parental responsibility for the child where parents are not married. This traditional view affects the relationship of children and their divorced father; complete severance of contact seems common. Burghes notes that 40 per cent of absent fathers lose all contact with their children after two years (Burghes, 1994, p. 41). Of the remainder perhaps the majority will experience infrequent contact or conflict over contact arrangements.

One of the great stresses for children and their separated parents can be the issue of abduction. In 1981, Agopian and Anderson found that in the USA parental child stealing was arising as a problem. There have been several notable cases in the 1990s in the UK and it seems likely that the European Union will have to develop some legislation to deal with this problem when abducted children are moved within the Union.

Stepparenting

By far the best analysis of stepparenting comes from the work of De'Ath and Slater (1992) for the National Stepfamily Association in their handbook, *Parenting Threads*. What this text does is to argue very clearly that stepparenting is unlike natural parenting, being a 'third step' in parenting. In exploring parent–child relations in re-married families, Hobart (1987) located three 'classes' of children. In the first class he located children of the re-marriage who were shared by the two parents, second class were the wife's unshared children and third class were the husband's unshared children.

Whilst becoming part of a 'new family' may be a relief for children in some ways, especially in regaining an outwardly 'normal family', there is a wide range of challenges to be faced. Robinson and Smith characterise this as a process involving numerous stages in each of which there are many transitions and transformations (1993, see Chapter 8). There may be conflicts between children and their stepparent, especially revolving around the extent to which the child and stepparent 'accept' each other and how far the child 'accepts' the adult taking on the role of 'mother' or 'father'. There may be disputes between the new partners in which children manipulate loyalties; there may be disputes between different 'classes' of children. Beyond this, there may be dispute and confusion about the roles of grandparents and previous spouses.

In 1983, Wadsworth *et al.* found children in stepfamilies and single parent families more likely to experience accidents in the first five years of life. Kiernan created something of a media storm in the early 1990s by suggesting that stepchildren do clearly suffer as a result of divorce and re-marriage and are more disadvantaged in some ways than children in single parent families (see Kiernan, 1992a and 1992b).

What sorts of things may lead to arguments in a 'new family' with children from two previous marriages?

Following several decades of high rates of divorce and re-marriage, the issue of re-parenting is becoming more important. Whilst there is virtually no preparation for parenting in the UK, there is little preparation for re-parenting across Western nations. It seems clear that this issue, especially in view of long-standing concerns about the behaviour of children in stepfamilies, requires urgent attention.

Grandparenting

Modern later life families involve a much longer period of grandparenting, and even possibly great grandparenting. Much has been written about 'the generation gap', many modern families simultaneously experience three generation gaps. First, there is the gap between the grandparental generation and their married adult children. Second, there is the gap between intimate partners and their adolescent or older children. Third, there is the gap between grandparents and grandchildren. It is easy for the parental generation to feel that they are 'the sandwich generation', finding themselves in disputes with both younger and older generations.

Many people are grandparents before they reach 65 years of age. 'Grandparents are in a unique position in the family network because they are not the parents of the younger generation but they have a vested interest in the development of the grandchild' (Brubaker, 1985, p. 71). Whilst many grandparents value being a grandparent, the transition to the role has no clear rites of passage, grandparents have to create and negotiate 'rules' about their conduct with both the adult child generation and the grandchildren.

> Ask ten grandparents what is involved in being a grandparent.

Connidis (1989) suggests that the grandparent role has a range of meanings. It can become a central activity in the older person's life, grandparents are seen as elders and grandparenthood creates a sense of immortality. In their relationships with children, grandparents can indulge and spoil children and, in some ways, relive life through grandchildren.

The transition to grandparenthood is often a middle-age phenomenon and Connidis argues (1989, pp. 3–4) that the age has changed little over the century whilst Crawford (1981) argues that grandparents tend to be younger, still working and far from 'disengaged' from society. What has certainly changed is the duration of the relationship and the health and social status of people when they become grandparents. Cunningham-Burley (1984) has looked at the transition to grandparenthood and the impact this has upon the lives of those involved, especially in family and career development.

> Ask ten grandchildren what they like about their grandparents.

In exploring work on grandparents, Troll (1983) suggests that they occupy a special location as 'The Family Watchdogs' by which he contends that contemporary grandparents serve to maintain family systems as wholes. Troll found that grandparental roles are both extremely important in many families and extremely diverse, perhaps even more diverse than parental roles. One key to understanding grandparenting at any instant is the developmental status of grandparents and grandchildren. Plainly, middle-aged grandparents relate to new-born babies rather differently than 70-year-old widowers and their adolescent grandchildren.

The role of grandparents does seem to be very rich and diverse and is very often far from the 'symbolic role' implied in popular culture. In the UK, recent research has found that grandmothers are major providers of care for pre-school children of working mothers (Kiernan and Wicks, 1990, p. 35). Connidis suggests that we can explore the nature of grandparenthood by focusing upon the meaning people attach to role behaviours associated with grandparenting and the degree of satisfaction for grandparents and grandchildren. There can be very different levels of activity and styles of grandparenting ranging from intense engagement in child care to remote and rarely visited (Connidis, 1989, pp. 60–70).

In some cultures, and sometimes debated in the UK, a non-related older person may be 'adopted' by a family to fill the vacant location of grandparent.

Some have gone so far as to suggest that such a strategy may provide a 'solution' for the care of young children and the 'excess' of older people.

Divorce and grandparenting

With the rise in divorce, so the nature of grandparenting has become fraught with difficulties. Upon a divorce, many fathers lose contact with their children, this implies that paternal grandparents may also lose contact, perhaps to their distress. Thus, changes by parents can create all kinds of complexities, rivalries and 'side taking'. Connidis has suggested that 'In the wake of divorce, grand-mothers make themselves available as stabilisers in an unsettled family' (1989, p. 65). Whilst this may be true, it may also be the case that one or more grandmothers may compete for this role.

With the increasing complexity of family practices and pathways, so the possible relationships between family members grow very rapidly indeed. In a re-marriage for both partners with children from both previous marriages there can be four grandmothers available. If the new partnership were to have children 'of their own', children in one household may end up having different 'classes' of grandparents.

Motherhood

The continuation of any society depends upon the quality of parenting; parenting is rarely shared equally and the major burden usually falls to women. This feature of motherhood has been at the very centre of many feminist critiques (see Trebilcot, 1984; Phoenix *et al.*, 1991). In exploring the negative evaluation of non-mothering, Letherby observes that 'In Western society, all women live their lives against a background of personal and cultural assump-tions that all women are or want to be mothers' (1994, p. 252). Ribbens observes how this affects the lives of non-mothers: 'Women who do not become mothers are also significantly affected by the centrality of childrearing for the identities of women' (1994, p. 1). Motherhood is not simply a bio-logically based status but is a considerable bundle of activities ranging from infant care and the hard physical work of cleaning and laundry through to the continual 'emotional work' of monitoring and supervising relationships with children and with partners. We leave half our adult population to face what Boulton has characterised as 'responsibility without bounds' (1983, p. 78), with little or no coherent preparation or support.

The study of motherhood and housework only became accepted academically in the 1970s and is still marginal. Richardson associates this neglect with the assumed naturalness of motherhood (1993, p. ix). Whilst the responsibility of caring for children falls generally to mothers, it is important to note that countries vary a great deal in the levels of support they provide for women. The UK compares rather poorly with the rest of the European Union in terms of maternity leave, the provision of paternity leave, the level of maternity benefits and other support for family living (see Brown, 1992; Cohen, 1993).

> Ask ten mothers what they think every woman 'should know' before becoming a mother.

Following pioneering critical work by various feminists, Ribbens has recently sought to develop a feminist sociology of motherhood relating to the ordinary everyday activities involved in mothering. In developing a perspective from which to work, Ribbens argues that we must be critical of the notion of 'the family', must not assume boundaries between the public and private but rather look at how these are actively constructed, and that we must recognise the centrality of childrearing in women's lives (1994, p. 34).

Price (1988) makes the point that motherhood is the key image that girls learn in childhood that influences all their life events, including when to have children, why and how. More to the point, many women have a paid job as well as, not instead of, their role as wife and mother. This 'dual burden' carried by women may be the main reason for what Price calls 'the devastating effects of motherhood' including very considerable physical, intellectual and emotional stress (1988, pp. 125–43). Boulton found that at least 40 per cent of working-class mothers were prone to depression (1983, p. 31). Several studies have revealed that more than 50 per cent of mothers of pre-school children show signs of moderate to severe mental distress.

Teenage motherhood

Lawson and Rhode observe that, 'In many cultures, over many centuries, teenage pregnancy and childbirth have been a normal reproductive pattern' (1993, p. 1). It is only recently that teenage motherhood has been seen as something of 'a problem'; this reflects what Lawson and Rhode identify as *The Politics of Pregnancy*, that is, the political struggle over the appropriate age and marital status in which childbearing is to be encouraged. What we see at work here is society expressing clear values concerning the age at which women should bear children. Such views often carry distinct racist overtones in perceiving Black teenage motherhood as even more problematic than White (see Phoenix, 1993). Clearly, modern societies, especially the UK and USA, fail to prepare young people adequately for parenthood. This means that social and educational preparation for parenthood lags far behind biological maturity.

Murcott (1980) has noted the irony of a general disapproval of teenage motherhood, especially if unmarried. In considering any cursory examination of girls' toys (dolls, pushchairs, prams, etc.), it is surprising that more girls do not conform to such a prevailing ideology and engage in reproduction and motherhood as teenagers.

Kiernan (1980) has explored evidence that women who bear children in their teens differ (in their own childhood, adolescent and adult experiences) from those who bear children later. The point is that early childbearing leads to less education, less good jobs, less stable marriages, and those who marry after teenage pregnancy tend to have more children than they intended.

Mothering and paid work

One of the direct consequences of a popular family ideology emphasising female caregiving and male breadwinning is that many women give up or change their paid work roles upon becoming mothers. In the UK, most female careers are interrupted by childbirth; only a tiny proportion return to their pre-birth jobs, and most experience downward mobility (Brannen and Moss, 1988, pp. 1–11). The UK experiences 'a distinctive pattern of employment for women – high levels among women before childbirth and for older women whose children were at school or grown up, but low levels for women with "pre-school" children' (Brannen and Moss, 1992, p. 109). Much of this female employment is also of a precarious part-time nature with few occupational rights.

> Explore the views of half a dozen people as to whether mothers of school-age children should take paid work.

The central issue is the assumption by employers and many mothers themselves that motherhood will be of a lower priority than paid work. Despite a widespread belief in the importance of 'the family', this reveals that families are regarded as secondary to economic activity. In a study of *New Mothers at Work*, Brannen and Moss (1988) observe a considerable range of difficulties facing women who wish both to take up paid work and mother their children.

Fatherhood

In most Western societies, fatherhood is far more a status than an activity compared to motherhood. Whilst there is certainly the responsibility of bread-winning associated with the status of fatherhood, the main responsibility for most of the unpaid parenting work is usually assigned to the mother. This is true not only in popular wisdom but also in terms of legislation, taxation and welfare agency practices which assume that women undertake the bulk of unpaid work in the home. Many commentators have detected changes in the roles and location of men in families, especially concerning fatherhood (see Lewis and O'Brien, 1987). Whilst there is much optimism, it remains true (especially in the UK) that both society generally and men individually perceive paid work as their primary contribution to family life.

O'Brien has suggested that we should move analysis of parenting away from a focus upon mothers to include fathers as well (1992). This is an important shift but we need to be aware that we know less about the realities of fatherhood than we do about motherhood. Fatherhood may be extremely varied: dual-career fathers, househusbands, stepfathers, military fathers, adolescent fathers, single fathers, custodial and non-custodial fathers, widowers and gay fathers.

Can men mother?

Despite predictions that the 'new man' was emerging in the 1980s and 1990s, most housework and child care is still undertaken by mothers (see Delphy and Leonard, 1992, Chapter 9). In many Western nations, it was unheard of for men to work in nurseries or other children's areas until recent decades. Things plainly have changed a lot in the last few decades, it is now acceptable for men to take roles in teaching, nursing, etc. It is also acceptable for men to nurture their own children and Russell (1983) has demonstrated that men can be perfectly competent caregivers.

That men take up paid work and provide at least the major part of family incomes should not be belittled, it is an important and valuable aspect of fatherhood. What has happened, however, is that the primary commitment of men tends to be to continuous paid employment. The primary commitment of women, however, tends to be to motherhood and child care with paid employment coming second. What this does is to ensure that men's interest in employment overrides any commitment they may have to parenting.

In asking 'Why men don't rear children', Polatnick in 1973 suggested the convincing answer is that men are all too aware of the costs of caring for children and are able to avoid those costs. The very term 'mothering' refers not only to an activity but also to a gender and many people find it difficult to comprehend any other approach to parenting. My favourite exam question is 'Can men mother?'; over many years, I have found that students have major difficulties teasing out the distinction between the activities of mothering and the gender associated with mothering.

> Make a list and see whether men can perform 'mothering' activities. If you believe men could perform the tasks, explain why they do not do them.

One simple solution to inequality in families is to effect changes in male paid work patterns. The simplest and most obvious change is to put families first. Putting families first need not destroy men's commitment to paid work. For women we see that putting families first very often enhances and develops a paid work commitment. It may mean that men work less and have broken careers; this is true of women and in modern societies seems perfectly acceptable. More than this, making male occupational careers more like those of females seems an obvious and simple recipe for moving towards gender equality in both paid work and families.

There is a further problem here relating to the 'female' nature of mothering. A major finding of the last fifty years is that there is a great deal of abuse within families, often perpetrated by men. Whilst women certainly can be violent and abusive, there are those who argue that male violence and aggression are such as to make men bad child carers. On the one hand, encouraging men to mother may put children at risk. On the other hand, however, it does seem possible that encouraging men to mother may be one important way of addressing images of male aggression and violence.

The future of parenting

Whilst there have been many who have bemoaned the failures of parents, from the Ancient Greeks right up to the latest analyst, the desire to parent children is common to the majority of the adult populations in all societies. This does not indicate that parenting is biologically programmed or non-problematic. On the contrary, societies go to great lengths to encourage people (especially women) to parent and then place those people in a variety of extremely difficult situations. These difficult situations range from the 24-hour care of the newborn to somehow balancing their children's respect for authority and property with an overwhelming individualistic materialism.

> Ask ten parents what things they would like to change about being a parent.

Modern technology has created new childhood wants and the rapid invasion of information technology (computing, satellite and cable television) has generated enormous new challenges for parents in the last few decades. Traditionally, societies expected parents to find ways of coping with new situations for children. This is expected to be achieved without any significant preparation, guidance or support. It is time for a radical rethink.

At the heart of any radical new approach must lie the recognition not only of the status and esteem of parenthood but also of the need for serious study so that we can begin to better prepare and guide parents in the near and distant future. This must be part of a new approach to family living which seeks to understand and address issues such as family abuse, divorce, poverty and ill health.

Suggested reading

Bjornberg, U. 1992: *European Parents in the 1990s: Contradictions and Comparisons*. New Jersey: Transaction.

De'Ath, E. and Slater, D. (eds) 1992: *Parenting Threads: Caring for Children When Couples Part*. London: National Stepfamily Association.

Lawson, A. and Rhode, D. L. 1993: *The Politics of Pregnancy: Adolescent Sexuality and Public Policy*. New Haven: Yale University Press.

Price, J. 1988: *Motherhood: What It Does to Your Mind*. London: Pandora.

Pugh, G. *et al.* 1994: *Confident Parents, Confident Children: Policy and Practice in Parent Education*. London: National Children's Bureau.

Ribbens, J. 1994: *Mothers and Their Children: A Feminist Sociology of Childrearing*. London: Sage.

Chapter 8

Putting families first

Introduction

The following chapter lays out an agenda for putting families first. Since we, as a society, value family living so much, a scientist of family life is clearly obligated to explore how to support and enhance families. Whilst this is a clear value position, it is important to realise that this value position is made explicit unlike earlier modernist family theorising. Modernist work asserts that 'the family' exists and, for example, that men are primarily breadwinners and that women are primarily nurturers. Whilst this is a clear value position, it is often not recognised as such because so many believe it to be 'true'.

A postmodernist approach to Family Studies does not assert what is 'true' but rather seeks evidence about what family life is actually like. In finding family lives to be enormously complex, Family Studies adopts the notion of family practices and pathways to encompass variation and diversity. A postmodern Family Studies has to deal with the problem of 'the family'. To place families at the centre but also avoid defining 'the family', the solution adopted is to avoid defining 'the

173

family' altogether and, where necessary, adopt the concept of Family Citizenship.

In seeking to put families first, there is a clear need to reorientate ourselves to give equal status to paid and unpaid work, especially parenting and housework. It is also clear that a great deal more attention needs to be paid to preparing people for, and supporting people in, family relations.

The future of families is certain: what remains to be seen is whether we will leave families alone to cope as best they can or decide to take a positive role and seek to put families first to enhance the quality of family lives, just as we have enhanced the quality of material living over recent decades.

Why put families first?

In developing his own argument for 'putting families first', Wicks commences from an essentially economic argument by observing that, 'If things do not change Britain will spend billions of pounds on family breakdown by the year 2000' (Wicks, 1994, p. 18). Whilst there are clear economic grounds and those which may be linked to particular political positions, it is important to realise that there are also clear sociological reasons why we should put families first.

Importance of family living

The determination of human beings to create and maintain the secure intimacy of family living should be taken as a signal that this is the single most important feature of human social existence. As the recent Commission on Social Justice reminded us, 'Families are the first social institutions children know and the means by which they are introduced to all the others' (1994, p. 311). The very centrality of family living to human social existence speaks very clearly of the need to do everything within our power to put families first.

It needs reiterating that the major part of the lives of the vast majority of citizens is oriented towards partnering and parenting. Whether we like it or not, these are major life preoccupations for virtually all citizens. Certainly there are those who, having spent one or two decades in families as children, may reject the idea of family living for the rest of their lives. Even for these people, it is not possible to avoid orientation towards belief systems, housing patterns, fashion and paid work systems that relate to family living.

Value placed on family living

When asked, the vast majority of people place family living at the top of their agenda of important life issues. I can think of few other topics or issues about which such large numbers of people would share similar views.

Ask ten people of all ages to list the five most important things in their lives.

In attempting to indicate what might be involved in developing a 'family perspective', Wicks argues that, 'The development of a "family perspective" within the policy making process is, perhaps, one step that all parties and groups concerned about the family might support' (1991, p. 182). One of the key vehicles in pursuing a family perspective in policy-making, adopted from the United States and proposed by the Study Commission on the Family, is that of 'Family Impact Statements'. Such statements are seen as involving assessments of:

1   The impact of the proposed policy on different family units, including one parent and dual worker families, for example.
2   The assumptions made about family life, including male and female roles.
3   The association between the new policy and existing related polices and the likely cumulative impacts of these measures.
4   The rights and responsibilities of families.
5   The intelligibility of the new policy – questions of access, complexity and so on.
6   The policy goals in relation to families and how these will be achieved, and procedures for monitoring and evaluation.

(see Wicks, 1991, pp. 181–2)

Families are the key transmitters of cultural values and the main models of both acceptable and unacceptable behaviours. We should not leave families to engage in this work alone but support them in developing basic human values around respect, tolerance, acceptance of diversity, equality, service, responsibility for others, truth, decency, honesty and co-operation.

Logic of Family Studies

Curiously, modernist family sociology often asserts that 'the family' is the most important thing of all yet supports a system that declines to interfere in 'the family' and often makes life unnecessarily difficult for those families that some-how fail to conform, such as having disabled parents, unemployed parents or dual-career parents. This hardly seems to be a reasonable means of supporting 'the most important thing of all'. More to the point, such an approach often denies the responsibilities of sociologists and others. In asserting the moral correctness of 'the family', such sociologists have been happy to label millions of families as somehow being 'problems' in experiencing abuse, unhappiness, divorce or single parenthood. In a similar vein, the Commission on Social Justice argues that, 'A strong community should support its families, rather than expect strong families to make up for the limitations of weak communities' (1994, p. 313).

Need to address family issues

Social scientists are often hesitant about discussing courses of action arising out of their theoretical work. In beginning to understand how the economy or human personalities work, economists and psychologists have not hesitated to 'apply' their work. The situation in Family Studies is the same. In beginning to shed light on what life in families is like, we face a wide range of urgent and pressing issues. It is my view that we should recognise divorce, single parenthood, abuse and poverty for common experiences that are often harmful and damaging. Many negative evaluations of divorce or single parenthood are supported, in part, by images and models of 'the family' offered by modernist family sociology.

Preliminaries

The majority of citizens in most Western societies either marry or engage in legally recognised cohabitation. One common feature of such intimate partner-ships is the bearing and raising of children. Whilst this can be a difficult and stressful process, parents do generally value and love their children and make tremendous sacrifices for them.

It should also be remembered that it is within these settings that adults buy the most expensive items in their lives, that is, housing, cars and other con-sumer goods. It is from families that the majority of paid workers emerge and return each day and families are one of the key means by which consumption is carried out.

Family lives, then, are very positively evaluated by the majority of our population. Family lives are also of huge economic significance. Modern Western nations have reached the late twentieth century with extraordinarily high levels of material wealth but also with extraordinarily high levels of material costs. The mid-twentieth century triumphs of 'welfare' and 'health care' seem to have dimmed a little as we find the persistence of child poverty, chronic sickness in all ages, the development of twentieth century diseases, even the decline of longevity in some nations.

A wide range of issues in families represent real cash costs. Consider the human costs, cash costs and lost production resulting from difficult children at school, marital disputes, marital violence and separation, divorce, related problems of addiction, housing, property disputes, the physical and sexual abuse of children. It is simple economic nonsense not to try to prevent these.

Policies for families rather than family policy

Many commentators have argued that the UK should develop a 'family policy'. The simple point is that we need policies for families rather than a distinct 'family policy'. All policies need to be oriented to the varied and diverse nature of families. The clearest way to achieve this is by asserting the notion of Family Citizenship to locate rights, duties and responsibilities with families as well as those which fall to individuals. In doing this, attention to a wide range of family practices and pathways needs to be incorporated.

The essence of successful family living is neither enforced dependency nor isolated individualism but a situation in which families and the state are interdependent. In this, we need to recognise that families are social and not natural and that it is the process of maintaining family living that matters rather than the formal structure or label. We need to also recognise that families distribute both material and non-material 'goods' and 'bads'; policies for families will therefore need to address material and non-material issues as being of equal priority.

We must recognise that the services performed by families vary significantly over time and we should offer appropriate continual preparation, support and assistance to improve the quality of these. This may be directed towards enhancing the ability of people to help themselves as well as the ability of people to help each other. As Coote *et al.* (1990) argued, we need to work with the grain of change and not oppose change that is already existent. Similarly, we should encourage, educate and facilitate rather than coerce.

Ask ten people for their ideas about policies to better support all families.

In the 1994 All Party Parliamentary Hearings on Parenting, one of the main conclusions revolved around the need to better co-ordinate policy and practice. This co-ordination was seen as required between central government departments as well as within local government and between central and local government. Perhaps one of the most important points was the argument for 'a single government department to be given the job of ensuring that the policies of other departments are favourable to families' (Soley, 1994, p. 6).

Short-, medium- and long-term perspectives

There is a very great deal that can be done in the short term, from legislating for paternity leave to demanding 'family friendly' policies in workplaces and all public institutions. It has to be recognised, however, that a great deal of the changes involved in putting families first require looking beyond the normal political horizon of the next election. It is very important indeed to develop long-term plans to re-prioritise family living and ensure that these are adopted by the short-term interests of political groupings.

Comparative and European perspective

There is a great deal to be learnt by exploring how various societies and cultures already put families first (see, for example, Kiely and Richardson, 1991). Across Europe there is a wealth of experience with potential alternative systems of child care, family benefits, paternity leave and so on. Above all else, the UK is now a European nation and must not be left behind, despite the best attempts of the 'anti-Europe' lobbies. The extent of literature on European Social Policy improved considerably in the mid-1990s and Hantrais has put the topic of European Family Policy on the agenda (see Hantrais, 1995, Chapter 5; Hantrais and Lebablier, 1996). Following this, Ditch *et al.* (1996a, 1996b) at the European Family Policy Observatory at the University of York have added extremely valuable European material.

Built environment

In many ways the physical environment, from the design of housing to rapidly evolving information technology, reflects social priorities that put materialism first and place families a very poor second. Whilst a very long-term view is needed, it is vital that the issue of putting families first is adopted by physical and structural planners and that, wherever possible, changes are made to the existing infrastructure to make family living easier.

A great deal of work needs to be done to orientate housing towards family needs both in the nature of housing markets and the details of construction. Information technology is developing at an astonishing pace and is certainly invading family homes. There is precious little consideration of the impact of this technology beyond the pornography and censorship debates. A significant amount of work needs to be done to make the wider environment more 'family friendly', and this certainly includes the kinds of issues taken up by 'Green' parties in the UK and Europe. In terms of environmental protection more comprehensive links need to be made between items such as car pollution, asthma and the costs of the ill health of asthmatic children for their families.

Discrimination and inequality

We need to recognise that many of the major forms of discrimination and inequality hinge around family life, from the invisibility of the disabled, the social exclusion of the poor, through to criticisms of Asian marriage systems. Many of the 'equality lobbies' have made little progress; putting families first offers the opportunity to develop equality in new ways.

> Who should be unequal: the poor, lesbians, children, Black people, women, Asian people, criminals, the disabled?

Recognising discrimination, inequality and social exclusion in families (see Commission of the European Communities, 1992) offers the opportunity to develop new approaches to a wide range of social ills. It seems unlikely that we will achieve gender equality by making women more like men, nor age equality by 'putting children first'. You may need to positively discriminate toward some group but you will always need to change the condition of the dominant group.

Work must start from a recognition of widespread variation and diversity in families by way of social class, ethnicity, material wealth, employment patterns through to examples such as disability, rural families, illiterate parents and children, the mentally ill, those in poverty and the homeless.

Work, paid and unpaid

Modernist family sociology whilst valuing 'the family' also values individualism and materialism. Many men work extremely hard to provide a decent living for their families only to find themselves strangers in their own homes. Parents are encouraged to exert authority, control and discipline over children on the basis of family love in a society that seems only to value wealth and material rewards. These things are unlikely to change overnight and indeed may be unchangeable. This should not, however, prevent us from exploring different approaches to understanding family living.

Parenting and housework

Our paid workers produce remarkable goods and services. Our unpaid workers, especially mothers and housewives, produce similarly remarkable goods and services. In attempting to develop a new approach to understanding family lives, it is absolutely vital that we begin to pay equal attention and respect to paid and unpaid work.

> Ask six men and six women if housework and motherhood are less important than paid work.

In putting families first, clearly, we should recognise the labour involved in child care and housework as proper work and it should be given no more or less priority than any other form of work. Whilst it is easier to think of domestic work such as cooking or laundry as somehow unimportant, Ribbens makes the important point that much of this work should be seen as invisible production. Mothers also take on the stress and responsibility of caring, coping and taking on a wide range of 'emotional work' that creates and sustains families (Ribbens, 1994, p. 59). Equality of recognition and respect between paid work and motherhood and housework should be developed; most obvious would be the end of discrimination in eligibility for welfare benefits.

Caring in families

We can all care better for our elders, our partners, our children and ourselves and we have a duty to care better. We also have, however, a right to expect training, support and help in caring better. In contributing to a better society, we certainly can and do have obligations as individuals but society itself (through both the state and influential organisations) has a prime obligation to facilitate that care. The 1994 All Party Parliamentary Hearings on Parenting (as reported in Soley, 1994, p. 8) identified three elements of the need to care for the carers:

1   Support for carers must be improved, including increased provision of day care and respite care. Social Services should assess carers and their needs.
2   Friendly employment practices, which make provision for carers, should be encouraged.
3   The earnings limit for invalid care allowance should be increased.

Wise and Stead observe that:

> Current community care policies which assume the 'natural' ability of families to provide care, seem to justify non-intervention by statutory services, except where families appear to be 'inadequate'.... This argument is spurious, since the state has no hesitation in intervening in other areas, such as education.
>
> (1985, p. 9)

The need for intervention is quite obvious in view of the extent and costs of domestic violence and marital breakdown. It is now time to construct a case to facilitate the best possible care within families.

We currently under-use a huge volume of potential caring from all kinds of people not 'connected' to families. Many single people, unemployed, disabled and elderly people might be willing to undertake caring if it was recognised and valued. Many families have needs around the care of children, elderly members, disabled members or the sick. Mobilising these resources, especially by developing systems of caring for the carers, would allow us both to strengthen community and keep more people independent.

Child care

Many writers on women's issues have focused upon the provision of child care. Whilst we need to be wary of child care becoming a 'dumping ground' whereby women become 'more equal to men', it is none the less true that good quality child care outside family homes may add considerably to the quality of family lives by both reducing stress on families and improving young people's long-term life chances (see Soley, 1994, p. 7). The Commission on Social Justice asserted that, 'Children are 100 per cent of the future. Investment in their life-chances is the best social and economic investment we can make. Key reforms include: Child care and nursery education for under-fives' (1994, p. 320).

The All Party Parliamentary Hearings on Parenting argued, as many before, for nursery education for all children and, more specifically, 'More high quality, affordable child care must be provided. Both under-fives, after school and holiday care are needed and a wide range of providers should be encouraged' (Soley, 1994, p. 8). Child care provision should be much more than simply making available nurseries, play schools and crèches. The key is to develop flexible child care systems that are available when needed (even 24-hour availability), where needed (both larger units and small distributed units), and how they are needed (two or three short sessions a week through to full-time respite care when a parent or sibling is seriously ill). Such child care may give respite to parents, perhaps caring for new-born or young children, and introduce children to the wider social world; it may also lay a firm foundation for later educational achievement.

Successive UK governments have avoided intervention in this area; a National Childcare Development Agency, as proposed by the Equal Opportunities Commission (1991a, pp. 14–15; 1991b, pp. 5–8), does seem an obvious way forward.

Care of the elderly

The declining condition of the very elderly, especially the sick and frail, is a matter of concern throughout Europe. In the UK, frail, dependent old people have been released from hospital into private nursing homes until the bulk of their 'savings' has been exhausted and their adult children then charged the fees. To see the care of the elderly only as an issue of resources and who should 'pay the bills' is absurd. It seems clear that an emphasis upon putting families first should concentrate upon empowering families. Enabling families to care would not only improve the condition of many old people but it would also enhance their dignity and reduce tensions between the generations. Baldock argues that there is a three-cornered battle over who will care for the elderly and who will pay for it (1993, p. 146); the three parties being the state, the elderly and current or potential carers. Whilst seeing the care of the elderly in this way is popular, it is essentially flawed because it reduces human relationships and the status of elderly people to crude economics. Motenko and Greenberg have argued that we should revise our perspective on later life, 'A perspective of old age as a time of continued, positive growth and change is proposed. Dependence is not a marker of decline and deterioration, but a necessary development for positive growth and enhancement of later-life family reciprocity' (1995, p. 382). The elements of such care systems include training, preparation, financial resources, equipment, health care provision and respite care.

Business and industry

At first sight it might seem that previous tirades against materialism leave me essentially unsympathetic to business and industry. This is simply not the case; rather, I want to see business and industries take up and extend their activities, most especially combining material and non-material aspects of their operation to build entirely new forms of enterprise. The development of successful medical science generated huge markets for business and industry in the areas of medical technology, hospital and clinic construction, drug manufacture and all kinds of goods and services. Just so, in my view, business and industry can play a significant and major role in Family Studies.

> Ask the manager of your local supermarket what he or she does to support families.

I see nothing wrong in collaborating with business and industry to understand the impact of computers in the home, making family travel safer, or making shopping with children easier. We can bring these tasks about immediately. Once you begin to think about the possibilities of putting families first, they reveal themselves as endless; so too, the opportunities for new products, new sales, better goods and services are huge. I am a sociologist, in a discipline with a traditional reputation for hostility to business and industry and yet I drive a car, wear clothes, buy toys, food and a wide range of services. I see nothing wrong in trying to make any product or service 'better' or more suited to 'family living' and see nothing wrong if this happens to make the goods or services more profitable.

> Write to the Director General of the Confederation of British Industry (CBI) and ask what he (or she?) will do to put families first.

Business and industry may put families first by shaping their activities to better suit the 'family needs' of their employees. Immediate ideas are flexible hours, more liberal attitudes to the difficulties of child care, on-site crèches or joint child care arrangements with other local businesses.

The guiding concern should be the minimisation of harm and the maximisation of benefit to 'family living'. At times this may mean that short-term sales are lost; both dentists and harassed parents would welcome the removal of sweets from supermarket checkouts. The long-term improvement in the health of children, lower dental costs, customer loyalty and so on may far outweigh short-term costs. I do believe that business and industry which clearly and publicly supports Family Studies and explores for themselves and in collaboration with social science 'the family dimension' will gain significant market advantages. As the policy succeeds and is imitated, 'the family dimension' will become a factor built into business planning.

Gender and paid work

Feminists have rightly identified gender inequality in paid work as one of the key forms of discrimination in modern societies. Brannen and Moss conclude that:

> While other countries have slowly begun to try to connect the world of employment and the world of parenthood, Britain has ignored the matter, remaining wedded to an outdated view about parenthood and child care. The time for change is long overdue.
>
> (1988, p. 168)

This issue is especially relevant among feminists who have long argued against the sole homemaker role for women and for integration into the male world of work. Landau argued that women's secondary place in the labour market is no solution to inequality but rather 'The solution is to follow strategies that promote equal responsibility between men and women for child-care and housework, rather than encouraging women to work only in the home or to make their double burden [of paid work and housework/child care] work' (1992, p. 47). The simplest and clearest solution here would be to insist that parents with pre-school children do exactly this, that is, put their families first. Women already do this in large numbers, it is time to encourage men to do so. On the one hand, fathers should be given parental leave on full wages or salary. On the other hand, mothers should be encouraged, if they wish, to maintain paid employment. In exploring the nature of working women and their families, Lerner suggests the need to put families first by concluding that, 'A consensus needs to be achieved. . . . Ultimately, what is needed is an approach that puts the families in the forefront and is responsive to the changes that confront them' (1994, p. 96).

List all the items about family life you would like to see included in the general activities of business and industry.

Again, carers of children should be legally entitled to care first for their children before paid work. In this way, time for child care during sickness, flexible hours to facilitate school delivery and out-of-hours care should be mandatory and free from gender bias. The Commission on Social Justice has argued that 'we need to empower women to share financial, as well as emotional and practical, responsibility for their children' and that 'we need to encourage and enable men to share the emotional and practical, as well as the financial, responsibilities of parenthood' (1994, p. 313).

Workplace family policies

Much paid employment conflicts with the needs of parents and children in the number of hours worked or the scheduling of those hours. We should insist upon the recognition of Family Citizenship in the workplace. The simple shift would be from employing individuals to employing members of citizen families and developing legislation that seeks to protect and enhance those citizen families. All employers should be encouraged by law to develop and deliver family policies within the workplace.

There are some examples of family friendly workplace policies in Europe, the USA and Australia, such as paid paternity leave, flexitime for carers (of children, the sick, the disabled and the elderly), and career break options (see Commission of the European Communities and the Belgian Ministry for Employment and Labour, 1992). As Pleck has noted, these tend to focus upon women and their familial roles; the shift to supporting families more widely demands that men be involved in the same way (1993).

The key change is to see employers moving away from merely running an enterprise and brought to a wider recognition of the location and role of that enterprise in the local community and the family lives of workers, residents, clients and customers. Such a wider recognition can occur with the provision of child care, links with local Family Associations and/or child care agencies and the provision of flexible work scheduling.

Production

It is time that we made clearer moral judgements about production. We already make some judgements about product safety and the moral implications of atomic power or arms production. Let us take on board the point about recognising both individuals and family citizens and ensuring that our production enhances Family Citizenship in all respects. Important are the local environment, the nature of paid work and the relationships of paid workers within their own families, the nature of products and their impact in enhancing families. We need to reconcile the 'family dimension' with 'profits' by introducing other criteria for buying or producing goods and services.

> Ask six working parents how their employers could improve the way paid work influences family life.

One area in which a good deal remains to be done is reconciling the interests of commercial enterprise and the interests of children. Too many products today seem to exploit children's naiveté and encourage consumption patterns that may damage both children and parents in the short, medium and long terms. We have to ask serious questions about television and video, computer games, snack foods, fashions and so on.

Wages and benefits

The obvious change would be in matching payments for labour, not only to effort, but to family responsibilities, and moving towards accepting and supporting the 'full costs' of caring within families, understanding that this changes over time with family development. Costs vary with the age of dependants (new-born, school-age, elderly) and conditions (healthy, impaired, sick). Again, this can warrant positive discrimination, say in investing in the children of single parents to seek to avoid later heavy social costs of ill health, abuse or delinquency.

This could be achieved by moving towards a unified wage and benefit system oriented towards citizen families. It remains the clearest indictment of the way we organise ourselves in modern Western societies that children born to poor parents experience impoverished childhoods. This can be in no one's best interests, certainly not those of poor parents and their children. We know, for example, that single parenthood is a key route into poverty for a large number of women and children in the UK. Whilst we should certainly seek to enable people to avoid single parenthood if they wish (by way of education, availability of support systems when family problems arise, etc.) we should also recognise the penalties paid by such citizen families and consciously discriminate in their favour to avoid poverty.

What is proposed here is a simple and clear device by which society might say to individual families, we recognise the work you do for society, we recognise that this falls outside the usual paid work, and we want to make sure that each parent receives sufficient income to properly care for all our children.

This could most easily be achieved by way of a Negative Income Tax system geared towards family living.

Family relations

Men and women

Coote *et al.* argued that families need strong, self-reliant women (1990, pp. 34–6). Whilst an important point, this needs to be treated carefully; we really do not want a situation where women become as aggressive and exploitative as men. The last thing we need is to leave patriarchy untouched and build instead a female version that is just as powerful and destructive of family relations. What we really need to do is to encourage women to be more self-reliant whilst also encouraging men to be less self-reliant. The All Party Parliamentary Hearings on Parenting concluded that, amongst other things, strengthening the role of fathers, especially by, 'Helping men to be involved with their children is one way of providing a positive sense of identity' in the battle to reduce youthful crime (Soley, 1994, p. 8). We need adults who, above all else, put all families first: not just their own families but all families.

Adults and children

Nearly all societies contain imbalances of power between generations. Equal opportunities must be sought for all generations. In some cases, this may well mean positive discrimination towards those most dependent. We need to ensure some equity of resources to generations, focusing especially on providing resources to the very young and the elderly. This is often seen as presenting the 'problem' of too few workers and too many dependants. This is, of course, part of the growing individualism and wish to ignore generational interdependence. We need to ensure, too, equity of resources within generations, addressing the problem of the very poor (and very rich) among the young and old.

Gender inequality and parenting

The single clearest inequality between the genders in contemporary societies relates to parenting. Most simply put, parenting is a primary activity for women and, at best, a secondary activity for men. The fact of childbirth does not mean that women are somehow best suited to shop for food, prepare meals, make beds, do the laundry or any of the other hundreds of elements of contemporary child care and housework.

The putting of families first can most obviously and clearly be achieved by confronting and dismantling the gendering of parenthood. It is also vital to prepare all citizens for future parenting, with or without partners, and seek to do all we can to avoid people parenting in poverty or other stressful conditions. The simplest and clearest way of achieving this is to aim to facilitate 'male mothering'. It should be our aim to achieve the position where we can no longer assume that it will be the female who takes responsibility for child care.

> Males: would you like to bring up children? If not, why do you expect women to do it?
> Females: would you like to be truly equal to men? If not, why not?

Conflict and abuse

It is vital to grasp that individuals are not the simple products of nature or nurture but are complex beings, often decent and honest but also capable of being devious, deceptive and abusive. Indeed, we sometimes applaud these mixtures in folk tales and popular media. We know that families distribute the 'bads' of conflict and abuse as well as the 'goods' of warmth, love and material comfort.

> Should we accept some family violence as a means of 'resolving disputes'?

We need to seek to understand and reduce the extent of family conflict and abuse as a matter of urgency. We may be able to reduce family abuse by making men more like women in breaking their work patterns for childrearing and placing them in situations of nurturance. Exposing more men to full-time childrearing may encourage 'female' virtues of co-operation and value placed upon non-material goods and skills.

Also needed is a readiness to support families in periods of stress and conflict, many of which are predictable, such as unemployment or the birth of a first child. Family members need to be willing to accept and value such support intended, as it should be, to prevent pain and harm rather than as 'interference'. It is also clear that in so far as conflict and abuse arise out of material poverty, we should be ready to provide material support in both long and short periods of crisis.

Marriage and divorce

Despite rising divorce rates, the wish to create and sustain intimate partnerships is clearly a major life preoccupation for nearly all adults. In view of this, it is shocking to see how little investment is made in preparing people for partnering and de-partnering.

Divorce represents huge human, social and economic costs. We know that divorce is linked to ill health, emotional disturbance, addictions and subsequent family poverty. Clearly, we need to make the processes and outcomes of divorce far less damaging to all involved.

Family conciliation and reconciliation are obviously important. It also seems very clear that we should seek to prevent people arriving at the situation of wishing to divorce not by making the process more difficult or painful but by doing all we can to support marriage and partnerships. The quality of intimate relationships is easily as important as the quality of paid work relationships. It is in the wider interests of society to prepare people for stable, long-term intimate partnerships.

Human services: prevention

Modern Western societies have generated a wide range of voluntary or state-based service delivery systems and professions. It has long been known that many of these overlap, compete, even conflict with one another. Added to this is the well-known argument that prevention is far better than cure. Utting, working within the Joseph Rowntree Foundation's priority on 'Supporting Families, Preventing Breakdown' spends a considerable section of his text exploring the means of prevention (Utting, 1995, pp. 54–71). Utting explores a wide range of current activities. These kinds of initiatives can be taken further to argue that the means to address, if not solve, many family problems is to encourage all human service systems to recognise and develop responses to Family Citizenship. This will involve putting families first and exploring what can be done to enhance the quality of family living whilst reducing negative aspects of family living. We need to orientate health, education, social work, law and policing much more towards the needs and interests of citizen families. I suggested some time ago that this might lead to the linking, even unification, of services and systems under local democratic control (Bernardes, 1988).

> List six ways in which human services could better support ordinary families.

Family life education

One of the main conclusions of the All Party Parliamentary Hearings on Parenting in 1994 was the need to engage in funding 'Relationship Education', especially in schools, noting that this required suitable training for teachers and outside educators as well as a renewed emphasis upon sex education (Soley, 1994, p. 6). Senior figures in the National Children's Bureau have long argued for a coherent policy for parent education. To some this might seem like an unaffordable luxury. In detailing an agenda for action, Pugh *et al.* (1994, p. 235) have developed a detailed suggestion for education for family life in schools, further education colleges and the Youth Service as well as clear support and care for prospective parents before they conceive a child. The key to grasping the importance of such an agenda lies in realising that ourselves having all been children once is no guarantee that we will make competent parents. Indeed, in view of emerging evidence of child abuse by parents and other forms of behaviour regarded as 'poor parenting', it seems clear that we need to rebuild all human service provision towards facilitating better family living. Clearly, the UK's National Curriculum should be fundamentally reoriented towards family living. In 1984, Pugh and De'Ath set out a very detailed case for Family Life Education on behalf of the National Children's Bureau. Education needs to be about preparing individuals to be decent citizens, to have decent relationships and partnerships. Family abuse, intimidation and discrimination all need to be tackled, not as 'additional items' but by reorienting the curriculum.

At the moment, much formal education seems to be about paid work and individual citizenship. We need to add unpaid work and Family Citizenship. Also needed, as Utting notes (1995, p. 57), is continuing education, not just for 'career changes' but, much more importantly, for family life changes (such as childbirth or the parenting of adolescent children) which involve all family members.

This education does not need to be paternalistic, formal or authoritarian. All schools have at hand a huge reservoir of expertise in the parents of their pupils. Moreover, there are very large commercial interests which profit from family consumption. Together, surely current parents and industry could better prepare all pupils for family living.

Health

Interestingly, the World Health Organisation developed a clear argument for prevention at a Conference held in 1984 that concluded, among other things, that:

> Much greater emphasis should be placed on primary and secondary prevention. This should include work in schools on the roles and responsibilities of marriage and parenthood, work with mothers who have young children, high risk families and people in mid life crises.
>
> (1986, p. 16)

The report drew upon the increasingly clear evidence that partnering, parenting and the stresses of family living have lasting impacts upon the health of family members. We also know that most family carers act as primary health workers and have an important role in health education and prevention.

At the simplest possible level it is vital to recognise that a great deal remains to be done about health in the Western nations. Whilst preventive work is an obvious, though often neglected step (see Townsend, 1988, pp. 1–27), another vital development is family oriented health provision. There is much American work that identifies the importance of families in health and the importance of health in family life (see Doherty and Campbell, 1988). In developing family education and preparation for partnering and parenting, there is a clear opportunity to prepare people for improved health.

Social work

The anti-discriminatory ethos of contemporary social work in the UK does not match beliefs about traditional family values and casework dealing with both 'family problems' and 'problem families'. Whilst it is plain that we should act to help those in trouble, the logic of social work seems fundamentally flawed. As the 1994 All Party Parliamentary Hearings on Parenting made clear, priority needs to be given to preventative work with families. Whilst priority was given to supporting voluntary sector organisations in this respect (Soley, 1994, p. 7), the first priority of statutory social work should be the support of all ordinary families to avoid, prevent or lessen the chances of 'problems' emerging. This requires a total and complete reorientation of social work practice. Current practice maintains the *status quo* of beliefs about traditional families and, as we see all too often, fails to even adequately deal with emerging problems, such as child sexual abuse.

Utting (1995, pp. 59–61) developed a clear argument for the role of a wide range of voluntary organisations, such as Relate and Home-Start in what he terms 'secondary prevention'. One of the major problems facing such organisations is that of inadequate funding which, in turn, relates to the extent to which multi-agency co-operation can be developed. It seems clear that a much more general priority of putting families first would begin to address both parts of this problem.

191

Law and crime

Simply put, all criminals have families that may be both part of the basis of criminal behaviour and significantly affected by the criminal justice system. Similarly, the victims of crime are members of families and their families can suffer just as much at the hands of criminals as do individual victims.

In the 1993 report, 'Crime and the Family', Utting *et al.* discussed an extensive 'family based delinquency prevention programme' (1993, p. 27). Included in this scheme were family planning and preparation by family life education in schools, antenatal and postnatal care, and a national mass media campaign on parent education. To support this, parental skills training, good quality child care and pre-school education must all be made available.

Utting argues that, 'No discussion of the scope for prevention would be complete without considering the ability of the law and the legal system to inhibit or exacerbate the more adverse consequences of family breakdown' (1995, p. 66). The way in which legislation and the legal system operates partly reflects and often partly influences community values about family life (such as marriage and divorce). It is within this context that many debates about the extent and nature of variation and diversity within families occurs (for example, debates about single parents or lesbian mothers). The law needs to recognise the rights of families, this would best be done through the notion of Family Citizenship being enshrined in legal practice.

Family Associations

Perhaps the most important point remaining to be made relates to the potential role of Family Associations in taking a major role in putting families first. Family Associations across much of Europe set out to address the needs of families as families (see Bernardes, 1995a and 1995b). In many European countries, these Associations play an important, at times even central, role in national policy debates about family life and related matters. The Union of Large and Young Families in the Flemish Community of Belgium covers the majority of the population and plays a major role in debates on child care, care of the elderly and welfare benefits for families.

Recent work in the UK (Bernardes, 1995a and 1995b) has revealed that there are very many more associations relating to family life than might have been expected. The majority of these are small, relatively recently formed (especially in the 1980s which seems to have been a boom time in founding such associations), and have very specific service aims relating to the needs of particular types of families and/or particular types of family needs. Research in the UK has not revealed any significant membership organisations on the model common in partner nations, exemplified by the Union of Large and Young Families in Belgium.

Whilst UK Family Associations are potentially valuable, there remain some major obstacles to development, the most important one of which is the highly segmented nature of the sector. There are many small isolated associations that are unaware of the activities of other associations; as a consequence, there seems to be a great deal of overlap and duplication of initiatives and innovation. Having said this, there are many associations undertaking an enormous range of activities in support of families that involve very large numbers of clients/families. The range of these activities is relatively under-researched and consequently poorly understood.

Family Associations are uniquely placed, even if somewhat under-developed in the UK. In many ways, Family Associations are the foremost experts on what families need and how those needs may be met. Such associations are already meeting a wide variety of perceived urgent needs of many kinds. There is an enormous amount of good practice and novel initiatives that meet needs in imaginative and efficient ways. Family Associations, if expanded to include a model of membership more like the European model, would be very well placed to play a crucial role in determining how to put families first. Family Associations, working on the basis of existing good practices, could survey what families feel would be valuable and determine how those perceived needs could be met.

Family lives in the future

I long ago became accustomed to being regarded as faintly odd, studying 'family life' is usually seen as rather dull, boring and even uninteresting. 'Family life' is thought of as being about (horror of horrors!) women and children, essentially non-economic subjects that do not directly involve trendy issues of social class, capitalist domination or revolution. 'Family living' is regarded as 'already understood' and as peripheral to 'real issues' in politics, business and industry and social science.

Perhaps all this is true. Perhaps 'out there' there are millions of stable, absolutely typical nuclear families rearing perfectly adjusted citizens who fall to the same tasks as their parents with hardly a murmur. Perhaps there is no marital strife, no separation, no divorce, no parental anguish, no childhood disabilities, no poverty, no child abuse, no parent–teenager gulfs, no adultery, no misery. Perhaps there are no hooligans, no drug addicts, no prostitutes or thieves. Perhaps none of these exist or if they do perhaps none of these ever had parents. Perhaps all these things happen to someone else and whilst we are each individually all right what happens to 'them' does not really matter. Perhaps 'the family' is alive and well and needs no more than the occasional glorification by a social scientist who does not care to look too closely. Perhaps *you* – as a child, teenager, adult, spouse, parent, old person – have always found 'family life' perfectly smooth and easy and free from any conflict or concern.

Western societies have developed and become modern, and perhaps postmodern, over the last few hundred years. Nowadays, many other societies are changing beyond all recognition within decades or less, skipping from pre-modern to postmodern conditions. These terms reflect primarily material and political culture. What is missing is any parallel development of our social structures. Societies do not 'evolve' in some 'natural' way. We have seen clearly enough that conflict, abuse, international war and genocide are as common in the twentieth century as ever. We have not allowed technology to 'evolve' in some 'natural' way but have taken an active role in its development, so we should take an active role in social development.

It is now time to recognise that ours are not the best possible societies, although they may not be among the worst either. We have simply failed to employ critical intellectual endeavour in those areas of life we think of as intensely 'private', that is, 'family lives'. It is time to change this. In the pursuit of such a change, my job as a scientist and academic is to generate the best possible 'new understandings' I can.

It is my belief that a new discipline requires a new and radical vision, no matter how inadequate and unimaginative that may be judged to be in years to come. At the same time, there is stark evidence that past responses to 'family problems' and 'problem families' have all been inadequate.

The most obvious thing to change is the general belief in 'the family' for a sensitivity to the existence of many different kinds of family practices and pathways. Many contemporary issues in families (abuse, divorce, single parent-hood), and about families (inequality, racism, etc.), arise as a direct result of individualism and materialism. We value healthy productive workers at the expense of their families. If children grow up believing that possessions and wealth are more important than families, then crimes to obtain wealth and power are hardly surprising.

Simply arguing to put families first, somehow 'over and above' individualism and materialism, is likely to fail. It is a common enough theme in religion, culture and political rhetoric. The strategy is to change the way in which we understand the world in the belief that this will change the world. It is with this in mind, that this chapter is dedicated to founding the discipline of Family Studies that will take Family Citizenship as its central vehicle and put families first.

Ours is a very rich society indeed, there is no developed society that needs any one of its citizens to ever be poor. By placing 'family living' at the focus of policy and all our activity, we could develop new mixes of paid and unpaid work, education, health and so on. By placing 'family living' as our goal we could begin to genuinely value our children and ensure a decent future for them all. Wildly cloud cuckoo land? Out of touch with the real world of business and industry? Like the vision of conquering diseases, I believe we should place 'family well-being' as a long-term goal and begin working towards it. In working towards such a goal, all sorts of items and issues will arise along the way that will improve and enhance our lives.

I have dared to hope, dared to dream. I have broken probably every convention or rule in social science; I have certainly rejected more or less all conventional wisdom about 'family life'. I have dared to open the sacred box and dared to reject the idea of 'the family'. I have dared to argue, as best I can, for the need to study and develop our understanding of 'family living'.

Clearly, families will keep on evolving, changing and rebuilding themselves whilst participants go on loving, hating and despising one another, sometimes all at the same time. Continual change in families is certain, it is for this reason that we must focus upon the varied and diverse family practices and pathways currently pursued. It is time to abandon faith in 'the family' and begin working instead towards improving some practices and pathways whilst discouraging others. It is obvious to me, for example, that we should seek to discourage conflict and abuse by encouraging preparation for partnering and parenting. This can be achieved by insisting, at every possible opportunity, that government, business and society are committed to taking action towards putting families first.

Suggested reading

Coote, A. *et al.* 1990: *The Family Way: A New Approach to Policy-Making.* London: Institute of Public Policy Research.

Elliot, F. R. 1996: *Gender, Family and Society.* Basingstoke: Macmillan.

Kiernan, K. and Wicks, M. 1990: *Family Change and Future Policy.* London: Family Policy Studies Centre.

Utting, D. *et al.* 1993: *Crime and the Family: Improving Child-Rearing and Preventing Delinquency.* London: Family Policy Studies Centre.

Whitfield, R. C. 1980: *Education for Family Life: Some New Policies for Child Care.* London: Hodder and Stoughton.

Glossary

Arranged marriage Term used to label a wide range of mate selection practices which involve more participants than the future marital pair. Participants may include parents, close kin, marriage brokers, religious functionaries, etc.

Class (social) A major group within society, usually thought of as defined by some common feature or interest.

Cohabitation Two people living together in a sexual relationship of some permanence, without being married to one another.

Conceptual frameworks A set of concepts that are linked or inter-related to generate something ranging from a descriptive to an explanatory framework.

***De facto* (divorce)** The point at which a marriage has broken down although not yet legally recognised.

***De jure* (divorce)** The point at which marriage breakdown is legally recognised and the marriage contract is terminated.

Deviance Infringing the informal norms or formal rules of society.

Differentiation The creation and maintenance of difference between (sets of) individuals.

Discourse Shared forms of speech or language that, by their nature, support and maintain certain sets of ideology rather than others.

Discrimination Treating one person or group of persons less favourably than another on the basis of some popularly understood grounds such as social class, race, colour, sexual orientation, age or national origins.

Dysfunctional The view that certain actions or events are harmful to the smooth functioning of a system. Note that this presumes both a system's view of societies and that all behaviours or events are either functional or dysfunctional.

Ethnic group (ethnicity) A group defined not only by common kinship but also by culture and religion.

Ethnocentricity The tendency to view another cultural group through the eyes of one's own culture, usually believing that the values of one's own culture are superior.

European Union Recently adopted term for the European Community. From January 1995, there have been 15 member nations: Austria, Belgium, Denmark, Eire, Finland, France, Germany, Greece, Italy, Luxembourg, The Netherlands, Portugal, Spain, Sweden and the United Kingdom.

Family, the (nuclear family) An ideal-type (see below) in social science, usually taken to imply two heterosexual parents with a small number of children where the husband is the breadwinner and the wife the caregiver. The very use of the term presupposes that a single form of 'the family' exists. Commentators often associate a wide range of 'normal' behaviours, such as the absence of violence or abuse, the central role and responsibility of parents in socialising (see below) their children, and indicate that such 'normal' families are both very common and of positive value to society.

Feminism A blanket term given to a wide range of academic and popular work that emphasises the need to recognise the location, contribution and equal importance of women in comparison to men.

Functionalism The view of society as a working system in which social phenomena can all be explained by their contribution to the survival of the system. Critical note: assumes existence of a single reality, a unified society and clearly defined social phenomena, such as 'the family'.

Ideal-type ('the family') An idea from Weberian sociology that attempts to define the essence of a phenomenon. Critical note: this approach assumes that a phenomenon does exist (the family) and instances can be distinguished (this is, 'a family' from a 'not a family').

Ideology Sets of ideas or beliefs that have consequences for social organisation or action.

Individualism (individuality) An emphasis upon individual action as opposed to collective action. Many cultures do not think so readily of themselves and their own personal interests before the interests of others.

Industrialisation The process whereby societies moved from pre-industrial forms to adopting the styles and practices appropriate to industrial production techniques (concentration in urban areas, cash wages, etc.).

Life course A perspective that sees human existence in terms of significant events that occur to individuals over time: birth, marriage, parenting, death.

Modernism (as distinct from postmodernism) A general belief that science and rationality have achieved stability, certainty and order in modern societies.

Negative Income Tax Term covering a wide variety of schemes which propose the integration of tax and benefits systems into a single system covering all citizens whether in paid work or not. Such a system should mean that many benefits could be paid without application procedures when income falls to a certain level or certain needs arise (e.g.: number of children, registered disability, etc.).

Patriarchy A system in which men possess and defend greater power and influence than women.

Positivism The view that the methods of the natural sciences (such as observation, measurement and experimentation) are appropriate in the social sciences, especially the emphasis upon facts and causes.

Postmodern (postmodernism, postmodernity) The view that some societies have moved beyond the certainty and order achieved by modernisation to a state characterised by uncertainty and disorder.

Romantic love The belief in romantic attachment between heterosexuals as the basis for contracting marriage ties.

Social structure Differing behaviours based upon beliefs about 'the way things are' which create and sustain differentiation within societies.

Socialisation The process whereby children develop from helpless infants to become adult members of society, often believed to centre on a process of 'learning' appropriate beliefs, behaviours and values, initially from parents and later schools and wider society.

Theory A general interpretation of relationships between events or phenomena in society. More generally, the means by which we 'explain' things that are initially inexplicable or for which popular explanations are deemed inadequate.

Universality The belief that 'the nuclear family' has a biological basis and therefore exists in all human societies.

Bibliography

Adams, B. N. and Cromwell, R. E. 1978: 'Morning and night people in the family: a preliminary statement'. *Family Co-ordinator*, 27, 1, 5–13.

Adams, R. N. 1971: 'An Inquiry Into The Nature Of The Family'. In A. S. Skolnick and J. H. Skolnick (eds), *The Family In Transition*. Boston: Little Brown, 73–82.

Adamson, P. (ed.) 1993: *The Progress of Nations: 1993*. New York: UNICEF.

Agnew, R. and Hugeley, S. 1989: 'Adolescent violence towards parents'. *Journal of Marriage and the Family*, 51, 3, 699–711.

Agopian, M. W. and Anderson, G. L. 1981: 'Characteristics of parental child stealing'. *Journal of Family Issues*, 2, 4, 471–83.

Ahrons, C. R. 1983: 'Divorce: A crisis of family transition and change'. In D. H. Olson and B. C. Miller (eds), *Family Studies Review Yearbook Volume 1*. Beverly Hills: Sage, 222–9.

Alanen, L. 1988: 'Rethinking childhood'. *Acta Sociologica*, 31, 1, 53–67.

Aldous, J. 1990: 'Specification and speculation concerning the politics of workplace family policies'. *Journal of Family Issues*, 11, 4, 355–67.

Alford, R. D. 1982: 'Intimacy and disputing styles within kin and nonkin relationships'. *Journal of Family Issues*, 3, 3, 361–74.

Allan, G. 1985: *Family Life: Domestic Roles and Social Organisation*. Oxford: Blackwell.

Allen, C. M. 1990: 'Women as perpetrators of child sexual abuse: recognition barriers'. In A. L. Horton *et al.*, *The Incest Perpetrator: A Family Member No-One Wants to Treat*. Beverly Hills: Sage, 108–25.

Allen, S. and Wolkowitz, C. 1987: *Home Working: Myths and Realities*. Basingstoke: Macmillan.

Almeida, R. V. 1994: *Expansions of Feminist Family Theory Through Diversity*. New York: Haworth Press.

Ambert, A. 1992: *The Effect of Children on Parents*. New York: Haworth Press.

Anderson, M. 1971: 'Introduction'. In M. Anderson (ed.), *Sociology of the Family: Selected Readings*. Harmondsworth: Penguin, 7–17.

—— 1980: *Approaches to the History of the Western Family, 1500–1914*. Basingstoke: Macmillan.

Archard, D. 1993: *Children: Rights and Childhood*. London: Routledge.

Aries, P. 1986: *Centuries of Childhood*. Harmondsworth: Penguin.

Armstrong, L. 1991: 'Surviving the incest industry'. *Trouble and Strife*, 21, 29–32.

Aronson, J. 1990: 'Women's perspectives on informal care of the elderly: public ideology and personal experience of giving and receiving care'. *Ageing and Society*, 10, 61–84.

Askham, J. 1984: *Identity and Stability in Marriage*. Cambridge: Cambridge University Press.

Backett, K. C. 1982: *Mothers and Fathers: A Study of the Development and Negotiation of Parental Behaviour*. London: Macmillan.

Badinter, E. 1981: *The Myth of Motherhood: An Historical View of the Maternal Instinct*. London: Souvenir.

Baldock, J. 1993: 'Old Age'. In R. Dallos and E. McLaughlin (eds), *Social Problems and the Family*. London: Sage, 123–53.

Ball, D. W. 1972: 'The "family" as a sociological problem: conceptualisation of the taken-for-granted as prologue to social problems analysis'. *Social Problems*, 19, 3, 295–307.

—— 1975: 'Privacy, publicity, deviance and control'. *Pacific Sociological Review*, 18, 3, 259–78.

Barrett, M. 1980: *Women's Oppression Today: Problems in Marxist Feminist Analysis*. London: Verso.

Barrett, M. and McIntosh, M. 1991 (Revised edition): *The Anti-Social Family*. London: Verso.

Beechey, V. 1979: 'On patriarchy'. *Feminist Review*, 3, 66–82.

Bender, D. R. 1967: 'A refinement of the concept of household: families, co-residence and domestic functions'. *American Anthropologist*, 69, 6, 493–504.

Beresford, B. 1994: *Positively Parents: Caring For A Severely Disabled Child*. University of York: HMSO for Social Policy Research Unit.

Berger, B. and Berger, P. L. 1983: *The War Over the Family: Capturing the Middle Ground*. London: Hutchinson.

Berger, P. L. and Kellner, H. 1971: 'Marriage and the construction of reality: an exercise in the microsociology of knowledge'. In B. R. Cosin (ed.), *School and Society: A Sociological Reader*. London: Routledge Kegan Paul and Open University Press, 23–31.

Berman, W. H. 1985: 'Continued attachment after legal divorce'. *Journal of Family Issues*, 6, 3, 375–92.

Bernard, J. 1942: *American Family Behaviour*. New York: Harper.

—— 1982 (Revised edition): *The Future of Marriage*. New Haven and London: Yale University Press.

Bernardes, J. 1981: 'Diversity within and alternatives to "the family": the development of an alternative theoretical approach'. Unpublished PhD Thesis, University of Hull.

—— 1985a: 'Do we really know what "the family" is?' In P. Close and R. Collins (eds), *Family and Economy in Modern Society*. Basingstoke: Macmillan, 192–211.

—— 1985b: '"Family ideology": identification and exploration'. *Sociological Review*, 33, 2, 275–97.

—— 1986a: 'Multidimensional developmental pathways: a proposal to facilitate the conceptualisation of "family diversity"'. *Sociological Review*, 34, 2, 590–610.

—— 1986b: 'In search of "the family": analysis of the 1981 UK census: a research note'. *Sociological Review*, 34, 4, 828–36.

—— 1987: 'Doing things with words: sociology and "family policy" debates'. *Sociological Review*, 35, 4, 679–702.

—— 1988: 'Founding the NEW "Family Studies"'. *Sociological Review*, 36, 1, 57–86.

—— 1990: 'The family in question'. *Social Studies Review*, 6, 1, 33–5.

—— 1991: 'Exploring Family Studies in the UK and European Community'. *European Research*, 2, 1, 16–19.

—— 1993: 'Responsibilities in studying postmodern families'. *Journal of Family Issues*, 14, 1, 35–49.

—— 1995a: 'Family Associations in the UK: a national research'. In International Centre for Family Studies, *Family Associations in Europe*. Milan: International Centre for Family Studies.

—— 1995b: *Family Organisations and Associations in the United Kingdom: A Directory*. London: Family Policy Studies Centre.

Bernardes, J. and Keddie, D. 1994: 'Family Citizenship and Family Associationism'. Unpublished paper presented to the Conference, 'Family Associations in Europe', Milan.

Bernier, J. C. 1990: 'Parental adjustment to a disabled child: a family systems perspective'. *Families in Society*, 1, 10, 589–96.

Biegel, D. E. *et al.* 1991: *Family Caregiving in Chronic Illness: Alzheimer's Disease, Cancer, Heart Disease, Mental Illness, and Stroke*. Newbury Park, California: Sage.

Bigner, J. J. and Bozett, F. W. 1989: 'Parenting by gay fathers'. *Marriage and Family Review*, 14, 3/4, 155–75.

Birdwhistell, R. L. 1966: 'The American family: some perspectives'. *Psychiatry*, 26, August, 203–12.

Bjornberg, U. 1992a: *European Parents in the 1990s: Contradictions and Comparisons*. New Jersey: Transaction.

—— 1992b: 'Parenting in transition'. In U. Bjornberg (ed.), *European Parents in the 1990s: Contradictions and Comparisons*. New Jersey: Transaction, 1–41.

Blaxter, M. 1981: *The Health of Children: A Review of Research on the Place of Health in the Cycle of Disadvantage*. London: Heinemann.

Blume, E. S. 1990: *Secret Survivors: Uncovering Incest and its After Effects in Women*. New York: Wiley.

Booth, T. and Booth, W. 1994: *Parenting Under Pressure: Mothers and Fathers With Learning Difficulties*. Buckingham: Open University.

Bott, E. 1964 (Revised edition): *Family and Social Network: Roles, Norms, and External Relationships in Ordinary Urban Families*. London: Tavistock.

Boulton, M. 1983: *On Being a Mother: A Study of Women with Pre-School Children*. London: Tavistock.

Bowlby, J. 1965: *Child Care and the Growth of Love*. Harmondsworth: Penguin.

Bowley, A. L. and Hogg, M. H. 1925: *Has Poverty Diminished?* London: King and Son.

Brannen, J. and Moss, P. 1988: *New Mothers at Work: Employment and Childcare*. London: Unwin.

—— 1992: 'British households after maternity leave'. In S. Lewis *et al.* (eds), *Dual Earner Households: International Perspectives*. London: Sage, 109–26.

Brannen, J. and O'Brien, M. 1995: *Childhood and Parenthood*. London: Institute of Education, University of London.

—— 1996: *Children in Families*. London: Falmer Press.

Brannen, J. and Wilson, G. 1987: *Give and Take in Families: Studies in Resource Distribution*. London: Allen and Unwin.

Brannen, J. *et al.* 1994: *Young People, Health and Family Life*. Buckingham: Open University Press.

Brim, O. G. and Ryff, C. D. 1980: 'On the properties of life events'. In P. B. Baltes and O. G. Brim (eds), *Life-Span Development and Behaviour Volume 3*. New York: Academic Press, 367–88.

Brock, L. J. and Jennings, G. H. 1993: 'What daughters in their 30s wish their mothers had told them'. *Family Relations*, 43, 1, 61–5.

Brown, J. C. 1992: 'Which way for family policy: choices for the 1990s'. In N. Manning and R. Page (eds), *Social Policy Review 4*. University of Kent: Social Policy Association, 154–74.

Brownmiller, S. 1976: *Against Our Will: Men, Women and Rape*. Harmondsworth: Penguin.

Brubaker, T. H. 1985: *Later Life Families*. Beverly Hills: Sage.

Buck, N. and Scott, J. 1994: 'Household and family change'. In N. Buck *et al.*, *Changing Households: The British Household Panel Survey 1990–1992*. University of Essex: ESRC Centre on Micro-Social Change, 61–82.

Buck, N. *et al.*, 1994: *Changing Households: The British Household Panel Survey 1990–1992*. University of Essex: ESRC Centre on Micro-Social Change.

Burgess, E. W. 1926: 'The family as a unity of interacting personalities'. *The Family*, 7, 1, 3–9.

Burghes, L. 1994: *Lone Parenthood and Family Disruption: The Outcomes For Children*. London: Family Policy Studies Centre.

Burgoyne, J. and Clark, D. 1981: 'Starting again? Problems and expectations in remarriage'. *Marriage Guidance*, 19, 7, 334–46.

—— 1985: 'You are what you eat: food and family reconstitution'. In A. Murcott (ed.), *The Sociology of Food and Eating*. Aldershot: Gower, 152–63.

Burr, W. R. *et al.* 1988: 'Epistemologies that lead to primary explanations in family science'. *Family Science Review*, 1, 3, 185–210.

Burris, B. H. 1986: 'Working mothers: the impact of occupational status on the family/work nexus'. *International Journal of Sociology and Social Policy*, 6, 2, 8–21.

Burton, L. 1975: *The Family Life of Sick Children: A Study of Families Coping with Chronic Childhood Disease*. London: Routledge and Kegan Paul.

Busfield, J. 1986: 'Ideologies and reproduction'. In M. P. M. Richards and P. Light (eds), *The Integration of the Child into a Social World*. Oxford: Polity, 11–36.

Bybee, R. W. 1979: 'Toward further understanding and reducing violence against youth in families'. *Journal of Social Issues*, 35, 2, 161–73.

Callan, V. J. and Noller, P. 1987: *Marriage and the Family*. New South Wales, Australia: Methuen.

Cashion, B. G. 1984: 'Female headed families: effects on children and clinical issues'. In D. H. Olson *et al.*, *Family Studies Review Yearbook, Volume 2*. Beverly Hills: Sage, 481–9.

Cates, J. A. *et al.* 1990: 'The effect of AIDS on the family system'. *Families in Society*, 71, 4, 195–201.

Central Statistical Office 1994: *Annual Abstract of Statistics – 1994*. London: HMSO.

—— 1996: *Social Trends: 26*. London: HMSO.

Chandler, J. 1991: *Women without Husbands: An Exploration of the Margins of Marriage*. Basingstoke: Macmillan.

Cheal, D. 1987: '"Showing them you love them": gift giving and the dialect of intimacy'. *Sociological Review*, 35, 1, 150–69.

—— 1988: 'The ritualisation of family ties'. *American Behavioural Scientist*, 31, 6, 632–43.

—— 1991: *Family and the State of Theory*. Hemel Hempstead: Harvester Wheatsheaf.

Chester, R. 1971: 'The duration of marriage to divorce'. *British Journal of Sociology*, 22, 2, 172–82.

Clark, D. (ed.) 1993: *The Sociology of Death*. Oxford: Blackwell.

Clarke, K. *et al.* 1994: *Losing Support: Children and the Child Support Act*. London: The Children's Society.

Cockett, M. and Tripp, J. 1994: *The Exeter Family Study: Family Breakdown and its Impact on Children*. Exeter: University of Exeter Press.

COFACE (Confederation of Family Organisations in the European Community) 1987: *Family Models and Social Legislation: Family Policies in the EEC Member States*. Brussels: COFACE.

—— 1989: *Families in a Frontier-Free Europe*. Brussels: COFACE.

Cogle, F. L. and Tasker, G. E. 1982: 'Children and housework'. *Family Relations*, 31, 3, 359–99.

Cohen, B. 1993: 'Childcare policy in the European Community: finding a place for children'. In R. Simpson and R. Walker (eds), *Europe – For Richer or Poorer?* London: Child Poverty Action Group, 64–77.

Cohen, B. and Fraser, N. 1991: *Childcare in a Modern Welfare System: Towards A New National Policy*. London: Institute for Public Policy Research.

Cohen, G. 1987: 'Introduction: the economy, the family, and the life course'. In G. Cohen (ed.), *Social Change and the Life Course*. London: Tavistock, 1–32.

Coleman, V. E. 1994: 'Lesbian battering: the relationship between personality and perpetration of violence'. *Violence and Victims*, 9, 2, 139–52.

Combes, G. and Schonveld, A. 1992: *Life Will Never Be The Same Again*. London: Health Education Authority.

Commission of the European Communities 1992: *The Community's Battle Against Social Exclusion*. European File 4/1992. Brussels: Commission of the European Communities, DG X.

—— 1993a: *New Ways of Working: The Challenge for Companies and Families*. Brussels: Commission of the European Communities.

—— 1993b: *Eurobarometer 39.0. The Europeans and the Family: Results of an Opinion Survey*. Brussels: Commission of the European Communities.

Commission of the European Communities and the Belgian Ministry for Employment and Labour 1992: *Europe '93 – Business and the Family: What Strategies to Bring Them Together*. Brussels: Commission of the European Communities.

Commission on Social Justice 1994: *Social Justice: Strategies for Social Renewal*. London: Vintage.

Community Education Development Centre 1992: *Preparation for Parenthood: Myth or Reality?* Coventry: Community Education Development Centre.

Connidis, I. A. 1989: *Family Ties and Ageing*. Toronto, Canada: Butterworths.

Cooper, D. 1971: *The Death of the Family*. London: Allen Lane.

Coote, A. *et al.* 1990: *The Family Way: A New Approach to Policy-Making*. London: Institute of Public Policy Research.

Cotterill, P. and Letherby, G. 1993: 'Reviewing the family album: empty spaces, hidden lives'. Unpublished paper presented to the 'British Sociological Association Family Studies Group', Staffordshire University, Sociology Division.

Coverman, S. 1985: 'Explaining husbands' participation in domestic labour'. *The Sociological Quarterly*, 26, 1, 81–97.

Cowan, C. P. *et al.* 1985: 'Transitions to parenthood: his, hers, and theirs'. *Journal of Family Issues*, 6, 4, 451–81.

Crawford, M. 1981: 'Not disengaged: grandparents in literature and reality, an empirical study in role satisfaction'. *Sociological Review*, 29, 3, 499–519.

Cuber, J. F. and Haroff, P. B. 1974: 'Five types of marriage'. In A. Skolnick and J. H. Skolnick (eds), *Intimacy, Family, and Society*. Boston: Little Brown, 313–25.

Cunningham-Burley, S. 1984: 'On telling the news: grandparenthood as an announceable event'. *International Journal of Sociology and Social Policy*, 4, 4, 52–77.

Dalley, G. 1996 (Second edition): *Ideologies of Caring: Rethinking Community and Collectivism*. London: Macmillan.

Dallos, R. and McLaughlin, E. 1993: *Social Problems and the Family*. London: Sage.

Dallos, R. and Sapsford, R. 1995: 'Patterns of diversity and lived reality'. In J. Muncie *et al.* (eds), *Understanding the Family*. London: Sage, 125–70.

Davies, J. (ed.) 1993: *The Family: Is It Just Another Lifestyle Choice?* London: Institute of Economic Affairs.

Davies, J. B. 1982: 'The transmission of alcohol problems in the family'. In J. Orford and J. Harwin (eds), *Alcohol and the Family*. London: Croom Helm, 73–87.

De'Ath, E. 1996: 'Family change: stepfamilies in context'. *Children and Society*, 10, 1, 80–82.

De'Ath, E. and Slater, D. (eds) 1992: *Parenting Threads: Caring for Children When Couples Part*. London: National Stepfamily Association.

Delphy, C. and Leonard, D. 1992: *Familiar Exploitation: A New Analysis of Marriage in Contemporary Western Societies*. Cambridge: Polity.

DeMaris, A. 1992: 'Male versus female initiation of aggression: the case of courtship violence'. In E. C. Viano (ed.), *Intimate Violence: Interdisciplinary Perspectives*. Washington: Hemisphere Publishing, 111–20.

Dennis, N. and Erdos, G. 1993: *Families Without Fatherhood*. London: IEA Health and Welfare Unit.

DeVault, M. L. 1991: *Feeding the Family: The Social Organisation of Caring as Gendered Work*. Chicago: University of Chicago Press.

Ditch, J. *et al.* 1996a: *A Synthesis of National Family Policies 1994*. York: University of York.

—— 1996b: *Developments in National Family Policies in 1994*. York: University of York.

Dobash, R. E. and Dobash, R. P. 1992: *Women, Violence and Social Change*. London: Routledge.

Doherty, W. J. and Campbell, T. L. 1988: *Families and Health*. Beverly Hills: Sage.

Doherty, W. J. and Whitehead, D. 1986: 'The social dynamics of cigarette smoking: a family systems perspective'. *Family Process*, 25, 3, 453–9.

Dominian, J. *et al.* 1991: *Marital Breakdown and the Health of the Nation*. London: One Plus One.

Donati, P. 1991: 'The development of European policies for the protection of families and children: problems and prospects'. Paper presented to the EEC Conference 'Children, Family and Society', Luxembourg, May.

—— 1993: 'Family movements and social policy in Europe today: the issue of inter-generational equity'. *Annales*, Part 3, 205–20.

—— 1994: 'Family Associations in Europe: a general outlook and typology'. In W. Dumon and T. Neulant (eds), *National Family Policies in the Member States of the European Union in 1992 and 1993*. Leuven-Brussels: European Observatory on National Family Policies, 42–65.

Dorn, N. *et al.* 1987: *Coping with a Nightmare: Family Feelings About Long-Term Drug Abuse*. London: Institute for Study of Drug Dependency.

Douglas, J. 1991: *Is My Child Hyperactive?* Harmondsworth: Penguin.

Driver, E. and Droisen, A. 1989: *Child Sexual Abuse: Feminist Perspectives*. Basingstoke: Macmillan.

Duncombe J. and Marsden D. 1995: '"Workaholics" and "Whingeing women": theorising intimacy and emotion work – the last frontier of gender inequality?' *Sociological Review*, 43, 1, 115–169.

Durham, M. 1985: 'Family, morality and the New Right'. *Parliamentary Affairs*, 38, 2, 180–91.

—— 1991: *Sex and Politics: The Family and Morality in the Thatcher Years*. Basingstoke: Macmillan.

Eastman, M. 1982: 'Granny battering: a hidden problem'. *Community Care*, 413, May, 12–13.

Eastman, M. and Sutton, M. 1982: 'Granny battering'. *Geriatric Medicine*, 12, 11, 11–15.

Eaton, M. 1986: *Justice for Women? Family, Court and Social Control*. Milton Keynes: Open University Press.

Elliot, F. R. 1996: *Gender, Family and Society*. Basingstoke: Macmillan.

Elliott, B. 1993: *Vision 2010: Families and Health Care*. Minneapolis: National Council on Family Relations.

Elliott, M. 1992: 'Tip of the iceberg?' *Social Work Today*, 23, 26, 12–13.

Equal Opportunities Commission 1991a: *The Key to Real Choice: An Action Plan for Child Care: A Discussion Paper*. Manchester: Equal Opportunities Commission.

—— 1991b: *The Key to Real Choice: An Action Plan for Child Care: Summary and Recommendations*. Manchester: Equal Opportunities Commission.

Estaugh, V. and Wheatley, J. 1990: *Family Planning and Family Well-Being*. London: Family Policy Studies Centre.

Eurostat 1995: *Eurostat Yearbook 1995: A Statistical Eye on Europe 1983–1993*. Luxembourg: Office of Official Publications of the European Communities.

Fagin, L. and Little, M. 1984: *The Forsaken Families*. Harmondsworth: Penguin.

Feminist Review (Special edition) 1988: 'Family secrets: child sexual abuse'. *Feminist Review*, 28.

Ferraro, K. J. *et al.* 1983: 'Problems of prisoners' families: the hidden costs of imprisonment'. *Journal of Family Issues*, 4, 4, 575–91.

Finch, J. 1983: *Married to the Job: Wives' Incorporation in Men's Work*. London: Allen and Unwin.

—— 1989: *Family Obligations and Social Change*. Cambridge: Polity.

—— 1996: 'Family responsibilities and rights'. In M. Bulmer and A. M. Rees (eds), *Citizenship Today: The Contemporary Relevance of T H Marshall*. London: UCL Press, 193–208.

Fine, M. A. 1993: 'Current approaches to understanding family diversity: an overview of the special issue'. *Family Relations*, 42, 3, 235–7.

Firestone, S. 1972: *The Dialectic of Sex: The Case for Feminist Revolution*. London: Paladin.

Fitzgerald, T. 1983: 'The New Right and the family'. In M. Loney *et al.* (eds), *Social Policy and Social Welfare*. Milton Keynes: Open University Press, 46–57.

Fletcher, B. C. 1983: 'Marital relationships as a cause of death: an analysis of occupational mortality and the hidden consequences of marriage – some UK data'. *Human Relations*, 36, 2, 123–34.

Fletcher, R. 1973 (Revised edition): *The Family and Marriage in Britain: An Analysis and Moral Assessment*. Harmondsworth: Penguin.

Flynn, C. P. 1990: 'Relationship violence by women: issues and implications'. *Family Relations*, 39, 2, 194–8.

Fox, K. D. and Nickols, S. Y. 1983: 'The time crunch: wife's employment and family work'. *Journal of Family Issues*, 4, 1, 61–82.

Foxcroft, D. R. and Lowe, G. 1995: 'Adolescent drinking, smoking and other substance use involvement: links with perceived family life'. *Journal of Adolescence*, 18, 2, 159–77.

Franks, H. 1990: *Mummy Doesn't Live Here Anymore*. London: Guild.

Friedman, D. E. 1990: 'Corporate response to family needs'. *Marriage and Family Review*, 15, 1/2, 77–98.

Gallie, D. 1994: 'Social consequences of long term unemployment in Britain'. In O. Benoit-Guilbot and D. Gallie (eds), *Long Term Unemployment*. London: Pinter, 121–36.

Gavron, H. 1966: *The Captive Wife: Conflicts of Housebound Mothers*. Harmondsworth: Penguin.

Gelles, R. J. 1995: *Contemporary Families: A Sociological View*. Thousand Oaks: Sage.

George, M. J. 1994: 'Riding the donkey backwards: men as the unacceptable victims of marital violence'. *Journal of Men's Studies*, 3, 2, 137–59.

Germain, C. B. 1994: 'Emerging conceptions of family development over the life course.' *Families in Society: The Journal of Contemporary Human Services*, 75, 5, 259–68.

Gibson, C. S. 1994: *Dissolving Wedlock*. London: Routledge.

Giddens, A. 1989: *Sociology*. Cambridge: Polity.

—— 1992: *The Transformation of Intimacy: Sexuality, Love and Eroticism in Modern Societies*. Cambridge: Polity.

Gilbert, L. A. 1993: *Two Careers/One Family: The Promise of Gender Equality*. London: Sage.

Gittins, D. 1993 (Second edition): *The Family in Question – Changing Households and Familiar Ideologies*. Basingstoke, Macmillan.

Glendenning, F. 1993: 'What is elder abuse and neglect?' In P. Decalmer and F. Glendenning (eds), *The Mistreatment of Elderly People*. London: Sage, 1–34.

Glenn, E. N. *et al.* 1994: *Mothering: Ideology, Experience, Agency*. London: Routledge.

Goldthorpe, J. E. 1987: *Family Life in Western Societies: A Historical Analysis of Family Relationships in Britain and North America*. Cambridge: Cambridge University Press.

Goode, W. J. 1970 (Revised edition): *World Revolution and Family Patterns*. New York: Free Press.

Gordon, T. 1994: *Single Women: On The Margins?* Basingstoke: Macmillan.

Gottman, J. S. 1989: 'Children of gay and lesbian parents'. *Marriage and Family Review*, 14, 3/4, 177–96.

Graham, H. 1993: *Hardship and Health in Women's Lives.* Hemel Hempstead: Harvester Wheatsheaf.

Grant, D. and Stitt, S. 1994: 'Primary food poverty in Europe'. Unpublished paper presented at the 'European Society of Medical Sociology Conference', Vienna, Austria.

Greengross, W. 1980: *Sex and the Handicapped Child.* Rugby: National Marriage Guidance Council.

Greer, G. 1971: *The Female Eunuch.* London: Paladin.

—— 1991: *The Change – Women, Ageing and the Menopause.* Harmondsworth: Penguin.

Gubman, G. D. and Tessler, R. C. 1987: 'The impact of mental illness on families: concepts and priorities'. *Journal of Family Issues*, 8, 2, 226–46.

Gubrium, J. F. and Holstein, J. A. 1990: *What Is Family?* Mountain View, California: Mayfield.

Hadley, J. 1987: 'Mum is not the Word'. *Community Care*, 685, 5 November, 24–6.

Hanson, B. G. 1991: 'Conceptualising contextual emotion: the grounds for "Supra-Rationality"'. *Diogenes*, 156, Winter, 33–47.

Hantrais, L. 1995: *Social Policy in the European Union.* Basingstoke: Macmillan.

Hantrais, L. and Lebablier, M-T. 1996: *Families and Family Policies in Europe.* London: Longman.

Harris, C. C. 1969: *The Family: An Introduction.* London: Allen and Unwin.

Hartmann, H. I. 1981: 'The family as the locus of gender, class, and political struggle: the example of housework'. *Signs*, 6, 3, 366–94.

Haskey, J. C. 1987: 'Divorce in the early years of marriage in England and Wales: results from a prospective study using linked records'. *Journal of Biosocial Science*, 19, 3, 255–71.

—— 1991: 'Estimated numbers and demographic characteristics of one-parent families in Great Britain'. *Population Trends*, 65, 35–45.

Heaton, T. B. and Albrecht, S. L. 1991: 'Stable unhappy marriages'. *Journal of Marriage and the Family*, 53, 3, 747–58.

Hey, V. *et al.* 1989: *Hidden Loss: Miscarriage and Ectopic Pregnancy.* London: Women's Press Ltd.

Hobart, C. 1987: 'Parent–child relations in remarried families'. *Journal of Family Issues*, 8, 3, 259–77.

Hobbs, N. *et al.* 1985: *Chronically Ill Children and Their Families: Problems, Prospects, and Proposals from the Vanderbilt Study.* San Francisco: Josey-Bass.

Hoghughi, M. and Richardson, G. 1990: 'The root of the problem'. *Community Care*, 25 October 1990.

Holland, P. 1992: *What is a Child? Popular Images of Childhood.* London: Virago.

Holt, J. 1974: *Escape from Childhood: The Needs and Rights of Children.* Harmondsworth: Penguin.

Hood, J. and Golden, S. 1979: 'Beating time/making time: the impact of work scheduling on men's family roles'. *Family Co-ordinator*, 28, 4, 575–82.

Howe, D. *et al.* 1992: *Half a Million Women: Mothers Who Lose Their Children by Adoption.* Harmondsworth: Penguin.

Ineichen, B. 1977: 'Youthful marriage: the vortex of disadvantage'. In R. Chester and J. Peel (eds), *Equalities and Inequalities in Family Life.* London: Academic Press, 53–69.

Ingoldsby, B. B. and Smith, S. (eds) 1995: *Families in Multicultural Perspective.* New York: Guilford.

Jackson, P. R. and Walsh, S. 1987: 'Unemployment and the family'. In D. Fryer and

P. Ullah (eds), *Unemployed People: Social and Psychological Perspectives*. Milton Keynes: Open University Press, 194–216.

Jackson, R. 1994: *Mothers Who Leave: Behind The Myth Of Women Without Their Children*. London: Pandora.

Jenks, C. 1982: 'Introduction: constituting the child'. In C. Jenks (ed.), *The Sociology of Childhood: Essential Readings*. London: Batsford, 9–24.

—— 1996: *Childhood*, London: Routledge.

Journal of Family Issues 1986 (Special issue): 'Death and the family'. *Journal of Family Issues*, 7, 3.

—— 1995 (Whole issue): 'Cultural diversity in American family life'. *Journal of Family Issues*, 16, 3.

Kazak, A. E. 1986: 'Families with physically handicapped children: social ecology and family systems'. *Family Process*, 25, 2, 265–81.

Keating, N. C. and Cole, P. 1980: 'What do I do with him 24 hours a day? Changes in the housewife role after retirement'. *Gerontologist*, 1, 84–9.

Kempson, E. *et al.* 1994: *Hard Times? How Poor Families Make Ends Meet*. London: Family Policy Studies Centre.

Khan, V. S. 1979: *Minority Families in Britain: Support and Stress*. Basingstoke: Macmillan.

Kiely, G. and Richardson, V. 1991: *Family Policy: European Perspectives*. Dublin, Eire: Family Studies Centre.

Kiernan, K. 1980: 'Teenage motherhood: associated factors and consequences: the experiences of a British birth cohort'. *Journal of Biosocial Science*, 12, 4, 393–405.

—— 1986: 'Teenage marriage and marital breakdown: a longitudinal study'. *Population Studies*, 40, 1, 35–54.

—— 1992a: 'The impact of family disruption in childhood on transitions made in young adult life'. *Population Studies*, 46, 2, 213–34.

—— 1992b: 'The impact of family disruption in childhood on transitions made in young adult life'. *ESRC Bulletin*, 51, September, 6–7.

Kiernan, K. and Estaugh, V. 1993: *Cohabitation: Extra-Marital Childbearing and Social Policy*. London: Family Policy Studies Centre.

Kiernan, K. and Wicks, M. 1990: *Family Change and Future Policy*. London: Family Policy Studies Centre.

Kinsey, A. C. *et al.* 1948: *Sexual Behaviour in the Human Male*. Philadelphia: Saunders.

Kinsey, A. C. *et al.* 1953: *Sexual Behaviour in the Human Female*. Philadelphia: Saunders.

Klein, D. M. and White, J. M. 1996: *Family Theories: An Introduction*. London: Sage.

Kline, S. 1993: *Out of the Garden: Toys, TV and Children's Culture in the Age of Marketing*. London: Verso.

Knox, D. and Wilson, K. 1978: 'The differences between having one and two children'. *Family Co-ordinator*, 27, 1, 23–5.

Kumar, V. 1993: *Poverty and Inequality in the UK: The Effects on Children*. London: National Children's Bureau.

La Fontaine, J. 1990: *Child Sexual Abuse*. Cambridge: Polity.

Laing, R. D. 1976: *The Politics of the Family and Other Essays*. Harmondsworth: Penguin.

Landau, R. 1992: 'On making "choices"'. *Feminist Issues*, 12, 2, 47–72.

LaRossa, R. and LaRossa, M. M. 1981: *Transition to Parenthood: How Infants Change Families*. London: Sage.

Laslett, P. 1982: 'Foreword'. In R. N. Rapoport *et al.* (eds), *Families in Britain*. London: Routledge, xi–xv.

Lawson, A. 1988: *Adultery: An Analysis of Love and Betrayal*. Oxford: Blackwell.

Lawson, A. and Rhode, D. L. 1993: *The Politics of Pregnancy: Adolescent Sexuality and Public Policy*. New Haven: Yale University Press.

Lees, S. 1986: *Losing Out: Sexuality and Adolescent Girls*. London: Hutchinson.

LeMasters, E. E. 1978: 'Folklore about parenthood'. In J. Savells and L. J. Cross (eds), *The Changing Family*. New York: Holt, Rinehart and Winston, 283–97.

Leonard, D. and Speakman, M. A. 1986: 'Women in the family: companions or caretakers'. In V. Beechey and E. Whitelegg (eds), *Women in Britain Today*. Milton Keynes: Open University Press, 8–76.

Lerner, J. V. 1994: *Working Women and Their Families*. London: Sage.

Leslie, G. R. and Richardson, A. H. 1961: 'Life cycle, career pattern and the decision to move'. *American Sociological Review*, 26, 4, 894–902.

Letellier, P. 1994: 'Gay and bisexual domestic violence victimisation: challenges to feminist theory and responses to violence'. *Violence and Victims*, 9, 2, 95–106.

Letherby, G. 1993: 'The meanings of miscarriage'. *Women's Studies International Forum*, 16, 2, 165–80.

—— 1994: 'Mother or not, mother or what?' *Women's Studies International Forum*, 17, 5, 525–32.

Levin, I. 1990: *How to Define Family. Family Reports, 17*. Uppsala, Sweden: University of Uppsala.

Levin, I. and Trost, J. 1992: 'Understanding the concept of family'. *Family Relations*, 41, 3, 348–51.

Levinson, D. 1989: *Family Violence in Cross-Cultural Perspective*. California: Sage.

Lewin, E. 1994: 'Negotiating lesbian motherhood: the dialectics of resistance and accommodation'. In E. N. Glenn *et al.* (eds), *Mothering: Ideology, Experience, Agency*. London: Routledge, 333–54.

Lewis, C. and O'Brien, M. 1987: *Reassessing Fatherhood: New Observations on Fathers and the Modern Family*. London: Sage.

Lewis, J. 1993: *Women and Social Policies in Europe: Women, Family and the State*. Aldershot: Elgar.

Lewis, S. *et al.* 1992: *Dual-Earner Families: International Perspectives*. London: Sage.

Lister, R. 1989: *The Female Citizen*. Liverpool: Liverpool University Press.

—— 1991: 'Citizenship engendered'. *Critical Social Policy*, 11, 2, 65–71.

Longfield, J. 1984: *Ask the Family: Shattering the Myths about Family Life*. London: Bedford Square Press.

Lovell, A. 1983: 'When a baby dies'. *New Society*, 65, 4 August, 167.

Lyons, R. F. *et al.* 1995: *Relationships in Chronic Illness and Disablity*. London: Sage.

McFadyen, A. *et al.* 1993: 'Ritual abuse: a definition'. *Child Abuse Review*, 2, 35–41.

McGlone, F. and Cronin, N. 1994: *A Crisis in Care? The Future of Family and State Care for Older People in the European Union*. London: Family Policy Studies Centre.

Macintyre, S. 1985: 'The management of food in pregnancy'. In A. Murcott, *The Sociology of Food and Eating*. Aldershot: Gower, 57–72.

McKenry, P. C. and Price, S. J. 1994: 'Families coping with problems and change'. In P. C. McKenry and S. J. Smith (eds), *Families and Change: Coping with Stressful Events*. London: Sage, 1–18.

Macklin, E. D. 1980: 'Nonmarital heterosexual cohabitation'. In A. Skolnick and J. H. Skolnick (eds), *Family In Transition*. Boston: Little Brown, 285–307.

Mannheim, K. 1972 (First published 1936): *Ideology and Utopia: An Introduction to the Sociology of Knowledge*. London: Routledge and Kegan Paul.

Manniche, E. 1991: *Marriage and Non-Marital Cohabitation in Denmark: Family Reports 20*. Uppsala, Sweden: Uppsala University.

Mansfield, P. and Collard, J. 1988: *The Beginning of the Rest of Your Life? A Portrait of Newly-Wed Marriage*. Basingstoke: Macmillan.

Marriage and Family Review 1985 (Special issue): 'Pets and the family'. *Marriage and Family Review*, 8, 3/4.

Marsden, D. 1969: *Mothers Alone: Poverty and the Fatherless Family*. Harmondsworth: Penguin.

Marsden, D. and Abrams, S. 1987: '"Liberators", "companions", "intruders" and "cuckoos in the nest": a sociology of caring relationships over the life cycle'. In P. Allatt *et al.* (eds), *Women and the Life Cycle: Transitions and Turning Points*. Basingstoke: Macmillan, 192–207.

Mason, J. 1986: 'Gender inequality in long term marriage: the negotiation and renegotiation of domestic and social organisation by married couples aged 50–70'. Paper presented at the 'British Sociological Association Annual Conference', Loughborough University.

—— 1987: 'A bed of roses? Women, marriage and inequality in later life'. In P. Allatt *et al.* (eds), *Women and the Life Cycle: Transitions and Turning Points*. Basingstoke: Macmillan, 90–105.

—— 1990: 'Reconstructing the public and the private: the home and marriage in later life'. In G. Allan and G. Crow (eds), *Home and Family: Creating the Domestic Sphere*. Basingstoke: Macmillan, 102–21.

Matrix Book Group 1984: *Making Space: Women and the Man Made Environment*. London: Pluto.

Mayer, J. E. 1967a: 'People's imagery of other families'. *Family Process*, 6, 1, 27–36.

—— 1967b: 'The invisibility of married life'. *New Society*, 230, 23 February, 272–3.

Meyer, C. J. and Rosenblatt, P. C. 1987: 'Feminist analysis of family textbooks'. *Journal of Family Issues*, 8, 2, 247–52.

Meyer, J. 1989: 'Guess who's coming to dinner this time? A study of gay intimate relationships and the support for those relationships'. *Marriage and Family Review*, 14, 3/4, 59–82.

Miller, B. 1979: 'Gay fathers and their children'. *Family Co-ordinator*, 28, 4, 543–52.

Mitchell, A. 1985: *Children in the Middle: Living through Divorce*. London: Tavistock.

Mitterauer, M. and Sieder, R. 1982: *The European Family: Patriarchy to Partnership from the Middle Ages to the Present*. Oxford: Blackwell.

Mooney, J. 1993: *Researching Domestic Violence – Centre for Criminology Occasional Paper*. London: Islington Council.

—— 1994: *The Hidden Figure: Domestic Violence in North London*. Middlesex: Middlesex University.

Moore, B. 1965: 'Thoughts on the future of the family'. In B. Moore, *Political Power and Social Theory: Seven Studies*. New York: Harper and Row, 160–78.

Morales, E. S. 1989: 'Ethnic minority families and minority gays and lesbians'. *Marriage and Family Review*, 14, 3/4, 217–39.

Morgan, D. H. J. 1975: *Social Theory and The Family*. London: Routledge and Kegan Paul.

—— 1985: *The Family, Politics and Social Theory*. London: Routledge and Kegan Paul.

—— 1996: *Family Connections: An Introduction to Family Studies*. Oxford: Polity.

Morrow, V. 1992: *Family Values: Accounting for Children's Contribution to the Domestic Economy*. Cambridge: Sociological Research Group, University of Cambridge.

—— 1993: '"Rarely seen and never heard?" Methodological and ethical considerations of researching children'. Unpublished paper presented at the 'British Sociological Association Annual Conference', University of Essex.

Motenko, A. K. and Greenberg, S. 1995: 'Reframing dependence in old age: a positive transition for families'. *Social Work*, 40, 3, 382–90.

Mott, F. L. and Haurin, R. J. 1982: 'Being an only child: effects on educational progression and career orientation'. *Journal of Family Issues*, 3, 4, 575–93.

Mount, F. 1982: *The Subversive Family: An Alternative History of Love and Marriage*. London: Jonathan Cape.

Muncie, J. *et al.* 1995: *Understanding the Family*. London: Sage.

Muncie, J. and Sapsford, R. 1995: 'Issues in the study of "the family"'. In J. Muncie *et al.* (eds), *Understanding the Family*, London: Sage, 7–37.

Murcott, A. 1980: 'The social construction of teenage pregnancy: a problem of ideologies of childhood and reproduction'. *Sociology of Health and Illness*, 2, 1, 1–23.

—— 1988: 'On the altered appetites of pregnancy: conceptions of food, body and person'. *Sociological Review*, 36, 4, 733–64.

Murdock, G. P. 1949: *Social Structure*. London: Collier Macmillan.

—— 1965: *Social Structure*. New York: Free Press.

Myrdal, A. and Klein, V. 1968 (Revised edition): *Women's Two Roles: Home and Work*. London: Routledge and Kegan Paul.

NCH 1993: *A Lost Generation? A Survey of the Problems Faced by Vulnerable Young Children Living on their Own*. London: NCH (formerly National Children's Home).

NCH Action For Children 1994: *Unequal Opportunities: Children With Disabilities and their Families Speak Out*. London: NCH Action For Children (formerly National Children's Home).

Neate, P. 1991: 'Elder abuse: home truths'. *Community Care*, 13 June.

Nickols, S. Y. and Metzen, E. J. 1982: 'Impact of wife's employment upon husband's housework'. *Journal of Family Issues*, 3, 2, 199–216.

Nilson, L. B. 1978: 'The social standing of a housewife'. *Journal of Marriage and the Family*, 40, 3, 541–8.

Noller, P. and Callan, V. 1991: *The Adolescent in the Family*. London: Routledge.

Nunnally, E. W. *et al.* (eds) 1988: *Troubled Relationships*. Newbury Park: Sage.

Oakley, A. 1974a: *The Sociology of Housework*. Oxford: Martin Robertson.

—— 1974b: *Housewife*. Harmondsworth: Penguin.

—— 1976: 'The family, marriage, and its relationship to illness'. In D. Tuckett, *An Introduction to Medical Sociology*. London: Tavistock, 74–109.

—— 1979: *From Here to Maternity: Becoming a Mother*. Harmondsworth: Penguin.

—— 1980: *Women Confined: Towards a Sociology of Childbirth*. Oxford: Martin Robertson.

—— 1981: *Subject Women*. London: Fontana.

Oates, K. 1982: 'Child abuse – a community concern'. In K. Oates (ed.), *Child Abuse: A Community Concern*. North Ryde, Australia: Butterworths, 1–12.

O'Brien, M. 1992: 'Changing conceptions of fatherhood'. In U. Bjornberg (ed.), *European Parents in the 1990s*. New Jersey: Transaction, 171–80.

—— 1995: 'Allocation of resources in households: children's perspectives'. *Sociological Review*, 43, 3, 501–17.

OPCS (Office of Population Censuses and Surveys) 1992a: *Census 1991 – Household Composition*. London: HMSO.

—— 1992b: *General Household Survey – 1991*. London: HMSO.

—— 1994: *Population Trends No 76, Summer 1994*. London: HMSO.

Orford, J. and Harwin, J. 1982: *Alcohol and the Family*. London: Croom Helm.

213

Palmer, C. E. and Noble, D. N. 1984: 'Child snatching: motivations, mechanisms and melodrama'. *Journal of Family Issues*, 5, 1, 27–45.

Parker, G. 1985: *With Due Care and Attention: A Review of Research on Informal Care*. London: Family Policy Studies Centre.

Parsons, T. 1971: 'The normal American family'. In B. N. Adams and T. Weirath (eds), *Readings on the Sociology of the Family*. Chicago: Markham, 53–66.

Pawson, R. 1993: 'Social mobility'. In D. H. J. Morgan and E. Stanley (eds), *Debates in Sociology*. Manchester: Manchester University Press, 26–51.

Pearce, H. F. 1993: *The Pretended Family: A Study of the Division of Domestic Labour in Lesbian Families*. Leicester: Faculty of Social Sciences, University of Leicester.

Penhale, B. 1993: 'The abuse of elderly people: considerations for practice'. *British Journal of Social Work*, 33, 2, 95–112.

Peterson, Y. 1979: 'The impact of physical disability on marital adjustment: a literature review'. *Family Co-ordinator*, 28, 1, 47–51.

Phoenix, A. 1991: *Young Mothers?* Cambridge: Polity.

—— 1993: 'The social construction of teenage motherhood: a black and white issue?' In A. Lawson and D. L. Rhode (eds), *The Politics of Pregnancy*. New Haven: Yale University Press, 74–97.

Phoenix, A. *et al.* 1991: *Motherhood: Meanings, Practices and Ideologies*. London: Sage.

Pickvance, C. G. and Pickvance, K. 1995: 'The role of family help in the housing decisions of young people'. *Sociological Review*, 43, 1, 123–49.

Pittman, F. S. 1985: 'Children of the rich'. *Family Process*, 24, 4, 461–72.

Pizzey, E. 1974: *Scream Quietly Or The Neighbours Will Hear*. Harmondsworth: Penguin.

Pleck, J. H. 1977: 'The work–family role system'. *Social Problems*, 24, 4, 417–27.

—— 1993: 'Are "family supportive" employer policies relevant to men'. In J. C. Hood (ed.), *Men, Work and Family*. London: Sage, 217–37.

Polatnick, M. 1973: 'Why men don't rear children: a power analysis'. *Berkeley Journal of Sociology*, 18, 45–86.

Pollock, L. A. 1983: *Forgotten Children: Parent–Child Relations from 1500 to 1900*. Cambridge: Cambridge University Press.

Power, T. G. and Parke, R. D. 1984: 'Social network factors and the transition to parenthood'. *Sex Roles*, 10, 11/12, 949–72.

Price, J. 1988: *Motherhood: What It Does to Your Mind*. London: Pandora.

Pugh, G. 1980: *Preparation for Parenthood: Some Current Initiatives and Thinking*. London: National Children's Bureau.

Pugh, G. and De'Ath, E. 1984: *The Needs of Parents. Practice and Policy in Parent Education*. Basingstoke, Macmillan.

Pugh, G. *et al.* 1994: *Confident Parents, Confident Children: Policy and Practice in Parent Education*. London: National Children's Bureau.

Ramey, J. 1978: 'Experimental family forms: the family of the future'. *Marriage and Family Review*, 1, 1, 1–9.

Rapoport, R. 1989: 'Ideologies about family forms: towards diversity'. In K. Boh *et al.* (eds), *Changing Patterns of European Family Life: A Comparative Analysis of 14 European Countries*. London: Routledge, 53–69.

Rapoport, R. and Rapoport, R. N. 1976 (Second edition): *Dual Career Families Re-Examined: New Integrations of Work and Family*. London: Robertson.

—— 1982: 'British families in transition'. In R. N. Rapoport *et al.* (eds), *Families in Britain*. London: Routledge, 475–99.

Rapoport, R. *et al.* 1977: *Fathers, Mothers and Others: Towards New Alliances.* London: Routledge and Kegan Paul.

Rapoport, R. N. *et al.* (eds) 1982: *Families in Britain.* London: Routledge and Kegan Paul.

Rees, A. M. 1996: 'T.H. Marshall and the progress of citizenship'. In M. Bulmer and A. M. Rees (eds), *Citizenship Today: The Contemporary Relevance of T H Marshall.* London: UCL Press, 1–23.

Reinisch, J. M. with Beasley, R. 1991: *The Kinsey Institute New Report on Sex.* Harmondsworth: Penguin.

Reiss, I. L. 1965: 'The universality of the family: a conceptual analysis'. *Journal of Marriage and the Family*, 27, 4, 443–51.

Ribbens, J. 1994: *Mothers and their Children: A Feminist Sociology of Childrearing.* London: Sage.

Richards, M. 1988: *Key Issues in Child Sexual Abuse: Some Lessons From Cleveland and Other Inquiries.* London: National Institute for Social Work.

Richardson, D. 1993: *Women, Motherhood and Childrearing.* Basingstoke: Macmillan.

Ricketts, W. and Achtenberg, R. 1989: 'Adoption and foster parenting for lesbians and gay men: creating new traditions in family'. *Marriage and Family Review*, 14, 3/4, 83–118.

Rimmer, L. and Wicks, M. 1981: 'The family today'. *MOST – Journal of Modern Studies Association*, 27, Autumn, 1–4.

Roberts, H. 1993: 'The women and class debate'. In D. H. J. Morgan and E. Stanley (eds), *Debates in Sociology.* Manchester: Manchester University Press, 52–70.

Roberts, M. 1991: *Living in a Man Made World: Gender Assumptions in Modern Housing Design.* London: Routledge.

Robinson, M. 1991: *Family Transformation Through Divorce and Remarriage: A Systemic Approach.* London: Routledge.

Robinson, M. and Smith, D. 1993: *Step by Step: Focus on Stepfamilies.* Hertfordshire: Harvester Wheatsheaf.

Rodger, J. J. 1995: 'Family policy or moral regulation?' *Critical Social Policy* 15, 1, 5–25.
—— 1996: *Family Life and Social Control: A Sociological Perspective.* London: Macmillan.

Rogge, J-U. 1989: 'The media in everyday family life: some biographical and typological aspects'. In E. Seiter *et al.* (eds), *Remote Control: Television, Audiences, and Cultural Power.* London: Routledge, 168–79.

Roll, J. 1986: *Babies and Money: Birth Trends and Costs.* London: Family Policy Studies Centre.
—— 1992: *Lone Parent Families in the European Community.* London: European Family and Social Policy Unit.

Roman, L. G. *et al.* 1988: *Becoming Feminine: The Politics of Popular Culture.* London: Falmer.

Root, J. 1984: *Pictures of Women: Sexuality.* London: Pandora.

Rosenblatt, P. C. and Burns, L. H. 1986: 'Long term effects of perinatal loss'. *Journal of Family Issues*, 7, 3, 237–54.

Rosenblatt, P. C. and Cunningham, M. R. 1976: 'Television watching and family tensions'. *Journal of Marriage and the Family*, 38, 1, 105–11.

Rossiter, C. and Wicks, M. 1982: *Crisis or Challenge? Family Care, Elderly People and Social Policy.* London: Study Commission on the Family.

Rothblum, E. D. and Cole, E. 1989: *Loving Boldly: Issues Facing Lesbians.* New York: Harrington.

215

Rothman, B. K. 1982: *In Labour: Women and Power in the Birthplace*. London: Junction Books.

Russell, G. 1983: *The Changing Role of Fathers*. Milton Keynes: Open University Press.

Scott, J. and Perren, K. 1994: 'The family album: reflections on personal and family life'. In N. Buck *et al.* (eds), *Changing Households*. University of Essex: ESRC Centre on Micro-Social Change, 263–90.

Searle-Chatterjee, M. and Sharma, U. 1994: *Contexualising Caste*. Oxford: Blackwell.

Segal, L. 1983: *What Is To Be Done About The Family?* Harmondsworth: Penguin.

Shelton, B. A. and John, D. 1993: 'Does marital status make a difference? Housework among married and cohabiting men and women'. *Journal of Family Issues*, 14, 3, 401–20.

Shipman, M. D. 1981 (Revised edition): *The Limitations of Social Research*. Harlow, Essex: Longman.

Shorter, E. 1975: *The Making of the Modern Family*. Glasgow: Fontana.

Sjoberg, G. *et al.* 1995: 'Family life and racial and ethnic diversity: an assessment of communitarianism, liberalism and conservatism'. *Journal of Family Issues*, 16, 3, 246–74.

Skolnick, A. 1978 (Second edition): *The Intimate Environment: Exploring Marriage and the Family*. Boston: Little Brown.

Skynner, R. and Cleese, J. 1983: *Families and How to Survive Them*. London: Methuen.

Smith, C. 1996: *Developing Parenting Programmes*. London: National Children's Bureau.

Smith, D. E. 1993: 'The standard North American family: SNAF as an ideological code'. *Journal of Family Issues*, 14, 1, 50–65.

Smith, D. S. 1993: 'The curious history of theorizing about the history of the Western nuclear family'. *Social Science History*, 17, 3, 325–53.

Smith, S. 1995: 'Family theory and multicultural family studies'. In B. B. Ingoldsby and S. Smith (eds), *Families in Multicultural Perspective*. New York: Guilford, 5–35.

Smlalek, R. N. Z. 1978: 'Observations on immediate reactions of families to Sudden Infant Death'. *Paediatrics*, 62, 2, 160–5.

Sobal, J. 1984: 'Marriage, obesity and dieting'. *Marriage and Family Review*, 7, 1/2, 115–39.

Soley, C. (Chair) 1994: *Report of the All Party Parliamentary Group on Parenting and the International Year of the Family*. London: Exploring Parenthood.

Spence, J. and Holland, P. 1991: *Family Snaps: The Meanings of Domestic Photography*. London: Virago.

Stacey, J. 1990: *Brave New Families: Stories of Domestic Upheaval in Late Twentieth Century America*. New York: Basic Books.

—— 1993: 'Good riddance to "the family": a response to David Popenoe'. *Journal of Marriage and the Family*, 55, 3, 545–7.

Steinglass, P. 1980: 'A life history model of the alcoholic family'. *Family Process*, 19, 3, 211–26.

Stitt, S. and Grant, D. 1993: 'Poverty research: A study using Rowntree's research imagination'. Unpublished paper presented at the 'British Sociological Association Conference', University of Essex.

Stones, C. 1994: *Focus on Families: Family Centres in Action*. Basingstoke: Macmillan.

Struckman-Johnson, C. and Struckman-Johnson, D. 1994: 'Men pressured and forced into sexual experience'. *Archives of Sexual Behaviour*, 23, 1, 93–114.

Sussman, M. B. 1973: *Non-Traditional Family Forms in the 1970's*. Minnesota: National Council on Family Relations.

—— 1975 (Special edition): 'The second experience: variant family forms and life styles'. *Family Co-ordinator*, 24, 4.

Sweeting, H. and West, P. 1995: 'Family life and health in adolescence: a role for culture in the health inequalities debate?' *Social Science and Medicine*, 40, 163–75.

Sydie, R. A. 1987: *Natural Women, Cultured Men: A Feminist Perspective on Sociological Theory*. Milton Keynes: Open University Press.

Szinovacz, M. E. 1980: 'Female retirement: effects on spousal roles and marital adjustment'. *Journal of Family Issues*, 1, 3, 423–40.

Thompson, L. and Walker, A. J. 1995: 'The place of feminism in Family Studies'. *Journal of Marriage and the Family*, 57, 4, 847–65.

Townsend, P. *et al.* 1988: *Inequalities in Health: The Black Report, The Health Divide*. Harmondsworth: Penguin.

Trebilcot, J. (ed.) 1984: *Mothering: Essays in Feminist Theory*. New Jersey: Rowan and Allanheld.

Troll, L. E. 1983: 'Grandparents: the family watchdogs'. In T. H. Brubaker (ed.), *Family Relationships in Later Life*. Beverly Hills: Sage, 63–74.

Trost, J. and Hultaker, O. 1986: 'Legal changes in the role of fathers: Swedish experiences'. *Marriage and Family Review*, 9, 3/4, 85–100.

Umberson, D. 1989: 'Parenting and well-being: the importance of context'. *Journal of Family Issues*, 10, 4, 427–39.

Unger, D. G. and Sussman, M. B. 1990: 'Introduction: a community perspective on families'. *Marriage and Family Review*, 15, 1/2, 1–18.

Utting, D. 1995: *Family and Parenthood: Supporting Families, Preventing Breakdown*. York: Joseph Rowntree Foundation.

Utting, D. *et al.* 1993: *Crime and the Family: Improving Child-rearing and Preventing Delinquency*. London: Family Policy Studies Centre.

Valadrez, J. J. and Clignet, R. 1984: 'Household work as an ordeal: culture of standard versus standardisation of culture'. *American Journal of Sociology*, 90, 3, 812–35.

Veevers, J. E. 1974: 'Voluntarily childless wives: an exploratory study'. In A. Skolnick and J. H. Skolnick (eds), *Intimacy, Family, and Society*. Boston: Little Brown, 501–10.

Ventura, J. 1987: 'The stresses of parenthood reexamined'. *Family Relations*, 36, 1, 26–9.

Wadsworth, J. *et al.* 1983: 'Family type and accidents in preschool children'. *Journal of Epidemiology and Community Health*, 37, 100–4.

Wallerstein, J. S. and Kelly, J. B. 1980: *Surviving the Breakup: How Children and Parents Cope with Divorce*. London: Grant MacIntyre.

Wedemeyer, N. V. 1986: 'Death is part of family life'. *Journal of Family Issues*, 7, 3, 235–6.

Weeks, J. 1986: *Family Studies: Information Needs and Resources*. Yorkshire: British Library.

—— 1991: *Sexuality and Its Discontents: Meanings, Myths and Modern Sexualities*. London: Routledge and Kegan Paul.

Westwood, S. 1984: *All Day Every Day: Factory and Family in the Making of Women's Lives*. London: Pluto.

Westwood, S. and Bhachu, P. 1988: 'Images and realities: our beliefs about Asian families are often selective, prejudiced and riddled with contradictions'. *New Society*, 6, 6 May, 20–2.

Wheelock, J. 1990: *Husbands At Home: The Domestic Economy in a Post-Industrial Society.* London: Routledge.

White, L. K. *et al.* 1985: 'The effect of marital disruption on child's attachment to parents'. *Journal of Family Issues,* 6, 1, 5–22.

Whitfield, R. C. 1980: *Education for Family Life: Some New Policies for Child Care.* London: Hodder and Stoughton.

—— 1983: *Family Structures, Lifestyles and the Care of Children.* Birmingham: University of Aston.

Wicks, M. 1978: *Old and Cold: Hypothermia and Social Policy.* London: Heinemann.

—— 1987: *A Future for All: Do We Need A Welfare State?* Harmondsworth: Penguin.

—— 1991: 'Family matters and public policy'. In M. Loney *et al.* (eds), *The State or the Market.* London: Sage, 169–83.

—— 1994: *The Active Society: Defending Welfare.* London: Fabian Discussion Papers No. 17.

Wikler, L. 1983: 'Chronic stresses of families of mentally retarded children'. In D. H. Olson and B. C. Miller (eds), *Family Studies Review Yearbook Volume 1.* Beverly Hills: Sage, 143–50.

Williamson, H. and Butler, I. 1995: 'Children speak: perspectives on their social worlds'. In J. Brannen and M. O'Brien (eds), *Childhood and Parenthood.* London: Institute of Education: University of London, 294–317.

Willmott, P. and Young, M. 1960: *Family and Class in a London Suburb.* London: Routledge and Kegan Paul.

Wilson, C. 1982: 'The impact on children'. In J. Orford and J. Harwin (eds), *Alcohol and the Family.* London: Croom Helm, 151–66.

Wilson, H. 1987: 'Parental supervision re-examined'. *British Journal of Criminology,* 27, 3, 275–301.

Winn, M. 1985 (Revised edition): *The Plug-In Drug.* Harmondsworth: Penguin.

Wise, V. and Stead, B. 1985: *Change or Choice: Community Care and Women as Carers.* London: Greater London Council.

Wolin, S. J. and Bennett, L. A. 1984: 'Family rituals'. *Family Process,* 23, 3, 401–20.

Woodroffe, C. *et al.* 1993: *Children, Teenagers and Health: The Key Data.* Buckingham: Open University Press.

World Health Organisation 1986: *Children and Family Breakdown.* Copenhagen: World Health Organisation.

Wyatt, G. E. *et al.* 1993: *Sexual Abuse and Consensual Sex: Women's Developmental Patterns and Outcomes.* London: Sage.

Young, M. and Willmott, P. 1957: *Family and Kinship in East London.* Harmondsworth: Penguin.

Zaretsky E. 1976: *Capitalism, the Family and Personal Life.* London: Pluto.

Zinn, M. B. and Eitzen, D. S. 1990 (Second edition): *Diversity in Families.* New York: Harper and Row.

Index

Department of Health 133
dependency ratio 21
DeVault, M. L. 44, 91, 104
developing nations 8, 85
diet 98, 101
disabled 12, 98, 179; employment 99;
    higher education 99
discrimination 61, 136, 179; ethnic 150;
    social class 150
Ditch, J. 100, 114, 178
divorce 3, 14, 17, 18, 68, 120, 121, 129,
    130, 138, 143, 144, 150, 151, 154,
    167, 176, 177, 189, 194;
    African-Caribbean 144; as solution
    121, 145; Asian 144; children 145,
    163, 164; contact arrangements 164;
    custody 145; *de facto* 143, 197; *de jure*
    143, 197; employment 145; housing
    145; income 145; poverty 145;
    psychological 145; transitions 145
Dobash, R. E. 52, 74, 104
Dobash, R. P. 52, 74, 104
Doherty, W. J. 90, 191
domestic labour debate 42
Dominian, J. 145
Donati, P. xiii, 63, 64, 67, 68
Dorn, N. 90
Douglas, J. 122
Driver, E.
Droisen, A. 75
drugs 88, 90, 98, 100, 101, 115, 129, 143
dual: burden of women 78; career 40,
    81, 139; work 28, 81, 150
Dumon, W. xiii
Duncombe, J. 78
Durham, M. 28, 38, 59, 70, 133

Eastman, M. 76
Eaton, M. 164
economic: active 21, 152; inactive 21
education 12, 105, 114, 189; attainment
    151; public school 12
Eitzen, D. S. 134, 153, 161
elderly 21, 182, 192
Elliot, F. R. 22, 44, 83, 100, 104, 195
Elliott, B. 98
Elliott, M. 72
engagement 127
Engels, F. 41

Equal Opportunities Commission 182
Erdos, G. 113, 123, 151
Estaugh, V. 136, 148, 158
ethnicity 12, 83, 86, 98, 134, 136, 138,
    150, 198
Europe 1, 2, 7, 12, 13, 14, 18, 22, 61, 62,
    63, 65, 68, 80, 83, 92, 102, 105, 114,
    124, 136, 137, 147, 155, 161, 164,
    168, 178, 179, 198
European Family Policy Observatory
    178
Eurostat 15, 16
exclusivity 127

Fagin, L. 82
families 127; 'the family' 2, 6, 9, 38, 45,
    149, 198; 'the family', abolish 43; 'the
    family', counting 9; 'the family',
    decline 154; 'the family', existence 2,
    54; 'the family', power of 3; 'the
    family', universality 6, 199; and
    crime 123; associations 68, 192;
    biology 6; breakdown 120;
    citizenship 63, 64, 67, 177, 185, 189,
    190, 192, 194; consumption 88, 176;
    cooking and meals 44; deviant 72;
    discourse 45; distributive systems 66;
    diversity 3, 8, 11, 12, 40, 41, 106,
    129, 135; dysfunctional 72; education
    2, 24, 65, 66, 142, 155, 177, 190,
    192; extended kin 87; external
    environment 71; history 7; impact of
    computing 94; importance 1, 175;
    international comparisons 13;
    intimate interior 71; invisibility 56;
    issues, costs of 177; language 5, 55;
    loyalty to 115; morality 4, 6; murder
    74; nuclear 5, 8, 10, 135, 150;
    obedience to 115; obligations 65; our
    familiarity 54; pathways 46, 47, 69,
    71, 86, 88, 116, 119, 151, 154; pet(s)
    79; photographs 92; pleasure and joy
    52; policies 14, 177; postmodern 38;
    poverty 18, 68, 101, 189; practices 63,
    64, 71, 80, 88, 89, 90, 91, 97, 109,
    116, 119; privacy 56; putting first
    173; rural extended 8; sense of
    normality 54; starting 127; theory
    29, 36, 37, 40, 41, 44; trends 15;

Rees, A. M. 63
Reinisch, J. M. 132
Reiss, I. L. 6
Relate 191
religion 3, 150
reproduction 132, 140, 146
restaurants 160
reward structure 78
Rhode, D. L. 172
Ribbens, J. 2, 32, 44, 47, 59, 81, 87, 109,
    167, 168, 172, 180
Richards, M. 72
Richardson, A. H. 80
Richardson, D. 167
Richardson, G. 75
Richardson, V. 178
Ricketts, W. 9
Rimmer, L. 9
rites of passage 47, 165
Roberts, H. 20
Roberts, M. 85
Robinson, M. 144, 147, 164
Rodger, J. J. 14, 35, 43
Rogge, J-U. 93
Roll, J. 18, 154
Roman, L. G. 129
romantic love 131, 134, 137, 142, 199
Root, J. 129, 131
Rosenblatt, P. C. 93, 136, 158
Rossiter, C. 102
Rothblum, E. D. 136
Rothman, B. K. 159
Russell, G. 170
Ryff, C. D. 106

Sami 55
Sapsford, R. 3, 41
Scandinavia 147, 155
Scanzoni, J. 144
Schonveld, A. 159
school 177; day 85; leaving age 128
Scott, J. 1, 15
Searle-Chatterjee, M. 86
Segal, L. 66
separation 151
sex 129, 132, 142, 146; activity 132; and
    politics 133; as a commodity 132;
    behaviour 132; consensual 75;
    education 158; erotic environment

132; experimentation 76; extra marital
    146; fun 146; girl's reputation 131;
    images 132; language 131; orientation
    150; plastic sexuality 132; roles 112;
    satisfaction 146; teenage 75; television
    94; transmitted diseases 132, 133
shanty towns 85
Sharma, U. 86
Shelton, B. A. 136
Shipman, M. D. 58
shopping 88, 91, 105; catalogues 88;
    centre 88, 129; channels 88;
    supermarket 88, 183
Shorter, E. 7
siblings: co-operation 118; competition
    118; intimidation 118; step 118
Sieder, R. 7
Sikhs 86
single parenting 3, 14, 18, 19, 28, 62, 68,
    113, 129, 150, 151, 176, 194; as
    solution 151; Black 150; Queen
    Victoria 151
singlehood 127, 129, 130, 151
Sjoberg, G. 13
Skolnick, A. 149
Skynner, R. 134
Slater, D. 156, 164, 172
Smith, C. 156
Smith, D. 56, 164
Smith, S. 29, 36, 37, 41, 43
Smlalek, R. N. Z. 158
snack foods 186
soap operas 131
Sobal, J. 98
social 110; class 19, 130, 134, 138, 150,
    197; class – underclass 20, 83;
    construction of reality 141; costs of
    de-partnering 142; divisions 161;
    events 130; networks 162; work 189,
    191
socialisation 30, 110, 149, 199
sociology 4, 106, 176; of childhood 106;
    of death 125; of work 77; political 51;
    responsibilities 57; theory 4; values
    58, 60
Soley, C. 178, 181, 182, 187, 190, 191
solidarity 134
South Africa 137
South America 92

Wilson, C. 89
Wilson, G. 45
Wilson, H. 122
Winn, M. 93
Wise, V. 181
Wolin, S. J. 117
Wolkowitz, C. 121
women: as senior partners 139; health
    101; magazines 129; refuges 43, 74
Woodroffe, C. 124
work paid 4, 12, 20, 77, 80, 85, 99, 121,
    169, 171, 174, 179, 184; family
    policies 83, 185; flexible hours 183;
    home work 121; retirement 84; roles
    80; shift work 121; women 78;
    workaholism 121

work unpaid 20, 77, 85, 121; caring 79;
    cooking 78, 91; emotion 78;
    housework 3, 77, 78, 88, 114, 136,
    167, 180; housework, as ordeal 78;
    housework, male contribution 78;
    housework, positive meanings 79;
    housework, social standing 78;
    shopping 78
World Health Organisation 190
Wyatt, G. E. 75

Young, M. 4, 19
youth culture 128

Zaretsky, E. 42
Zinn, M. B. 134, 153, 161